Unlocking the
Adoption Files

Unlocking the Adoption Files

Paul Sachdev

Lexington Books

D.C. Heath and Company/Lexington, Massachusetts/Toronto

Library of Congress Cataloging-in-Publication Data

Sachdev, Paul.
    Unlocking the adoption files / Paul Sachdev.
      p.   cm.
    Bibliography: p.
    Includes index.
    ISBN 0-669-20975-9 (alk. paper)
    1. Adoption—Canada.   2. Adoptees—Canada—Identification.
  3. Adoption—Law and legislation—Canada. 4. Social surveys—Canada.   I. Title.
HV875.58.C2S23   1989
362.7'34—dc20   89-12300
                                                    CIP

Published simultaneously in Canada
Printed in the United States of America
International Standard Book Number: 0-669-20975-9
Library of Congress Catalog Card Number: 89-12300

The paper used in this publication meets the minimum requirements of
American National Standard for Information Sciences—Permanence of
Paper for Printed Library Materials, ANSI Z39.48-1984.∞™

Year and number of this printing:

89 90 91 92 10 9 8 7 6 5 4 3 2 1

To my beloved parents whose unfailing love and sacrifices taught me the value of parenthood.

Contents

Tables

Foreword

The Civil Rights Movement in the 1960s initially concerned with the civil rights of racial minorities, had a broader effect. It sensitized other minority groups in the population to the possibility of redressing the inequities they faced. It made the community at large more perceptive to the claims of social minorities for the need for change in their behalf.

One minority group responding to the changing climate of social opinion was the population of adoptees. Adult adoptees had, for some time, felt deprived of their right to greater knowledge about their biological origins. Adoption policies dictated and implemented a clear, unequivocal break between the family of origin of adoptees and the family in which they were subsequently reared. The issuance of a new birth certificate symbolized a second birth to the adopted parents, declaring the psychological and social nonexistence of any previous relationship to the adoptees' biological parents. Contact with biological parents and access to their records was discouraged by adoptive policy ideology and supported by legal regulations making each contact difficult except in unusual circumstances. As a consequence some percentages of adoptees encountered difficulties in developing a clear sense of identity in the absence of detailed knowledge about their biological background.

A second minority affected by agency policy were of biological parents who surrendered their child for adoption. Adoption policy prohibited subsequent contact with the adopted child and the adoptive family. Some percentage of this group of biological parents had never fully resolved the decision to surrender and felt a desire, if not a need, to learn more of what had happened to the child they gave up for adoption.

A movement initially inaugurated by adoptees and subsequently joined by biological parents developed in the 1960s in response to the changing zeitgeist regarding the rights of minorities.

The movement, which continued to grow through the 1970s and 1980s in numbers and visibility, sparked, if not a revolution, at least a radical change in adoption agency policy and associated legal regulations. It is known as the open adoption movement. It centered on unlocking the adoption files, making background information more accessible to adoptees and making possible actual contact between biological parents and their subsequently adopted child.

By now the movement has produced a modest body of literature on the responses, outcomes, and problems associated with the changes that have been introduced. The literature includes personal accounts by adoptees of their individual experiences in genealogical research and, in some instances, their actual meetings with biological parents.

A second group of reports includes mail questionnaire studies of opinions and attitudes of biological parents, adoptees, and adoptive parents relating to opening adoption files and searching for each other. A third group of studies was conducted by child welfare researchers. This generally involved interviews with nonrandomly identified groups of adoptees who volunteered to share their experiences with the researchers. These adoptees made up a convenience sample that might or might not have been representative of adoptees generally.

The study reported here by Professor Paul Sachdev presents a research project that, in some essential, consequential ways, differs from what was previously available in the literature regarding these questions. It is a notable contribution in that, because of its more rigorous methodology, its findings are clearly likely to have greater validity and general applicability than previous reports and personal accounts.

Professor Sachdev's report is based on a randomly selected group of respondents. The four significant groups of participants in the adoption event are sampled for personal interviews—adoptees, adoptive parents, biological parents, and adoption agency social workers. The extended personal interviews were structured in an interview schedule formulated, tested, and revised in terms of adoption theory and a through review of the literature. The interview schedule included a sizable number of open-ended questions, permitting a measure of individuality in response.

Sensitive that participants in the adoptive event might differ in their responses as a function of the period during which the adoption took place, Professor Sachdev took the desirable precaution of sampling historically. A group of study participants had adopted in 1958, other groups in 1968 and 1978.

Further, because previous research indicated clear gender differences in "open adoption" and "search" concerns and activity, Professor Sachdev gave clear visibility to gender considerations in the research design.

As a consequence of these notably desirable research considerations and that the total group of research participants is, by interview study standards, a fairly large group, results of the research response here can be confidently recommended to the attention of the many disciplines involved in adoption proceedings—social workers, doctors, lawyers, legislators. The report is written in a way that makes its findings easily and interestingly accessible to all those personally involved in adoption—adoptees, adopters, and birth parents.

The foreword is designed to suggest that the following report is worth the reader's time and effort. We clearly believe this to be the case.

Alfred Kadushin
Julia C. Lathrop,
Distinguished Professor of
Social Work

Acknowledgments

Several people to whom I feel indebted were involved in bringing this study to fruition and to list them all is not without the risk of inadvertently slighting some. Yet the contributions of certain individuals must be acknowledged. I am especially grateful for the most generous support and assistance I received from the staff of the Department of Social Services in an eastern province of Canada,[1] where this study was conducted. In particular, I thank the following officials: Hon. Tom Hickey (former minister of Social Services); Hon. Charles Brett (former minister of Social Services); Mr. George Pope (assistant deputy minister of Social Services). Without their extraordinary cooperation I never would have had a sample. Mr. Gilbert Pike, the former deputy minister of Social Services, extended himself beyond all measures in facilitating this research. I am also grateful to him for releasing some of the finest adoption workers from the department to work as interviewers for the research study.

For years, I have considered Robert K. Crocker of the Institute for Educational Research and Development at Memorial University the expert on research methodology and analysis of the most intricate data. He has been a tremendous help in every phase of the research study—from conceptualization of the problem to data collection and data analysis. I am deeply appreciative of Bob for making himself available at my convenience. Two renowned experts in adoption, Ben Jaffee and Alfred Kadushin, provided their generous and most helpful comments on instrumentation. To Dr. Kadushin, my mentor at the University of Wisconsin, I remain immensely indebted for providing an enviable model of scholarship and style of thinking that have enriched my professional development.

I doubt whether I could have ventured into this massive research project if I had not had the generous support and encouragement of Dr. J. Victor Thompson, then-director of the School of Social Work at Memorial University. He greatly facilitated the study and the writing of the manuscript

---

[1]The name of the province is kept confidential to safeguard anonymity of the respondents.

in a number of ways, one of which was release time from teaching. In addition, he provided substantial editorial assistance and many perceptive comments on the draft. I am eternally grateful to him.

In effect, it was the generous three-year grant from the National Welfare Grants Program of Health and Welfare, Canada, that started the research study. Mr. J. Evariste Thréault, Consultant Welfare Grants, encouraged me to develop the idea for the study on the topic, for which I extend my sincere gratitude to him.

Most of all, the hundreds of adoptive parents, birth mothers, adopted persons, and social work personnel deserve the most appreciation for their overwhelming responsiveness to my imposition on their time and stamina in answering lengthy and sometimes intricate questions. Their insightful comments and suggestions have proven immensely useful in drafting policy recommendations. Undoubtedly, without their generous cooperation I would have known little on the subject. I am particularly grateful to birth mothers, who endured painful memories during recall and provided a rare insight into their postadoption experience.

My special thanks to the diligent secretarial staff that responded to my importuning with humor and who, through efficient typing, turned my messy revisions into an intelligible manuscript.

Sudarshan, my wife, of course deserves the most thanks of all for sparing me from household responsibilities and for providing many helpful ideas and critiques.

Finally, while I acknowledge the input of ideas and comments from many sources, I alone am responsible for the views expressed in the book.

Paul Sachdev

Introduction

This book describes the members of the adoption rectangle—adoptive parents, birth mothers, adoptees, and social work personnel—and their attitudes toward opening adoption records. The impetus for the study was provided by the need of adoption agencies and departments for secure guidelines to develop a rational policy for handling requests for adoption information from adoptees and birth parents. For some time, social agencies have been under pressure from activist adoptee and birth parent groups and professional people to revise traditional policies on sharing information and facilitating reunions between consenting parties. The activist movement that gained strength in Canada and the United States has in recent years seriously challenged the current adoptive arrangements based on permanent secrecy.

Earlier Pioneers

Jean Paton's successful search for her birth mother in the early 1950s represented the earliest challenge to the institutional arrangements of adoptive kinship based on permanent anonymity. Her book, *The Adopted Break Silence*, was in every sense a pioneering effort describing the experience and anguish of adopted persons permanently separated through administrative and legal fiat from their biological roots. Audacious at the time, it outraged social work professionals, but it heralded the emergence of a social movement of the adopted for institutional reform. Paton organized an adoptee group, Orphan Voyage, that provided adoptees access to each other. Two decades later, in 1971, another adoptee and pioneer, Florence Fisher, formed Adoptees Liberty Movement Association (ALMA) to provide a wider forum to previously hidden and silent adoptees for mutual support and for promoting reunions with their birth parents. Two years later, in 1973, her book, *The Search for Anna Fisher*, narrated the

story of her relentless and exhausting struggle against obdurate bureau-
cracy to unveil her past. Her daring story kindled latent desire in many
adoptees and catalyzed the advance of the adoptee movement. Spurred by
the civil rights movement in the 1960s and encouraged by her successful
story, adoptees in record numbers started to rally under the banner of
ALMA. In Jean Paton's prophetic words, adoptees had indeed broken the
silence. ALMA is one of the largest national adoptee groups in the United
States, but many regional and national adoptee associations also have
sprung up with the common goals of providing mutual support and
achieving an abolition of secrecy surrounding unsealed adoption records.
In Canada the two most common adoptee groups with similar aims are
Parent Finders, with branches in six provinces, and the Canadian Adoptees Reform Association of British Columbia.

Mounting Inquiries from Adoptees

The number of adult adoptees seeking information about or contact with
a birth parent has increased severalfold since Jean Paton and Florence
Fisher knocked at the doors of adoption agencies. A few statistics will
illustrate this trend. In Ontario, in one year following the establishment of
a passive Adoption Disclosure Register in June 1979, six hundred adult
adoptees entered their names with the Ministry of Community and Social
Services (personal communication) and more than two thousand registered
in one month after the Ontario government set up an active Adoption
Disclosure Register in July of 1987 (The Globe and Mail, August 15,
1987, A8). About 660 requests a year are received from adoptees by the
Ministry of Social Services in British Columbia (Ministry of Social Services
and Housing, 1984). In Newfoundland, where the release of adoption
information is prohibited, the Department of Social Services received
thirty-six inquires in 1980. This number swelled to 101 in 1983. In one
month alone in 1984 the department received sixty requests (Dawe 1984).
In 1976, the Saskatchewan Department of Social Services received requests
for identifying information or a reunion from ninety-five participants in
adoption. This number peaked to 620 in 1985 (personal communication).
Similar trends exist in the United States. In Minnesota, for example,
within two years after liberalization of its adoption laws, 679 requests
from adoptees were received by the Minnesota Department of Public
Welfare (Weidell 1980). The Child Welfare League of American (CWLA)
reported that during 1975 more than three thousand adult adoptees contacted 155 agencies in the United States for information on their family
background (Jones 1976). Since the first national registry, International
Soundex Reunion Registry, was founded in 1975, there have been more

than forty-three thousand registrations and 1,750 matches (Gonyo and Watson 1988). In response to mounting demand for information or re-union, more than twenty-seven states currently operate public registries.

Female vs. Male Adoptees

One observation uniformly made by most studies is that female adoptees far outnumber male adoptees in their desire to seek genealogical information or reunion (Boult 1987; Day 1979; Farber 1977; Gonyo and Watson 1988; Kowal and Schilling 1985; Lithgow 1980; McWhinnie 1969; Rosenzweig-Smith 1988; Simpson et al. 1981; Sorosky et al. 1978; Stevenson 1976; Thompson et al. 1978; Tingley 1978; Triseliotis 1984; Weidell 1980; Yellin et al. 1983). In 1980-81 Triadoption Library, Inc. conducted a nationwide survey of search and support organizations and the kind of individuals who contacted them. It found that in twenty-two of the participating groups, four times as many women as men sought help in their search (Collins et al. 1981). These investigators attribute the high proportion of female adoptees seeking their origins to the fact that women as childbearers accord high value to family lineage and regard ancestry as highly significant for biological continuity.

Birth Mothers' Rights

Birth mothers are also beginning to assert their rights to know about or meet the children they relinquished. Like adoptees, birth mothers have organized themselves into a single large activist group in the United States called Concerned United Birthparents (CUB) with chapters in more than twenty-five states. Through their newsletter, *Communicator*, birth mothers advocate reformation of existing adoption policies in favor of a more open system that recognizes adoption as a kinship system to which each set of parents makes contribution toward the well-being of the adopted child. In Canada, the equivalent group is Birth Parent/Relative Group of Canada, with headquarters in Calgary, Alberta.

   Although birth mothers are returning to social agencies for information about or contact with the relinquished child, their number is far less than that of adult adoptees. Even fewer seek help in making contact with the adopted child. According to the survey by Child Welfare League of America, cited earlier, in 1975 an average of ten birth parents requested information, compared with nearly twenty adoptees (Jones 1976). In the Triadoption survey, birth parents constituted one-third (32.9 percent) of those who contacted search groups, as contrasted with fifty-six percent adoptees (Collins et al. 1981). Over half (53 percent) of the returning birth parents were interested in nonidentifying information only, while only 37 percent of them sought the agency's help in locating or identifying the adopted child. International Soundex Reunion Registry in Washington reported twice as many adoptees registered as birth parents in 1975 (Gonyo and Watson 1988). In Saskatchewan, of the adoption participants who request identifying information, only one-third come from birth parents (Ministry of Social Services and Housing 1984). In another Canadian study conducted by the Children's Aid Society of Metropolitan Toronto, the authors observed that the ratio of inquiries received by the agency from adult adoptees and birth parents during the three-year period from July 1, 1979 to June 30, 1982, was consistently 3:1 (Stoneman et al. 1985). Many investigators are unanimous in their observation that birth mothers are reluctant to initiate contact, however much they might desire, because of their fear of being intrusive or being mis-understood by the adopted person and his or her parents. But they are eager to meet when requested by the adoptee (Sachdev 1989; Sorosky et al. 1978; Sullivan 1977). In Saskatchewan, where searches are undertaken at the request of adult adoptees, only one-third of birth mothers contacted did not agree to a meeting (Dawe 1984). In the United States the CWLA survey noted that about four-fifths of biological parents who were located and contacted agreed to a meeting with the adopted child; only 14 percent of them did not want to meet. Similar observations were made by the Children's Home Society of California study. It reported that when birth parents were asked if they were interested in making contact with the children they relinquished, only 26 percent showed no interest in such reunion because they thought "it was not fair to intrude on the adoptive parents' privacy" (Jones 1976, 68) The Adoptee's Liberty Movement Association (ALMA) reported that in nearly five thousand reunions consummated through its efforts in 1980, the percentage of birth mothers rejecting reunions constituted only 2 percent (Dusky 1979). Similarly, in 1986, the first year following enactment of the Adult Adoptees Information Act in New Zealand, birth mothers who registered their veto prohibiting the release of their identity constituted less than 2 percent (personal communication).

Professionals Speak Out

Professionals are also calling for reform in existing adoption practices. David Kirk, a Canadian sociologist and himself an adoptive parent, challenged the 'as if born' myth with his 1964 release of *Shared Fate* and in 1981 he identified contradictions and role dilemmas in the institution of adoption, which he declared was in need of reform (Kirk 1964; 1981). In early 1976, the Child Welfare League of America recommended that its member agencies alert the relinquishing and adopting parents that secrecy of information cannot be permanently guaranteed to them (CWLA 1976). More recently, some professionals have proposed a more radical change, in the direction of a completely open adoption, especially for older adopted children (Borgman 1982; Groth et al. 1987; Pannor and Baran 1984). Open adoption, these advocates maintain, eliminates role conflicts of the adoption parties and recognizes birth parents as partners with active involvement in the adoption process.

Legislative Activities

As a result of pressure from activist adoptee and birth parents groups and professional people, adoption agencies in North America are becoming increasingly sensitive to the need for reevaluating current policies concerning adoption disclosure. In some jurisdictions in Canada and the United States adoption agencies have taken certain steps and others are contemplating such moves toward liberalizing adoption policies. But these changes have not followed a uniform pattern. Most provinces in Canada have a policy under which adoption departments permit the release of nonidentifying information regarding the child's background to adoptive parents and adopted adults. Nine provinces summarize general information on adoptees to birth parents upon request. However, more controversial practice involves the sharing of identifying information. At the time of this writing five provinces (Alberta, British Columbia, Manitoba, New Brunswick, Nova Scotia) maintain a passive adoption disclosure registry that permits exchange of identifying information and direct contact, provided both parties have voluntarily registered consent. Three provinces (Manitoba, Ontario, Saskatchewan) operate an active/passive registry that undertakes searches for birth parents on behalf of adopted adults only. However, the birth parent's consent is required before disclosing her or his identity. North West Territories searches for the unregistered birth parent at the request of the adoptee if the adoptive parents' consent is obtained. Quebec is the only province that operates a fully active search and intermediary system under which searches are conducted on behalf of either searching party. In the United States nine states (California, Colorado, Florida, Hawaii, Louisiana, New York, Oklahoma, Oregon, Texas) operate mutual consent voluntary passive registry and eleven states (Alabama, Connecticut, Georgia, Kansas, Kentucky, Minnesota, Nebraska, New Jersey, North Dakota, South Dakota, Wisconsin) have set up an active/passive and intermediary procedure. Tennessee is the only state with an active registry for adopted siblings only who are separated by adoption. All in all, by 1985 some thirty-five states had enacted laws permitting the release of adoption information. However, variations existed in terms of the nature of information (that is, identifying, nonidentifying, or medical), the prerequisites of age and consent to disclosure, the relative emphasis on the rights of the adoptee or birth parent, and the extent of the adoption agencies' involvement in facilitating searches (Herrington 1986).

Impetus for the Study

There has been no known systematic study that provided the basis for revision of disclosure policies in the aforementioned jurisdictions. Mostly, policies and procedures were introduced using a commonsense approach, more likely in response to lobbying by activist groups, or on the basis of a trendy model. In a few areas, administrators and policy makers invited feedback from interested constituents. The great variability and the truncated nature of these policy changes provided impetus for this comprehensive study involving a random sample of three hundred members of the adoption rectangle. This three-year-study, conducted in an eastern province of Canada, provided material for this book.

The social agencies' dilemma in unsealing adoption records and revising adoptive arrangements stems from the enormous difficulty in effectively harmonizing the guarantees and conflicting rights of the involved parties in such a way that one's advantage does not injure the interests and rights of another. The issues involved in the controversy and the opening of sealed records are the focus of discussion in the first chapter.

1
The Nature of the Controversy

The center of the debate is the permanent secrecy and anonymity that have been the hallmark of contemporary adoption practice. Such secrecy is a relatively recent development, however. Historically, in most ancient societies of Egypt, Greece, and Rome, adoption was an open informal exchange between kin members in ways that permitted continued and frequent contact between the two families. In that sense, adoption would create for the child an additional parental relationship, rather than a substitute relationship (Kadushin and Martin 1988). There was no legal precedent for adoption in North America. Thus, the first adoption law passed in Massachusetts in 1851 introduced for the first time the concept of permanent anonymity by providing "legal and complete severance of the relationships between child and biological parents" (Kadushin and Martin 1988, p. 535). The law became the model for most English speaking North American states and some other Western European countries. Adoption in most jurisdictions has followed a practice of sealing the court records and the child's original birth certificate after the adoption is decreed, preventing inspection by all parties involved. This practice has long been supported by adoption agencies. Adoptive parents, too, have found the sealed adoption records advantageous, as they serve their interests. However, activist groups of adoptees and birth parents find permanent concealment most offensive to their interests. In the following pages are perceptions of members of the adoption rectangle (adoption agencies, adoptive parents, birth parents, and adoptees) regarding the sealed records policy. Their views are based mainly on case studies of individuals, personal experiences, fictional beliefs, and limited research.

Adoption Agencies

Adoption agencies contend that confidentiality of adoption records maximizes the interests and needs of all parties to the adoption. It offers the biological mother an effective safeguard against the possible emotional trauma and the disruption of subsequently formed relationships that might result from the appearance of the child she surrendered or the adoptive parents. It also protects adoptive parents from confrontation with the biological mother and the inherent risk of interference with the child's integration into the new family. Furthermore, the assurance of anonymity decreases the birth mother's resistance to the idea of surrendering her child for adoption, thereby maintaining the supply of infants for childless couples. It also makes adoptive applicants feel less apprehensive about adopting children through agencies, thus making agency adoption a more attractive and viable alternative to gray or black markets. Sealed records are also viewed as helping the adoptee to develop psychologically stable relationships with the adoptive parents and to safeguard him or her against possible psychological distress that might result from stigmatizing or embarrassing disclosure about the birth parents or birth circumstances.

Agencies maintain that sealing adoption records serves to reinforce the "as if" concept for the parties involved in the adoption. The adoptive parents, for instance, like to believe the child never had any other parents, but belongs to them "as if" of their own blood. The birth mother likes to pretend she never had a child whom she relinquished. The 'as if' doctrine makes it easier for the adoptee to identify with the adoptive parents as though they were "real" forebears.

In fact, the practice of sealing records has been premised on certain assumptions and convictions among social workers. First, they promoted the adoptive couples' myth of rebirth of the child by altering the child's original birth certificate because they believed this illusion was crucial for the childless couples to accept adoption as a non-biological means of acquiring parenthood. Second, they were convinced that blood ties are not crucial to human psychological well-being (Clothier 1943)—that a person can be grafted onto the family tree of others and if transplanted early in desirable surroundings, he can develop into a healthy individual. Third, although social workers considered it desirable that adoptive parents "tell" the child, they did not anticipate that the revelation of his adoption status would activate a quest for his biological heritage. It was assumed that given the love and security of the adoptive home, the adoptee would fulfill an overall parent-child relationship and be able to resolve any identity concerns without the involvement of the biological parent. Fourth, they assumed the birth mother wanted to sever all ties with the relinquished child and would never wish to reestablish contact.

Adoptive Parents

Most experts have agreed that adoptive parents generally feel threatened by unsealing adoption records (Burke 1975; Geissinger 1984; Kadushin and Martin 1988; Lifton 1979; Pannor and Nerlove 1977; Triseliotis 1973). They fear the child's interest in his or her biological parents may result in the loss of love and loyalty. To them the relationship between their child and the birth parents is no more than a biological accident and they feel it is, in fact, they who have fulfilled the obligations and responsibilities of parents and provided the child with love and guidance. They may, therefore, interpret the adoptee's interest in the genetic parents as failure in their parenting role. Since they were offered guarantees of permanent confidentiality at adoption, they view any attempt at liberalization of adoption statutes as betrayal of the adoption agencies' pledge. They fear that reestablishment of their child's ties with the biological parents can seriously undermine the child's assimilation into the new family. This, in their view, is an infringement on their fundamental rights to enjoy the conditions necessary to rear the adopted child, the right that natural parents take for granted (Burke 1975; Carter 1978).

There are some recent indications that adoptive parents' antagonistic attitudes are beginning to relax, given the lessened stigma associated with illegitimacy, infertility, and increased acceptance of transracial and older children as adoptees. For example, a study conducted by the Children's Home Society of California (1977) involving completed questionnaires from three hundred adult adoptees, one hundred biological parents, and one hundred adoptive parents found that 64 percent of adoptive parents approved of their adult children's or their birth parents' desire to search for each other. Another study in California, by Sorosky et al. (1978) surveyed the attitudes of 170 adoptive parents who volunteered in group sessions and noted that there was a general shift in their outlook on open adoption with increased acceptance of the reality. More recently, Feigelman and Silverman (1986), like Sorosky, et al., reported that in their sample of 372 adoptive parents contacted through mailed questionnaires, three-fifths endorsed the idea of their children learning about and making contact with their birth parents.

Birth Parents

During the 1950s and 1960s, when out-of-wedlock pregnancy was frowned upon, young girls would find it advantageous to disappear to escape the stigma of illegitimacy and start their lives anew. This self-imposed anonymity reinforced social workers' conviction that birth mothers wanted to permanently close doors to their past. But volley of personal accounts on search and reunion that have appeared in recent years do not seem to support that long-held assumption about birth mothers. Their biographies and narrations reveal that the birth mother never really forgets the child she relinquished and has deep interest in knowing what becomes of him or her (Dusky 1979; Lifton 1979; Marcus 1981; Musser 1979). One of the few studies that investigated the feelings and attitudes of birth mothers years after relinquishment was conducted by Sorosky et al. (1978). On the basis of detailed personal interviews with thirty-eight mothers who responded to their newspaper advertisement, the authors concluded that "feelings of loss, pain, and mourning continued to be felt by the majority of birth mothers . . . . An overwhelming majority. . . . expressed an interest in knowing what kind of person their children had grown up to be" (p. 54). Ninety-five percent wanted the information about themselves updated in the agency files.

The results of two more recent studies done in Australia and in Canada concurred with those obtained by Sorosky et al. The Australian study, involving 213 birth mothers who relinquished a first child some thirty years previously found that an overwhelming majority—93.6 percent—felt a sense of loss in varying degrees over the period (Winkler and Keppel 1984). The Canadian study conducted by the Children's Aid Society of Metropolitan Toronto on 172 birth mothers who contacted the agency's Post Adoption Service Unit between 1979 and 1982 reported that 67 percent wanted some knowledge of the child relinquished some twenty-five years previously (Stoneman et al. 1985). Sachdev (1988) conducted a study of fifty-seven birth mothers in Ontario, Canada who reunited with their adult children and concluded that 70.2 percent of them continued to experience feelings of loss, pain, and grief till the day they met their child, forty years or more after relinquishment. A large number of birth mothers are searching and even a larger majority would like to search for the surrendered child. But they are restrained by respect for the privacy of the adoptive parents and adopted child and fear of disruption their contact may cause them. Eighty-two percent of the birth mothers interviewed in Sorosky et al.'s study (1978) said they would be receptive to a reunion if their child, upon reaching adulthood, wished it. A more recent study by Deykin et al. (1984), conducted among 334 birth mothers who were members of the Concerned United Birthparents, reported that a vast majority—96 percent—had considered searching and two-thirds had actually undertaken a search for their relinquished child.

Many birth mothers say they were not aware of the contractual arrangement assuring them of permanent confidentiality and contend that such contract was the mental construct of social workers who assumed they wanted to be anonymous. In the Children's Home Society of California study birth mothers were asked if they felt the agency made a contract with them for keeping their identity permanently secret. More than half—53 percent—said no. Birth mothers feel the so-called "contract" not only cut them off from the past but also made them invisible. Thus, for birth mothers it was a two-sided message—it protected them but at the same time warned them to stay away.

Many birth mothers say they experience emotional conflicts such as anger, grief, and guilt in the aftermath of adoption. They also have nagging doubts about their decision and often wonder about the child, but as advised by their social worker, they pretend his or her nonexistence. Thus, like an adopted child, the birth mother also is forced to play "the adoption game" and to lead a life of split existence. Birth mothers accept that they have lost the child forever, but contend that unsealed records are a step toward a meaningful relationship with their child, and a chance to resolve their guilt feelings and uncertainties about their child's feelings toward them.

Birth mothers also challenge legislatures' contentions that disclosure of their identities could inhibit the decision of a large number of mothers to surrender their babies for adoption. They cite examples of Finland, Scotland, and Israel, where adoption is practiced as effectively without confidential statutes. Some birth mothers claim that in reality the preservation of the right of confidentiality is promoted to protect the interest of adoptive parents, and that they were never given the option of whether to remain anonymous. (Jones 1976).

Of course, it is possible there are some birth mothers for whom anonymity is an important prerequisite to their decision to surrender their babies and who would not favor intrusion by their relinquished child (Feigelman and Silverman 1986).

Adopted Persons

Activist adoptees see sealed records as an affront to human dignity and to civil rights. They question the falsification of birth certificates, which they see as deception in the adoptive parent-child relationship, and challenge the psychological validity of the "veil" between their past and present lives as symbolized in the practice of sealing the records. These measures, they contend, force them to play the adoption game silently and repress their quest to know their genetic roots (Lifton 1979). According to adoption game rules they must consider their birth parents dead or nonexistent, and believe the adoptive parents are their real parents. The adoptees see the rejection of biological process of their origins a travesty of their existence and the legal system that promotes these fictional beliefs.

Activist adoptee groups also challenge statutes favoring confidentiality of adoption records on the grounds that they violate the principle of equal protection under the constitution and are, therefore, discriminatory, since nonadoptees are not required to obtain a court order to gain access to their birth records and other background information (Anderson 1977; Burke 1975; Prager et al. 1973). They also see it as ironic that while the illegitimate child's rights are upheld they as adoptees are denied equal status even though they are expected to carry the responsibilities and obligations of all citizens (Payne 1977; Scheppers 1975). Adoptee groups also contend that the constitutional validity of confidentiality is based on dubious criteria of preserving the interest and welfare of adoptees, who in fact are psychologically harmed by denied access to the facts of their natural heritage. It is also argued that by denying this access, the state creates potential medical problems and exposes them to the risk of unwittingly committing incest.

Adoptees' desire to open adoption records is also defended on the grounds that denial of such access constitutes a violation of their right to possible inheritance or benefits from their natural parents (Carter 1978).

While adoptees acknowledge the importance of confidentiality statutes in protecting adoptive parents' autonomy and privacy necessary to raise the child, they question the rationale supporting permanent confidentiality. In other words, it is understandable that confidentiality can enable the development of stable parent-child relationships and preserve the adoptive family unit when adoptees are children. But the conditions justifying such protection are no longer operative once children reach adulthood. Adoptees contend that as adults they do not need the same parental protection and control and therefore the state's interest in protecting adoptive parents' autonomy ceases to be compelling.

Adoptees also argue that because they were not party to the adoption agreement they should not be made to suffer the consequences of the decision to isolate them from their own birth history. They contend that opportunities provided by open adoption to learn about or seek contact with their genetic parents should not alter the nature and the intensity of the relationship with their adoptive parents. It is possible that this relationship can be strengthened once the adoptee has fulfilled his desire.

Quest for Identity

The most significant factor that generated the current controversy is the recognition by professionals that knowledge of one's heritage is a necessary part of identity formation. This is no less true for an adoptee. A number of studies on child development report that an individual ignorant of his biological heritage is seriously limited in the psychological dimension of identity. These studies further assert that it is not only natural but also desirable for a young adult to have curiosity about his forebears (Colon 1973; Douvan and Adelson 1966; Freud 1958; Horrocks and Weinberg 1970; Schumuck 1965; Smart and Smart 1972). Erikson (1968), for instance, considers it crucial in normal personality development that individuals develop a sense of identity derived from linkage or identification with one's past and any interference with this process is likely to result in identity confusion. Burke (1975) contends that a person's healthy, productive life is largely determined by incorporation into his personality of the knowledge about his cultural and biological origins. The significance of this fact is increasingly demonstrated by the recent struggle of many racial and ethnic groups for rediscovery and maintenance of their histories.

Some investigators contend that the struggle for self-identity in an adoptee is largely attributable to a need to integrate into his or her personality two sets of parents—adoptive parents and birth parents, who are generally obscure. Having failed in this process, an adoptee experiences emotional conflicts and anxieties (Clothier 1943; Costin 1963; Fisher 1972; Hubbard 1947; Mann 1976). Sorosky, et al. (1975) reviewed literature related to identity conflicts among adoptees and concluded that the lack of continuity with the past and of knowledge about origins results in "identity lacunae". In Alex Haley's highly acclaimed book *Roots*, the account of one black American's search for his ancestral African tribe strikes a forceful parallel with adoptees' desire to return to their genetic and historical origins (Haley 1976).

Adolescence and Curiosity

Rautman (1959) and Schechter (1965) suggest that an individual's identity begins to occur between the ages of three and six years, the period of Oedipal conflicts, and it is during adolescence that questions about one's origins are greatly intensified. Interest is focused on biological aspects. Other theorists seem to agree with this notion. Offord et al. (1969), for example, maintain that an adolescent adoptee has an acute identity problem and quite frequently wrestles with the question of who the real parents are and why they gave him or her up. At times the adoptee may identify with fantasized biological parents. An adolescent adoptee's confusion about his or her genetic roots is variously characterized as "genealogical bewilderment" by Sants (1965) and "roaming phenomenon" by Paul Toussieng (1962). Gawronski et al. (1974) noted that while genealogical bewilderment was common to most adoptees in their sample, latency and adolescence marked the development of curiosity about their genealogical past and pregnancy was the occasion when it was most intensely felt. Adult adoptees in the Triseliotis study also reported that as adolescents they were obsessed with the questions about their adoption and their genetic parents. More recently these observations were confirmed by Sorosky et al. (1978), in their extensive review of literature on adolescent development. The authors explain why during adolescence adoptees experience the greatest sense of curiosity by suggesting that during this phase of life "the heightened interests in sexuality make the adoptee more aware of how the human race and its characteristics are transmitted from generation to generation" (p. 113). An adolescent adoptee's concern about committing incest or inheriting disease may also reinforce curiosity about biological origins (Burke 1975).

While all children during adolescence experience in varying degrees problems of identity formation, adopted adolescents are particularly vulnerable to interference with development of self-identify because of their sense of deprivation of rootedness and linkage with their biological past (American Academy of Pediatrics 1971; Anglim 1965; Barinbaum 1974; Frisk 1964; Lion 1976; Livermore 1961; Mech 1973; Reynolds and Chiappise 1975; Schoenberg 1974; Sorosky et al. 1975; Starr 1976). Kornitzer (1971) notes that in the case of an adopted adolescent, the process of identity formation is impaired by the knowledge that "an essential part of himself has been cut off and remains on the other side of the adoption barrier" (p. 45). However, a comprehensive and methodologically sound study by Stein and Hoopes (1985) challenges the assertion of these investigators that adoptive status impinges on the process of identity formation during adolescence. In their sample of ninety-one adopted and nonadopted adolescents, the authors concluded that "adopted subjects showed no deficits in functioning on measures of overall identity when compared to their nonadopted counterparts" (p. 34). A similar conclusion was reached in an earlier study of identity crises in adoptees and nonadoptees aged eighteen to twenty-five. Norvell and Guy (1977) compared self-concept scores of the two groups and found no significant differences between. Their conclusion: "Adoptive status itself cannot produce a negative identity. If negative elements become incorporated in the adolescent's identity, they more likely than not stemmed from problems within the home" (p 445).

Kadushin (1978) reviewed literature on adoption disclosure and found support for the earlier findings, but also noted that adoptees' psychological need to know their genealogical background continues into adulthood. Certain periods of turmoil or significant life events involving family such as death, birth, marriage, separation, divorce, and so on propel them to act on their desire to seek access to confidential adoption records. Lawrence (1976), for example, affirmed through personal interviews with two hundred adult adoptees the presence of a compelling quest for information about their heritage. Jaffee (1974), too, noted in his sample of adult adoptees that many of them wanted more and complete knowledge of their origins.

Ample evidence in the literature suggests that an adoptee's desire to know his biological roots is not idle curiosity of individuals who are psychologically and socially impaired, as contended by some writers (Hubbard 1947; Jaffee and Fanshel 1970; Kowal and Schilling 1985; Lemon

1959; McWhinnie 1969; Simon and Senturia 1966), but is nearly a universal phenomenon in normal personality development (American Academy of Pediatrics 1971; Burke 1975; Day 1979; Gawronski et al. 1974; Hoopes et al. 1970; Jones 1976; Kadushin 1978; Kirk 1981; Krugman 1964; Lifton 1979; Sorosky et al. 1975; Thompson et al. 1978; Triseliotis 1973). One of the major studies designed to explore adult adoptees motivation to seek information about their origins was done by John Triseliotis in Scotland. He studied seventy adult adoptees who wrote or called Registrar House in Edinburgh in 1969 and 1970 for their original birth certificates. In most cases, Triseliotis found that the impulse to seek genealogical information and to search for birth parents was activated by "some deeply felt psychological need and rarely was it related to a matter-of-fact attitude" (Triseliotis 1973, 154). These findings were confirmed by a more recent American study by Kowal and Schillings (1985). The authors noted in their sample of 110 adult adoptees who contacted adoption agencies or an adoptee search group in two midwestern cities that for "most of them" the decision to search for their biological parents was not precipitous, but a well-thought-out step.

The intensity of desire varies with each individual person. Some adoptees may have an apparent disinterest in seeking knowledge about or contact with their biological parents, while others may manifest their interest more compulsively (Blum 1976; Gorman 1975; Sorosky et al. 1978). More significantly, despite the ubiquity of interest in genealogy, very few adoptees actually seek access to identifying adoption information and even fewer seek personal contact with their genetic parents (Feigelman and Silverman 1986; Triseliotis 1980). After reviewing trends in Scotland, England, and Wales, Triseliotis (1984) commented, "Adoptees are not bursting to gain access to their original birth records on reaching the age of eighteen. The fact is that in spite of all the publicity of recent years, access to birth records is still a minority response among adoptees" (p. 49). In Scotland, for example, where birth records have been unsealed since 1925, less than one-tenth of eligible nonrelative adoptees have so far sought access. Likewise, during the six years following the implementation of Section 26 of the Children Act 1975 in England and Wales, those who applied for access to birth records represented approximately 0.3 percent of adopted adults in that country (Triseliotis 1984). Of those applicants, only about one in five had any interest in actually meeting their biological parents. Two other British studies reached a similar conclusion. McWhinnic (1969), for instance, found that many adoptees in her retrospective study simply wished to observe their biological parents without being observed by them. Raynor (1980) interviewed forty-nine adopted children placed by the National Adoption Society and found that 78 percent had no interest whatsoever in meeting their birth families.

The Children's Home Society of California (1977) study noted that 38 percent of the responding adult adoptees admitted to have "rarely" or never thought of searching for their biological parents. During the three-year period following the repeal of adoption secrecy in Minnesota, 332 adult adoptees applied for access; only 12 percent of them made contact with their birth parents (Weidell 1980). Weider (1978) noted in his clinical observation of adoptees that their desire to search was in fact a wish to know about, not to reunite with, the genetic parents. These findings also were corroborated by more recent American studies. In a survey of 129 adoptive parents with children aged eighteen or older, Feigelman and Silverman (1983) reported that while curiosity to know about birth parents was widespread, only 20 percent of adoptees asked to see their birth records and even fewer (4 percent) had already contacted their birth parents. Stein and Hoopes (1985) found that although desire for background information was present among all fifty adoptees they studied, only 32 percent actually wished to search. It is, however, possible that the number of adoptees seeking information about or contact with their birth parents will increase as attitudes toward disclosure relax. A social environment that provides legitimacy to the expression of a desire they might have learned to repress may encourage them to come forward.

Adoptees' Quest and Adoptive Experience

Some experts on adoption hypothesized a correlation between adoptees' quest for origins with their adjustment in adoptive home life (Bernard 1953; McWhinnie 1969; Paton 1954; Raynor 1980). According to them, adoptees who are curious about their genealogy have generally unhappy and poor relationship with their adoptive parents. More recent studies do not support this viewpoint but maintain that while all adoptees generally are interested in learning about their biological heritage irrespective of their adoptive experience, the amount and kind of information sought may differ with each adoptee depending upon the degree of satisfaction with the adoptive relationship. For instance, Triseliotis (1973) noted in his sample of adult adoptees that those with a satisfactory adoptive home life were merely interested in background information, while those dissatisfied with their adoptive family relationships tended to seek reunions with their biological parents. A similar conclusion was reached by a Canadian study that concluded that the quality of adoption experience does not determine adoptees' desire to search for their genetic parents but does influence the expectations and goals they hope to accomplish from reunions. Adoptees with positive adoption experiences are content with genealogical information to complete their identities, while those with poor experience seek a closer relationship with the genetic family (Thompson et al. 1978). In

Great Britain, Raynor (1980) interviewed 105 adoptees (adopted by foster parents and by adoptive parents) and found that of the twenty-three who showed interest in contacting their birth parents, nearly 40 percent were dissatisfied with their adoption.

Adoptees who seek reunion with their birth parents also are distinguished from nonsearchers as being older, poorer in self-esteem (Aumend and Barrett 1984; Feigelman and Silverman 1983; Lamski 1980; Raynor 1980; Sobol and Cardiff 1983), dissatisfied with the amount of background information they receive (Aumend and Barrett 1984; Lamski 1980; Raynor 1980), and troubled with more self-doubts (Lifton 1979). Some evidence suggests that searchers are more emotionally and socially maladjusted and have greater learning difficulties in school than nonsearchers (Feigelman and Silverman 1983). They feel less positively about their adoptive parents and their adoptive status and report being less overall happy in their lives than do nonsearchers (Aumend and Barrett 1984).

Significantly few adoptees seek a lasting relationship with their birth mothers (Burke 1975). Kowal and Schilling (1985) found that only 15 percent of the searchers in their sample were hoping to achieve a sense of belonging or a surrogate family and most of them sought background information to fulfill an existential need. Rosenzweig-Smith (1988) studied (through a mailed questionnaire) the motivations of thirty-one adoptees who contacted Children's Home Society of New Jersey. The author observed that two primary reasons of adoptees for contacting their birth parent were to obtain background information and to "fill a void" (p. 417). A follow-up study of 157 reunions (Sachdev 1988) in Ontario, Canada, confirmed the findings of these studies. He noted that of 107 adult adoptees who met their birth mothers, only one-fifth (19.8 percent) described the relationship as mother-child and almost three-fourths (73.2 percent) felt they were friends or mere acquaintances. However, it is observed that regardless of adoptees' reactions to knowledge of or actual encounter with their birth parents, they seem to have benefited psychologically from learning the identity of their birth parents and of themselves (Simpson et al. 1981; Triseliotis 1973). Burke (1975) reviewed literature on reunion experiences and concluded, "Even those adoptees who do not like what they discover or fail to find a hoped for emotional relationship can benefit from learning the truth" (p. 1203).

Critique of the Literature

A closer examination of the studies reviewed amply suggests that the bulk of them are methodologically flawed and scientifically deficient. Some of these pitfalls are identified as follows:

1. Most literature on identity conflicts among adoptees consists of formulations based on clinical observations of a limited number of cases. Concepts such as "genealogical bewilderment", "identity lacunae", and "roaming phenomenon" used to assess identity concerns are, in most instances, psychoanalytically oriented without empirical validation. Similarly, a number of them (such as Clothier, Costin, Frisk, Hubbard, Kornitzer, Schoenberg) make sweeping generalizations without providing any scientific basis.

2. For the most part, particularly in earlier writings, authors (such as Dusky, Fisher, Lifton, Marcus, Musser, Paton) present anecdotal reports based on their personal experiences as well as those of other individuals. In most instances, their statements are rhetorical and lack scientific validity. It is significant to note that several of these authors are activists in the disclosure movement and advocates of open adoption records.

3. Almost all available research studies are based on a highly select sample of volunteers obtained through media appeals, (such as, Boult, Sorosky, et al., Gawronski et al., Children's Home Society of California, Lamski, Winkler and Keppel), captive clients of social agencies (such as Lion and Gillon, Kowal and Schilling, McWhinnie, Rosenzweig-Smith, Stevenson, Stoneman et al, Thompson, Triseliotis, Weidell), or members of activist groups (such as Feigelman and Silverman, Deykin et al., Kowal and Schilling, Sobol and Cardiff). With such a high selection bias the respondents in these studies can hardly be typical of the members of the adoption triangle in general. Interestingly, several of these studies (such as McWhinnie, Sorosky et al., Triseliotis), notwithstanding their unrepresentativeness, are frequently quoted in the literature as the guiding hand.

4. Not only do these research investigations suffer from faulty sampling design, but also their conclusions are based on extremely small sample size. This is particularly true of the studies that explored the outcome of reunions. For example, Triseliotis used a sample of four in Edinburgh; Stevenson, eleven in British Columbia; Lion et al., seven adoptees in Israel; Thompson, four in Toronto; Simpson et al., ten adoptees in Minnesota; and Depp, ten in Richmond, Virginia.

5. The research studies largely addressed the issues of identity concerns of adoptees and the experience of the parties involved in reunions. They did not explore the specific question concerning attitudes of the members of the adoption rectangle toward unseal-

ing adoption records and the attendant conflicts, or they explored the issue superficially, leaving out the nuances.

6. Finally, most of these studies relied on mailed questionnaires as a method of obtaining information from their respondents. The exceptions were the studies by Raynor, Sorosky et al., Stoneman et al., and Triseliotis. Experts agree that the survey method is highly limited on eliciting information on matters involving feelings, attitudes, and motives (Babbie 1986; Bailey 1987; Selltiz et al. 1981).

However, for all the methodological weaknesses, the studies reviewed in this chapter served to highlight key issues and themes, in particular the psychosocial conflicts inherent in unsealing adoption records.

2
Why the Study and How
It Was Done

I n light of the methodological limitations of earlier research investigations and a lack of systematic examination of the perspectives of the
adoption rectangle on adoption disclosure, this study attempted to
focus on the following important issues. First, it explored in depth the
attitudes of all parties involved—adoptive parents, adopted persons, birth
mothers, and social workers—toward liberalizing current policy on secrecy in adoption. It examined the issue of adoption disclosure from its
myriad facets relevant to the controversy. It included potential conflicts of
rights and interests that might result from changes in sealed-record status.
Second, the study examined attitudes of adoptive parents and birth mothers representing three and two different age groups, respectively, to permit
comparison of changes in attitudes over time. It also compares the perception among adoptees by gender, which very few studies have attempted.
Third, the three hundred sample respondents were selected randomly from
the records of the Department of Social Services in an eastern province of
Canada.[1] Thus, the views expressed in this study are representative and
form a better base for policy consideration than those solicited from
interest or pressure groups or through a task force, the approach employed by some provincial governments in Canada (such as British Columbia, Ontario, and Saskatchewan). The latter approach is likely to
encourage the participation of small but vocal minorities and, possibly,
zealots. Fourth, the information was gathered through personal interviews,
a technique considered more appropriate for complex, emotionally laden
subjects that may not otherwise be accessible through survey methods
(Kinsey et al. 1953; Rubin and Babbie, 1989; Selltiz et al. 1981). Nondirective probes were used to obtain more than simple for-and-against an-

---

[1]To safeguard the pledge of confidentiality given by the department to adoptive parents and
birth parents at adoption, the names of the eligible respondents were revealed to the research
team only after the social workers of the department identified and contacted each respondent and obtained explicit consent to participate in the study.

swers. Fifth, based on opinions expressed by respondents, the study offers guidelines for developing a cohesive policy on request-for-adoption information.[2]

Process of Inquiry

This being the first study of its kind, each process in the research design, from conceptualization of the problem areas to the method of data collection, had to be learned and relearned. At times, we had to invent the wheel, especially in developing strategies for locating and contacting birth mothers.

We gained a wide-angle perspective and captured nuances of the issue by going through several anecdotes and personal accounts of adoptees, birth mothers, and adoptive parents. We examined legal cases, state bills and legislations, task force reports, scientific literature, briefs, and articles by members of the adoption triangle, and attended presentations at national and international adoption conferences. We also sought consultations with experts in the field. The questions that formed the basis of the research inquiry were as follows:

1. What motivates adoptees to seek information about or meet their biological parents?
2. Does the quality of the adoptive experience affect the intensity of the adoptees' quest for their origins?
3. How do adoptive parents react to adoptees' interest in their biological parents?
4. Do birth mothers really wish to forget the child they relinquished or do they wish reunification?
5. Should adoption departments or agencies allow the sharing of identifying/nonidentifying/medical information between adoptees and their birth relatives (that is, birth mother, father, siblings), and between adoptive parents and birth parents?
6. Should information exchange be unrestricted or subject to conditions such as age and consent of the parties involved?
7. How do members of the adoption triangle view the adoption registry system and the role of adoption departments or agencies as counselors and as intermediaries in facilitating reunions between two consenting parties?

---

[2]In a South African follow-up study of eighty-two adult adoptees contacted through mailed questionnaires, Boult (1987) commented in the conclusion of her study, "The results showed that not even the most detailed questionnaire can ever substitute for in-depth interviews. . . ." (p. 217).

For social work personnel a separate set of questions was framed. In addition to questions five through seven, they were asked questions concerning their reactions to new responsibilities and tasks that might arise from changes in the adoption policy:

1. What kinds of new services might be needed to deal with requests from returning adoptees and birth parents?
2. In what way would the new policy affect the staffing need of the department?
3. To what extent is the social work staff receptive to changes in the adoption policy?
4. What kind of difficulties do you foresee that might affect the successful implementation of the new policy?
5. How do you see the role of the School of Social Work (at the provincial university) in facilitating the implementation of the new policy?

The investigation was pursued by a four-pronged research process—sampling, instrumentation, data collection, and data analysis.

Sampling

The study sample comprised a combined total of three hundred respondents from four constituencies—adoptive parents (N=152), birth mothers (N=78), adopted adults (N=53), and social work personnel (N=17). The criteria used to select sample cases in each group are as follows.

Adoptive Parents

Adoptive parents were studied via a time series or historical method by randomly selecting 152 respondents from three periods of adoption—1958, 1968, and 1978—to permit comparison of changes in attitudes, if any, over time. Because there were not enough cases in a given year that met the study criteria, it was necessary to draw sample respondents from the year preceding or following the study year. Thus, the resultant sample size available for analysis was respectively forty-seven, fifty-one, and fifty-four from the adoption periods 1957-59, 1968-69, and 1978. For the purpose of ease, the study years are referred to in this study as 1958, 1968, and 1978.

The sampled parents adopted a child one year old or younger through the provincial Department of Social Services. Four groups of adopting parents were excluded from the sampling frame: native Indian parents,

American service personnel who adopted in the province, relative or foster parents, and those in the northernmost region of the province. Native Indians numbering 3,225 in total population of the province in 1982 were excluded because of the different adoption practice known as 'custom adoption.' Under that system a child is placed with a relative directly by the mother and there is no time requirement for legalizing the adoption. Very rarely has the adoption of children among native Indians gone through the department in the usual way. As in custom adoption, participants in the relative and foster-parent-adoptions have considerable prior knowledge of each other. Thus, the concerns of these parents and those of their adopted children are not the same as that of the parents who adopt an infant under a department policy based on secrecy and confidentiality. The rationale to exclude parents who adopted older children was based on the consideration that a child who is not adopted before his first birthday is likely to have lived in the home of his biological or substitute mother before adoption and thus can carry the memories of his origins.

The northern half of the province was excluded from the study sample for reasons of geographic inaccessibility, small population (about 6 percent of the province's population), and travel costs. It was felt that inclusion in the sample of a few cases from this region would involve time and money highly disproportionate to the gains. Finally, the study was restricted to Anglo-Saxon population with British heritage because of overwhelming representation—over 92 percent—in the province's population (Statistics Canada, 1983, 2).

Three Adoption Periods. The decision to sample three adoption periods was motivated by the consideration that the open records policy would likely arouse greater anxiety and concern among the older adoptive parents (1958 and 1968 adoption year) than among the younger parents (1978 adoption year). Children adopted in the year 1958 had attained at least legal age at follow-up and, as adults, their interest in genealogical information had to be taken seriously. This possibility carries with it a great potential for activating their parents' apprehension and fear of losing the child's love and loyalty. In this sense, the issue of opening sealed records is very real, immediate, and relevant to the 1958 adoptive parents.

The 1968 adoptive parents were also likely to react to the issue with a great deal of alarm. Their adopted children had reached early adolescence at the time of the interviews, the period when identity concerns are intensified. Their heightened interest in self-identity, coupled with other developmental changes during adolescence, such as efforts to assert their independence, could trigger latent anxiety in adoptive parents over the possibility of separation and loss of the adopted child. Thus, for this group also, the issue of open records could have immediate relevancy.

The 1978 adoptive parents were included in the sample to ascertain their reactions to unsealed adoption records even though their children were still very young at the time of the interviews, which somewhat removed them from the issue and its implications. It is assumed that individuals tend to intellectualize the phenomenon and feel impassioned about it to the extent that they are at a distance from the situation of concern. Thus, we anticipated that unlike the 1958 and 1968 parents, the 1978 parents would be more rational in their views and provide a greater degree of objective perspective. We were, however, cognizant that it was not possible to ascertain whether their views could be attributed to their being remote from the problem or their being younger, more educated, and more informed than their older cohorts (that is, 1958 and 1968 parents).

Interview with Adoptive Mothers. It was decided to interview mostly adoptive mothers for the following reasons: First, given the agencies' requirement that the decision to adopt should be mutual between the adopting couples, the literature appears silent on the question of the relative participation of each spouse. However, since concerns around fertility and sterility seem to be more crucial to women it is surmised that the initiative to adopt, to a large extent, comes from the female spouse (Kornitzer 1976).

Second, the research evidence shows that more female than male adoptees seek information about their genealogy. Also, trial interviews with adoptive fathers confirmed our assumption that adoptive mothers were more knowledgeable about the genealogical concerns of their children than the fathers.

Finally, and perhaps more significantly, the ease of seeking adoptive mothers' participation provided additional justification for our decision. We found that mothers were far more cooperative and amenable to the study than were fathers. In addition, fewer mothers than fathers were working outside the home so it made them more accessible for interviews.

However, to ascertain the degree of congruence in the husband-wife views on adoption disclosure and their knowledge of the adoptee's interest in his birth parents, we interviewed twelve adoptive fathers. It was noted that fathers consistently held more conservative positions on the issue than did adoptive mothers, a finding supported by earlier investigators. Feigelman and Silverman (1983), for example, found in their sample of 372 adoptive families who mostly adopted transracially, that mothers were far more favorably disposed to adoptees' rights to know about and have contact with birth parents than were fathers. In a South African study of eighty-two adoptees, Boult (1987) found that adoptive fathers felt more threatened than did their spouses by the prospect of losing their children's love and loyalty. We recognize that these observations are tentative because of the limited sample of fathers and therefore are by no means conclusive; they nevertheless underscore the need for a further research investigation to gain understanding of whose views on the unsealed adoption records are likely to prevail in case of sharp differences.

Birth Mothers

A sample of seventy-eight birth mothers who relinquished their babies for adoption in the years 1968 (N = 39) and 1978 (N = 39) was drawn randomly using the selection processes similar to those followed in selecting the adoptive parents. Birth mothers in the 1958 adoption year were not included because there was little or no identifying information on them, rendering their location extremely difficult. Typical information in department files on birth mothers who relinquished children in 1958 would read: "Mary, the biological mother, placed the child, John, for adoption on 15 December 1958. The child was delivered in St. Clare's Mercy Hospital. Mary was staying with her aunt in town." The records of the department progressively improved in gathering and recording social histories from 1967 on.

There were three reasons why we sampled only birth mothers. First, for the most part, at least in the 1960s and 1970s, the decision to relinquish the child was made by the birth mother, whereas the birth father was involved only peripherally if at all. Historically, adoption agencies and departments have sought the birth mother's consent to adoption and regard her as one of the principals in the adoption decree. This practice was recently upheld by the Divisional Court of Ontario, which ruled that "casual fornicators" do not qualify as parents for the purpose of adoption, thus affirming that adoption agencies are under no obligation to inform the birth father or even get his consent (The Globe and Mail, April 2, 1988). Second, agency records generally contain information on birth mothers but are highly deficient on birth fathers. This leaves the most likely option for the searching adoptee to find his birth father through the birth mother. Third, the literature shows that in most cases, interested adoptees first search out their birth mothers before they meet other birth relatives.

Adoptees

Fifty-three adoptees who were at least nineteen years old, the age of majority in the province of the study, were contacted through the 1958 adoptive parents, the only feasible source to draw a random sample of adoptees. Forty-seven parents who participated in the study were asked their permission to contact their adult son or daughter. We made the request at the termination of the interview in the hope that the parent had understood the nature of the study and that a rapport had been established, optimizing the likelihood of cooperation. This approach also signified to them that we did not wish to contact their child surreptitiously. Direct contact with adopted persons was also undesirable because we did not know if they had been told of their adoptive status. The final decision to participate in the study rested with the adoptee, notwithstanding the parents' permission.

In addition to forty-seven parents who were involved in the study, we approached twelve additional 1958 adoptive parents in the sampling frame for permission to interview their children to complete the required sample size of 53. These parents were not interviewed; however, we explained the purpose and nature of the study to gain their cooperation.

More than four-fifths (82.2 percent) of the adoptive parents gave permission for contact with their adopted children. Of the sixteen parents (17.8 percent) who did not give permission, eleven were antagonistic to the study and refused to be interviewed. The remaining five parents who agreed to be interviewed, but refused permission for their adopted child, said the child had never shown any interest in the genetic parents and the discussion on the subject might ignite the child's curiosity. This mother typified their discomfort:

> I wouldn't want Linda[3] to be asked to take part in this study because she's never mentioned her mother or father and I wouldn't want her to start off fresh thinking of these things. As far as she's concerned I'm her mother and Keith's her father and I would like it to stay that way.

Interestingly, four of these parents were themselves opposed to unsealed records, while one parent expressed weak support for it. One confided in us her efforts to suppress her children's desire ever to gain information about or to make contact with birth parents.

> We told our adopted children that the information was sealed and could never be opened. Since then they never showed any interest.

We had no way of verifying these mothers' claims. In one instance, however, our hunch about the discrepancy between adoptive mothers' perception and the adoptee's interest was confirmed unwittingly when during the interview with the mother, her adopted son unexpectedly arrived home and overheard the exchange. He told the interviewer he had

---

[3]The real names are concealed in order to protect the identity of the respondents.

long been very curious about his genetic parents and volunteered to take part in this study. The encounter caused great embarrassment to the adoptive mother and some discomfort to the interviewer.

Adoption Workers

Social workers' bias in the assessment of adoptive parents has been well documented in studies on the selection process. These studies note a great disparity in the workers' decisions on applicants' suitability as parents not only across agencies but also within a given agency (Brieland 1984). Workers are influenced in the decision making by their attitudes toward certain classes of applicants, by their own concept of family, and values regarding parenting standards (Bradly 1966; Brieland 1959; Brown 1980). In recognition of social workers' potential influence on policy implementation it was considered desirable to examine the attitudes and perceptions of this fourth element in the adoption equation. We wanted to ascertain whether social work personnel responsible for policy making, as well as those working on the frontline, were receptive to more openness in adoption.

In the four regional offices of the provincial Department of Social Services there were about thirty workers who, for at least three years of their professional career, had been involved in adoption services. Of those, eleven adoption workers were selected to be interviewed in the two major regions of the province. In addition, we interviewed the three most senior officials having policy formulation and managerial responsibilities (minister, deputy minister, and assistant deputy minister of Social Services) and three administrators (child welfare director, assistant child welfare director, and adoption coordinator). In short a total of seventeen social work personnel were interviewed.

Determination of Sample Size

Although there was generally no rational way to determine the sample size for the study, our decision was not entirely arbitrary. Four considerations guided the sample size. First, there is some agreement among statisticians that $N \geq 30$ represents a cut-off point between small and large samples. That is, a randomly selected sample size of thirty and more tends to approximate normality of distribution (Blalock 1960; Champion 1970). More specifically, since each subsample in the study is as large or larger than the requisite thirty, and since the sample drawn will be essentially random, it should be possible to repose a degree of confidence in the generalizations of the study findings. Second, we also wanted to make sure that an adequate number of cases was available for subdivision into different response categories. Thus, we decided to draw a sample some-what larger than thirty for each cohort. Third, since the total number of adoptions completed in each study year varied, showing a steady increase from 1958 to 1978, it was considered desirable that our sample size for each group of adoptive parents reflect the variability of the population. Thus, our random sampling is disproportionate in that a larger number of cases was sampled from 1978 adoption year than from the 1968 or 1958 adoption year. Fourth, the maximum limit on the sample size was deter-mined by the time factor. That is, once past the minimum number needed, we continued to sample from the sampling frames and interviewed cases until June 30, 1985, the cut-off point for the data collection phase.

In recapitulation, the study sample is composed of three subsamples totaling 152 adoptive parents from three adoption periods—1958, 1968, 1978; two subgroups of birth mothers from two adoption periods—1968, 1978—totaling seventy-eight; and fifty-three adult adoptees and seventeen social services personnel, thus providing three hundred respondents for this study. Table 2–1 summarizes the sampling scheme for the four groups.

An examination of table 2–1 reveals the following important facets of the sampling outcome. First, we were able to locate and interview more than two-thirds (67.3 percent) of the eligible adoptive parents despite that the department had had no contact with them since they adopted a child some twenty-five years previously. Only eighteen parents (8 percent) were not identified. Second, it was not surprising that we lost to follow-up some one-third (35.9 percent) of the birth mothers who had either moved out of the province (17.6 percent) or who could not be identified (18.3 percent). This observation is significant given the secrecy and stigma asso-ciated with out-of-wedlock births in the 1960s, compelling many unwed mothers to hide. Once they married, which many of them did subsequent to relinquishment, identification became even more difficult because of new names. Two birth mothers were located but were not interviewed because contact with them was considered risky in view of the circum-stances of the pregnancy—rape in one case and psychiatric problems in the other. Third, we were also pleased with the rate of contact with adoptees, which was 59 percent of the potential cases, given that their availability to the study was contingent upon permission of the 1958 parents. Only a little over one-tenth (12.2 percent) could not be identified.

We lost potential respondents (13.7 percent adoptive parents; 17.6 percent birth mothers; 5.5 percent adoptees) mainly through moves out of the province. This was expected, however, in a province where a de-pressed economy and high unemployment rates force many people to leave each year in search of job opportunities in mainland Canada and the United States.

Table 2–1
Summary of Respondents Obtained and Number of Interviews Completed

	Adoptive Parents				Birth Mothers			Adoptees 1957-59	Social Work Personnel
	1957-59	1958-69	1978	Total	1957-69	1977-78	Total		
	(1958)	(1968)	(1978)		(1968)	(1978)		(1957-59)	
Total number of cases that met study criteria	90	99	86	275	99	86	185	90	30
Cases located and interviewed	48	50	54	152 [67.3%]	39	39	78 [51%]	53 [59%]	17
Cases not interviewed Reasons:									
–Moved out of province	17	8	6	31 [13.7%]	20	7	27 [17.6%]	5 [5.5%]	—
–Address unknown	11	7	—	18 [8.0%]	20	8	28 [18.3%]	11 [12.2%]	—
–Problem cases	—	—	1*	1 [0.4%]	2**	—	2 [1.3%]	—	—
–Deceased	3	—	—	3 [1.3%]	—	—	—	—	—
–Refusal	11	6	4	21 [9.3%]	6	12	18 [11.8%]	21***	—
Not needed for study and not interviewed due to time limitation	—	28	21	49	12	20	32	—	13

* = Psychiatric problem
** = 1 = Rape case; 1 = psychiatric problem
*** = 11 = Adoptive parents refused to participate in study
5 = Adoptive parents refused permission
5 = Adoptees refused to participate

A far more significant facet of the sampling outcome, in our view, was the low rate of refusal among the eligible adoptive parents and birth mothers, which was less then 10 percent and 12 percent respectively. Only five adoptees declined our invitation to participate. The chief reason given by more than half the adoptive parents was that they feared the study might stimulate policy changes. This was typified by this comment by a 1958 adoptive mother: "There is nothing wrong with the way the things are; we don't want to open a can of worms." Four 1968 adoptive parents, or one-fifth, were afraid that knowledge of their participation might precipitate genealogical curiosity among their adopted children. One 1968 adoptive father did not allow his spouse to participate because he was not convinced of our guarantees of confidentiality. Four 1958 adoptive mothers said they were too old to withstand the strain of the interview and another two felt they would be embarrassed by their inability to answer questions intelligently.

Of the birth mothers who refused to participate in the study, ten (eight 1978 and two 1968 birth mothers) were concerned that the interview would dredge up painful memories of the child and the adoption. Four birth mothers were afraid of inadvertent discovery by their husbands or boyfriends of their pregnancy before marriage and another four said their male partners were opposed to their participation, fearing the interview would stir up their past. The reasons advanced by unconsenting adoptees included their desire to avoid the subject ("I do not want to talk about my adoption and I'm happy with my adoptive parents"); lack of interest in genealogical background ("I never thought of my biological parents"), or the possibilities of being misunderstood by the adoptive parents ("It would hurt my mom").

Sample Bias

To ascertain the degree of sample bias, we compared the characteristics of the eligible cases unavailable to the study with those of the sample obtained and noted that both groups did not differ on age, income, education, and sex of the adopted child. However, our sample of adoptees was weighted in favor of females (N = 38) with a ratio of five females to two male adoptees (N = 15). This contrasts with a ratio of three females to two male infants adopted through the department in 1958-59. The disproportionately low representation of male adoptees could be attributed to several factors, chief among them being their moves out of the province because of poor job opportunities. We believe any possibility of sampling bias is offset by the larger-than-required sample size, which almost approximated the population size, the rich quality of data, the variability in responses obtained, and the candor of the respondents. However, one caveat is in order. With attitudes toward adoption disclosure changing in response to societal values and the increased exposure to the issue, it would be unrealistic for any study of the adoption triad to claim broad generalizations of its findings, especially to future participants.

We have every reason to feel satisfied with the rate of identification of eligible cases and their participation in the study as it compares well with the rates achieved in earlier follow-up studies in adoption. For example, two interview studies that followed up members of the adoption triad after a twenty-one to thirty year hiatus, a period comparable to this study, lost over 40 percent of the potential respondents through moves, lack of identification, or refusal (Jaffee and Fanshel 1970; Raynor 1980). Sample attrition was just as high—fourteen to forty-five percent—even in studies involving a shorter time interval, from eighteen months (MacDonnell 1981) to three years (Grow and Shapiro 1974). Similarly, of 204 families contacted seven years after they had adopted transracially, 35 percent were not available to the study conducted by Simon and Altstein (1981) either because they could not be reached or they refused to participate. Weidell (1980) surveyed the profile of adult adoptees who filed requests with the Minnesota Department of Public Welfare for access to their original birth certificates under the revised policy enacted in 1977. She reported that during the first two years, between 1977 and 1979, the department was unsuccessful in locating and identifying 37 percent of birth mothers.

The Province's Unique Sociocultural Conditions

In view of the low response rate achieved by earlier investigators, we feel convinced that our follow-up success was attributable to two main factors. First, the province, with its unique overlapping network characterized by strong institutional kinship and socioculturally congruent neighborhood, made it possible to locate even the most obscure respondents. Families have strong ties to church and group membership and extensive social connectedness, which make them less mobile. Because of their unassuming and charitable nature, the people of this province place almost instant trust in strangers and often do not hesitate to confide in them. One interviewer who traveled extensively throughout the province to locate and identify eligible respondents recorded this in her logbook:

> Usually few or no questions were asked about my identity or my reasons for checking names and addresses. People seemed quite free in giving even the most personal information about others when requested.

Another interviewer related a similar experience during her efforts to locate a 1978 adoptive parent.

I called similar names in the telephone directory, but every time I reached the wrong party. Finally I called the adoptive father's brother, who told me the adoptive parents number was unlisted but he did not remember it. He, however, suggested that I call his mother, who unreservedly gave me the adoptive parents' phone number without wondering why I wanted to reach her son.

Another interviewer made a similar observation:

I visited the last known address for a 1959 adoptive parent, but no one was home. I then inquired from the next-door neighbor. This middle-aged woman asked me in and volunteered a whole lot of information, without prompting, regarding the adoptive mother's involvement with another man, her subsequent divorce, and her daughter's illegitimate pregnancy. The adoptive mother had since moved to a city on the West Coast.

Convinced of the unique sociocultural situations of this province as a significant desiderata for locating potential respondents, we believe a similar study conducted in a large urban metropolis may not yield as satisfactory follow-up outcomes.

Second, while the social connectedness and close-knit nature of the locale greatly facilitated tracking of the selected respondents, it was the persistent and inexorable efforts of the interviewers that catalyzed the follow-up outcomes. The following excerpts from the logbook of the interviewers illustrate the amount of effort exerted to minimize sample attrition.

There was no phone in the birth mother's home. I drove two hours to contact her only to discover that she had moved to Montreal. A month later I learned that she had come back and was living in the area. I finally succeeded in making contact with her. She agreed to participate but was not in a position to be available for an interview because she needed someone to tend her two small children. I made an arrangement with a friend of mine who babysat them while I completed the interview.

There was no listing for the last known address of this 1958 adoptive parent but the telephone directory had several—about two dozen— similar names. I called all of them but none turned up the right party. I called the province Teachers Association (R was once employed as a teacher), but without success. Finally, I called one of their references who knew where Mrs. M. lived. I called but reached the adoptive father who, after knowing my identity and the purpose of my call, became highly upset and abusive and accused me of being intrusive. I kept my cool and assured him of the project's confidentiality. He then agreed for me to visit and explain to them the purpose of the study, which I did. The adoptive mother apologized for her husband's outburst. She agreed to an interview.

Instrumentation

Three separate interview schedules were prepared and presented for adoptive parents, birth mothers, and adoptees. Each schedule comprised core questions on adoption disclosure, uniformly asked of all respondents. The schedules differed from each other in terms of specific questions relevant to a particular group. For example, the adoptive parents' schedule contained a set of questions to examine their relationship with the adopted child and their perceptions of and reactions to the child's interest in the birth family. The birth mothers' schedule asked questions about the decision regarding relinquishment and postplacement experiences. The adoptees' schedule contained questions on their relationship with adoptive parents during growing up, reaction to adoptive status, interest in learning about or meeting with birth parents, and perception of adoptive parents' reactions.

The schedules combined open-ended and fixed alternative questions totaling 150 items and subitems to permit both a spontaneous response and specific uniform information. The open-ended questions were also intended to allow free and full response to questions dealing with feelings, perceptions, and motivations. To lead the respondent to answer more fully and with greater specificity, the schedules contained nondirective probe questions. The questions were worded in a manner that more nearly approached that of social conversation and exchange of information rather than a question-answer process. A detailed instruction sheet containing rules and directions for interviewers on the techniques of asking questions and on nondirective probes was also developed.

The schedules were pretested using a convenience sample of five to seven cases in each of the four groups, but those having similar characteristics to the respondents in the final study. Flaws such as ambiguously worded or double-barreled questions, uncommon terms, unclear or redundant questions, confusing question order, and inadequate response categories were identified. Respondents were asked to provide a critical analysis of all aspects of the schedule, including their understanding of the various questions and any omissions.

Data Collection

Data collection proceeded in three phases: (a) recruitment and training of interviewers; (b) locating and identifying eligible respondents; and (c) information gathering.

A. Recruitment and Training of Interviewers

Six experienced and professionally trained female social workers were selected from among those highly recommended by the Department of Social Services. It was felt that tracing of prospective respondents, particularly birth mothers, would involve "detective" work, and a woman interviewer would raise less suspicion and inquisition. Following on our conviction that cooperation of the respondents and elicitation of valid information hinged upon trained and skillful interviewers, the workers were given six weeks of training in the art of in-depth research interviewing, gathering reliable information, and coding responses. Reliability checks and ways of dealing with potential problems during the search procedures were dealt with through the use of role plays and simulated interviews with facsimile respondents. Finally, interviews with real respondents during the pretest were monitored and used for learning purposes.

B. Locating Respondents

Any study involving the follow-up of respondents who are not captive faces the difficult task of locating and identifying its sample. But the task of location in this study was more onerous and arduous because of elapsed time—up to twenty years—since respondents' last contact with the department. Marriage, remarriage, death, and movement of potential respondents out of the community made their identification extremely difficult. The social stigma associated with out-of-wedlock births, at least in the 1960s, put an extra burden on us to safeguard the anonymity of birth mothers. This required us to take circuitous routes. Further, earlier records of the department contained scant identifying information on adoptive and birth parents, which provided little helpful search avenues. It was not uncommon to find case histories on the 1958 or 1968 parents with nonspecific details such as "Mr. & Mrs. M. have four siblings (but no names and addresses) and Mr. M. was working as a carpenter" (but no name of the employer) or "Mary (birth mother) is staying with relatives until the delivery and placement of the child." The department record keeping improved considerably in the later years, making the location of 1978 parents relatively easier.

The key principles that guided our search efforts were persistence, perseverance, ingenuity, presence of mind, and a bit of humor. We employed all imaginable avenues, including the respondent's relatives, persons with similar surnames in the community, former employers, neighbors, and personal references to locate respondents. At times we followed trails to other provinces. To avoid inadvertent breach of confidentiality, our exploratory contact, which in most instances was via a telephone call, was extremely brief and nonspecific. Under no circumstances did we divulge our identity, the purpose of the call, or any reference to adoption unless we confirmed the identity of the person called. If the responding party happened to be someone other than the one being sought and insisted on the interviewer's identity and the purpose of the call, the interviewer would simply give her first name and state that she was a "friend," "acquaintance," "fellow employee," or "former school mate," depending on the background information of the respondent. This technique proved effective in locating the 1968 or 1978 adoptive mothers. However, to approach the potential 1958 adoptive mothers who were in their sixties or older, the interviewer could not possibly pose herself a "friend" or a "fellow employee" because of age difference without raising serious suspicion. Instead, she feigned that she was visiting from the mainland and the adopting couples were old friends of her parents who had lost contact with them over the years; she dutifully promised her mother that during her visit to this province she would try to find out their whereabouts so that her mother could write to her "friend."

These were some of the reasons we invented to avoid disclosure of our identity. To our great relief not once were our reasons challenged, nor were we forced into a position necessitating the revelation of our identity to the person other than the respondent. We had learned during the trial phase that the chances of successful contact were optimal if adoptive mothers were first approached, since fathers tended to subject us to more intensive scrutiny. It was true that adoptive mothers invariably discussed our invitation with their husbands before agreeing to an interview.

In the location of birth mothers, the most frequent search avenues used were their mothers and siblings. Since these birth mothers were almost the same age as the interviewers, they were inquired about using their first names and the interviewer posed as the birth mother's "high school mate" or a "fellow employee" as appropriate. In the case of a 1968 birth mother (most were married) it would seem odd and perhaps incredulous if the "friend" or the "fellow employee" had no knowledge of her marriage. To make the story more credible, the interviewer would pretend astonishment and offer an excuse for her ignorance: "I had been away for the past twelve years and had not been home for a while so I didn't know that she got married. I was in the area and wanted to see my 'friend' before I left the province again." In the event the interviewer was faced with an inquisitive relative who insisted on a full name she would disengage herself by saying she did not want to ruin the surprise for her "friend." In most instances, the relative furnished the whereabouts of the birth mother and offered unsolicited additional background information. It should be pointed out that our respondents were told about the artifice and strategy we employed in locating them. They appreciated our efforts to protect the unwarranted disclosure of their identity and the purpose of our approach. In a few cases our exploratory contact was through a visit to neighbors at the last known address of the respondent. This was done when telephone contact was not feasible and all other search avenues had been exhausted. We found the neighbors incredibly generous in offering helpful leads, which resulted in the identification of 10 percent of the cases. In some instances, neighbors invited interviewers in and gave unsolicited, detailed information about the family and the marital history of the potential respondent.

Respondents Identified. Once the respondent was located and identified, the interviewer made sure she or he was free to talk before broaching the purpose of the call. She also said she had a personal letter addressed to the respondent from the deputy minister of Social Services explaining the raison d'etre of the study. The letter was intended to establish authenticity of the interviewer and legitimacy of the research project. Some adoptive parents asked the interviewer to call back when their children were in school. Several birth mothers wanted to be reached by phone at work or at their parents' home.

The interviewer offered minimum information about the study on the phone, but sought to meet the respondent using what Bailey (1987) calls "positive approach," which does not ask the respondent's permission to drop in, an approach analogous to a door salesman's inquiry. At times, the interviewer was confronted with serial cancellation of appointments, but she did not give up until it became clear there was no way to overcome the respondent's resistance.

The initial reaction of birth mothers to our telephone contact was predictably one of shock and bewilderment. Some suspected something ominous had happened to the relinquished child; others feared their child was seeking contact with them. Adoptive parents reacted with less anxiety but were generally apprehensive about the possibility that the biological mother or Parent Finders (a national search and support group) acting on her behalf was attempting to seek contact with the child.

Face-to-Face Contact. We found that a personal meeting with respondents proved more effective than a plea on the phone for eliciting their participation. The meeting allowed us to fully explain the purpose of the study and to assuage any concerns. It also enabled the interviewer to reinforce the legitimacy of her identity and present the personalized letter from the deputy minister urging participation. The birth mothers' resistance to participation stemmed from their primary concern for anonymity, as they feared we might discuss the study findings in the media and divulge their identity. They referred to the growing number of such programs on television in recent years featuring members of the adoption triad. They also expressed concern that the interview would activate painful memories about the pregnancy and the child, which they had tried to suppress all these years.

Adoptive parents' concerns did not relate so much to the disclosure of their identity as it did to their children's becoming aware of their views on the issue, especially if they were opposed to access of adoption information. While most adoptive parents, especially younger ones, were appreciative of the opportunity to express their views on this important policy decision, they rather wished the issue had never surfaced for debate. Some feared the study might recommend changes in the current sealed-record status. The face-to-face approach enabled us to cut through a respondent's resistance and change the initial negative or "I'm not sure" reply to consent to participate. This occurred in more than one-third of the cases. The following excerpt from the logbook of one interviewer illustrates the efficacy of our approach.

> At my persistent urging Mrs. H., a 1968 adoptive mother, finally agreed to see me at her house. After I arrived, I met Mr. H. and soon realized that both were relentlessly against the study. Their objections ranged from the poor rationale and dubious utility of the study to their concern for confidentiality. After two and one half hours of discussion Mr. H. was convinced that the department was making a right choice in soliciting adoptive parents' views on an important issue such as this and they would like to be a part of the study.

Selected Problems during Locating Phase. Although the training program helped prepare interviewers to anticipate every conceivable problematic and sensitive situation and how to deal with it, a few situations were not predicted. They could have proved calamitous for the project had it not been for the presence of mind of the interviewers. Some examples:

> I phoned the sister-in-law of 1958 adoptive parents and said that I was looking for Mr. & Mrs. T, who were good friends of my parents. She told me the T's had died more than six years ago and was astonished that my parents wouldn't know about it. I was embarrassed but said the T's and my parents had lost contact with each other since they moved out of the province years ago. She seemed satisfied with my explanation and I terminated the conversation after expressing my sympathy.

> Mrs. B's (a 1968 adoptive mother) phone had been disconnected since my last conversation with her. So I went to her house at the address shown in the file to make an appointment for the interview. To my dismay Mr. & Mrs. B had moved and the guys who had rented the place were drunk. When I asked them about the B's they started being uncivil and grossly indecent. I managed to get out, and was able to obtain the new address of the B's.

> Mrs. S (a 1968 adoptive mother) agreed that I could visit her to explain the purpose of the study. When I arrived I was surprised to see Mr. S at

home. He was steaming in anger and went into a rage and became abusive. He yelled and shouted that I did not have respect for the adoptive parents' rights of confidentiality. He accused that the study was instituted for political motives and threatened that he would lodge a complaint to the Premier and write to local newspapers about the department's insensitivity toward confidentiality. I kept my cool and managed to calm him down. I was able to make him understand the purpose of the study and the opportunity it presents to adoptive parents to have their input. Mr. S apologized for his outburst and proceeded to show me pictures of his adopted children. Mr. and Mrs. S promised they would think it over. Although they decided against participation in the study, Mr. S at least did not make good on his threat. It was a big relief.

C. Gathering of Data

Information was gathered by face-to-face, in-depth interviews using a semistructured and thoroughly pretested interview schedule. The majority of interviews with adoptive parents were conducted in their own homes and most frequently when their children were in school, in bed, or out of the home. This was done to avoid detection of their parents' participation in the study or their views on the issue. Unlike adoptive parents, most birth mothers elected to be interviewed outside their homes, preferably in the office, to avoid detection by their friends and relatives. A few birth mothers were interviewed in a restaurant, a car, or in the interviewer's home. Adoptees were interviewed generally in their homes or at the university office. Each interview took two and one half to three hours in length.

One of the approaches that proved effective in minimizing "don't know" responses was to ask respondents to tune in to the situation or the person's feelings. The instruction sheet proved an effective measure to promote greater uniformity among interviewers in asking questions. Respondents, especially older adoptive parents, found helpful the question cards with multiple alternatives or situations. They could examine all alternatives at once in their relative strength as many times as they wished before selecting the most appropriate answer.

To safeguard against misrepresentation, incomplete reporting, or distortion of the data, all interviews were unobtrusively recorded verbatim by a portable tape recorder and a tiny microphone placed out of view to avoid distraction. Only five respondents resisted the use of a tape recorder. Interestingly, all five respondents refused the same interviewer to tape record interviews. When we found that it was the same interviewer who had expressed serious reservations during the training session about using a recording device, we felt convinced that the respondents' refusal was not caused by their uneasiness but probably by the interviewer's personal bias. The length and richness of the information obtained show that the tape recording had little or very transient effect on the respondents. Only three 1958 adoptive mothers said they were conscious of the tape recorder throughout the interview. "I forgot all about it shortly after we began talking" or "I didn't even know it was there," was the typical comment made by the rest of the respondents. That many respondents were able to display their emotions with utmost candor and a majority of birth mothers wept during the recall of their experiences provides further evidence that the tape recorder did not interfere with spontaneity and forthrightness of their responses.

In addition to the accurate recording of the responses, the interview tapes were also of great value in monitoring data collection, contingency cleaning, and assessing the reliability of the information received and coded. Once the interview was completed, the interviewer replayed the tape and converted the discursive interview material in a codebook providing preestablished categories. The author then compared the transcripts of each interview with the completed codebook and noted such things as inconsistencies and improper categorization. The author also listened to every second interview tape to check for emphasis, omissions, and faulty question wording. In 81.2 percent of the categorized items there was complete concurrence between the interviewer/coder and the author. Differences were resolved by discussion with the interviewer and if necessary by listening to the tape with an independent interviewer. Four adoptive mothers and one adoptee were contacted again to clarify their answers. All five respondents, to our pleasant surprise, were appreciative of the fact that we were so meticulous and thorough in reporting their responses.

Data Analysis

Data are presented using frequencies and percentages. We believe, however, that numbers do not tell the whole story; that is, they do not capture the nuances of attitudes, feelings, and perceptions. Therefore, to interpret the responses fully, we went beyond the simple for-and-against answers and explored the respondents' underlying motives. To highlight certain positions or attitudes, vignettes from the respondents' statements were used.

Still, percentages were used to demonstrate differences between groups and within subgroups. But to determine whether the difference was significant and did not occur by chance, it was necessary to calculate the sampling error associated with the response. For responses expressed in percentages, the sampling error for a simple random sample is represented

$$D = 1.96 \sqrt{\frac{PQ}{n} \left(\frac{1\text{-}n}{N}\right)}$$

Where D = percent sampling error
   PQ = percentages in the two response categories, agree/disagree
   n = sample size
   N = population size
   1.96 = standard score corresponding to the .95 level of confidence

The error may be interpreted as meaning that the percentage response for the entire population would be expected to be within plus or minus D of the sample value, ninety-five times out of one hundred. For example, if D is 5 percent for a given sample, we can say with 95 percent confidence that the population value will lie within plus or minus 5 percent of the sample value presented in a table of data. It should be noted that the percent errors were calculated using the total number of cases that met the study criteria as the population size, N, as shown in table 2–1. As an illustration, the sampling error within which the response of the entire population of 275 adoptive parents on the given question is likely to deviate from the percentage response of the sample adoptive parents in table 4–1 is ± 4.9 percent.

Furthermore, for comparison of responses between two or more groups on a single response category, agree/agree, or disagree/disagree, the percent error was expressed by the formula.

$$D_1 - D_2 = \sqrt{D_1^2 + D_2^2}$$

Where $D_1 - D_2$ = percent error between two groups on a similar response category, agree/agree; disagree/disagree

   D_1^2 = sampling error in group 1
   D_2^2 = sample error in group 2

For example, the sampling error at 95 percent confidence level for the adoptive parents' and birth mothers' responses on a response category, agree/agree in table 4–1, is ± 7.3 percent.

Given the constraints of time and resources and the sensitivity of the subject area, every conceivable effort was made to promote the randomness of the samples. Also, all possible measures were taken to improve the reliability and validity of the information gathered. It is hoped readers will place their confidence in the study findings.

Summary and Conclusion

The study was undertaken to examine the attitudes of all parties involved in the adoption—adoptive parents, adopted adults, birth mothers, and social workers—toward liberalizing current policy on secrecy in adoption.

It also explored potential conflicts of rights and interests that might result from the changes in sealed-record statutes. The purpose was to generate policy guidelines for dealing with requests from returning adoptees and birth parents for adoption information. The study, the first of its kind, involved three hundred randomly selected adoptive parents (N=152), birth mothers (N=78), adoptees (N=53), and adoption personnel (N=17) from the records of the provincial Department of Social Services in an eastern province of Canada. The sample parents were Anglo-Saxons who adopted a child one year old or younger through the department. Adoptions by relatives or by foster parents were excluded from the study because unlike nonrelative adoptions, the participants in these adoptions have considerable prior knowledge of each other.

Adoptive parents and birth mothers were studied via a time series or historical method by selecting respondents from three different adoption periods: 1958, 1968, and 1978. The selection of birth mothers was confined to two adoption periods, 1968 and 1978, because little or no identifying information was available on the birth mothers who relinquished children in the year 1958. This selection procedure permitted comparison of changes in attitudes, if any, over time. It was assumed that the open-records policy was likely to arouse greater anxiety and concern among older adoptive parents than among the younger parents. The children of adoptive parents in the 1958 adoption period had attained adulthood at the time of the study. Their interest in genealogical information was likely to activate among adoptive parents a fear of losing their allegiance. Children adopted in 1968 had reached adolescence, the period when identity concerns are intensified, which could trigger latent anxiety in adoptive parents. By contrast, 1978 adoptive parents were far removed from the issue and its implications since their children were still very young at the time of the interviews (1984-85) and thus would tend to intellectualize the phenomenon.

Adoptive mothers were mostly interviewed because of their greater knowledge of the adopted child's genealogical concerns and, most importantly, their greater accessibility to interviews than that of adoptive fathers. Twelve fathers, however, were randomly selected and interviewed to ascertain the degree of congruence in the husband-wife views. It was noted that fathers consistently held more conservative positions on the adoption disclosure policy than did their spouses. Only birth mothers were sampled for three reasons: they consented to the adoption decree, adoptees prefer establishing contact with the birth mother before they contact the birth father, and there was virtually no information available in the department's records on birth fathers.

Adoptees, who were at least nineteen years old, were contacted through the 1958 adoptive parents and interviewed. Adoption personnel included eleven social workers in adoption services in the four regional offices of the Provincial Department of Social Services and six senior officials and administrators involved in policy making.

Given the sensitive nature of the subject, the secrecy surrounding out-of-wedlock births in the 1960s, and the protracted time interval for follow-ups extending over twenty-five years, the rate of contact with the potential respondents was very high compared to earlier follow-up studies in adoption. Of the eligible respondents, fewer than twelve percent of adoptive parents, one-tenth of birth mothers, and six percent adoptees refused to participate. The high response rate was largely attributed to persistent and imaginative search efforts and intensive training of the female interviewers. At times, in our efforts to trace eligible respondents, we followed trails to other provinces in the country. A personalized letter from the deputy minister of Social Services explaining the raison d'etre of the study and urging cooperation also proved helpful in eliciting the participation of the respondents.

The information was gathered through in-depth interviews using a semistructured interview schedules containing 150 question items and sub-items. All interviews were tape-recorded and lasted about two and one-half to three hours. The discursive interview material was converted in a code book providing preestablished categories. There was complete concurrence in 81.2 percent of the categorized items between the interviewer/coder and the author. Differences in the 19 percent of the coded items were resolved by discussion with the interviewer and if necessary with an independent rater.

3
About the Samples

This chapter provides a brief sociodemographic profile of the adoptive parents, birth mothers, and adoptees who form the study population as a prelude to our examination of their views on the issue of opening adoption records.

Adoptive Parents

The 1958 parents were less homogeneous in sociodemographic characteristics than were the 1968 and 1978 parents (see table 3–1). The wide variability of the 1958 parents was attributed largely to the flexible and liberal selection criteria employed by the Department of Social Services in the 1950s and early 1960s. As the ratio of adoptive applicants to available white nonhandicapped infants tipped in favor of infants available for adoption in the 1970s, the department followed a more strict recruitment policy, which resulted in the selection of a more homogeneous population of parents. Thus, we see that the 1958 adoptive mothers in our sample had a wider age range (twenty-one to forty-nine years) at the time of adoption than did the 1968 and 1978 mothers, who were between twenty-one to thirty-nine years at adoption. In other words, the 1968 1978 mothers were younger, with more than one-half being under thirty, compared with the 1958 mothers, who represented a little over one-third (37.8 percent) in that category. Regarding their age at the interview, the three groups of adoptive mothers represented the modal age between fifty-three to sixty-four years (1958); forty-one to forty-six years (1968); and under thirty-five years (1978). Five 1958 adoptive mothers were sixty-five years and older.

Our adoptive families were not atypical with regard to the number of children they had either through adoption or born naturally to them. Consistent with the norm of large family size in the study province, at least up until 1970s, all three groups had up to five living children each;

Table 3–1
Selected Demographic Characteristics of Adoptive Parents
(percentages)

Characteristics	N =	1958 (45)	1968 (46)	1978 (49)	All Mothers (140)
Age at Adoption*					
Younger than 25		17.8	15.2	2.1	11.4
25–29		20.0	39.1	57.1	39.3
30–34		24.4	23.9	24.5	24.4
35–39		26.7	21.8	16.3	21.4
40–44		8.9			2.8
45–49		2.2			0.7
Age at Interview*					
Younger than 35		-	4.3	1.2	22.9
35–40		4.4	26.1	30.6	20.7
41–46		6.7	47.8	8.2	20.7
47–52		15.5	19.6	–	11.4
53–58		33.3	2.2	–	11.4
59–64		29.0	–	–	9.3
65 +		11.1	–	–	3.6
Number of Living Children	N =	(48)	(50)	(54)	(152)
1–2		62.5	58.0	77.8	66.4
3–5		35.5	38.0	22.2	31.6
6–8		–	4.0	–	1.3
9 +		2.1	–	–	0.7
Number of Biological Children					
0		72.9	54.0	70.4	65.8
1–2		18.7	36.0	22.2	25.6
3–5		6.3	10.0	7.4	7.9
9		2.1	–	–	0.7
Number of Adopted Children					
1		47.9	40.0	64.8	51.3
2		33.3	52.0	27.8	37.5
3		18.8	6.0	7.4	10.5
4		–	2.0	–	0.7
Educational Status Eighth grade or less	N =	(45) 31.3 [32.6]**	(46) 12.0 [16.0]	(49) 11.1 [11.1]	
Some high school or completed high school		52.1 [45.7]	48.0 [28.0]	35.2 [24.1]	
Technical training but not high school		– [–]	– [2.0]	1.9 [1.9]	

Table 3–1
Selected Demographic Characteristics of Adoptive Parents (Cont.)
(percentages)

Characteristics	N =	1958 (45)	1968 (46)	1978 (49)	All Mothers (140)
Technical training after high school		6.3 [10.9]	16.0 [20.0]	22.2 [29.6]	
Some university or university graduate		10.4 [10.9]	18.0 [24.0]	27.8 [25.9]	
Master's or post-graduate degree		– [–]	6.0 [10.0]	1.9 [2.7]	

*These data pertain to adoptive mothers only.
**Figures in brackets represent adoptive fathers' status.

two-thirds (66.4 percent) of all parents had at least two. One 1958 parent had nine children and one 1968 parent had eight. More than one-quarter each of the 1958 (27.1 percent) and 1978 (29.6 percent) couples and less than one half (46.0 percent) of the 1968 were fertile, but elected to add to the family by adoption. It seems adoption as a procedure for achieving parenthood was favored by both fertile and infertile parents, as nearly one-half (48.7 percent) of all parents adopted at least two children.

Considering the divorce rate of about 1 percent in this province in 1985, the last year of the interview, our sample families seem to have had stability in their marriages as only one parent in each of the 1958 and 1968 groups was divorced and two 1958 parents were separated at the time of the interview. Seven 1958 mothers and two 1968 mothers had lost their husbands via death.

The 1958 adoptive mothers were less educated than those in the 1968 and 1978 groups, while the 1978 mothers were slightly better educated than those in either of the older groups. For example, while the highest educational achievement was high school or less for most 1958 adoptive mothers (83.4 percent), this was true for three-fifths (60 percent) of the 1968 mothers and less than half (46.3 percent) for the 1978 mothers. Similarly, of those who had experienced some university education the 1978 adoptive mothers comprised the highest proportion (29.7 percent), followed by the 1968 mothers, who constituted one-fourth; only one-tenth of the 1958 mothers had attended a university. Adoptive fathers were better educated than their spouses except in the 1958 group. The 1978 fathers were slightly more educated than those in the 1968 group, but only in terms of post high school training. The difference between their educational attainment disappears when compared on college education.

Congruent with their educational attainment, more fathers in the 1968 and 1978 groups held high-status occupations such as professional, semiprofessional, or managerial positions, than those in the 1958 group. A large majority of wives in each group (57 to 63 percent) were currently or once employed as secretaries or manual workers. One-fifth of the 1958 mothers and one-tenth of the 1968 mothers never worked outside the home.

In view of the educational and occupational levels of our adoptive parents it was expected that economically, these parents belonged to a lower-middle to middle income bracket. It should be noted that the real income used here as a measure of economic status is misleading, since most families in these rural areas supplement their income by noncash sources such as produce from land and sea.

Birth Mothers

The *1968 birth mothers* were between the ages of twenty-nine to thirty-nine, with nearly three-fourths (71.8 percent) of them in the thirty-to-thirty-four age category (see table 3–2). Their mean age at interview was 32.4 years. More than four-fifths were married and living with their husbands, while one-tenth had been divorced and one was separated.

One-half (51.3 percent) of the 1968 birth mothers experienced at least three pregnancies after the surrender of the first child, with 13 percent of them having occurred out of wedlock.

The *1978 birth mothers* ranged in age from eighteen to thirty, with nearly two-thirds (64.1 percent) being in the twenty to twenty-four age bracket. Their mean age at the interview was 24.3 years. A little over one-third (36 percent) were married and two birth mothers were separated and the rest (59 percent) were single at the time of the interview. It was interesting to note that marriages of the birth mothers seemed less stable than those of the adoptive parents.

A little less than one-half (46.2 percent) of the 1978 birth mothers have had up to four pregnancies since relinquishment of the first child. Almost one-quarter (22.6 percent) of these occurred out of wedlock.

Almost the same proportion of birth mothers in both groups (10.3 percent and 12.8 percent) placed up to three children for adoption. The two groups belonged to the area's two major religions—Protestant and

Table 3–2
Selected Demographic Characteristics of Birth Mothers
(percentages)

Characteristics	N =	1968 (39)	1978 (39)
Marital Status			
Married		82.1	35.9
Separated		2.6	5.1
Divorced		10.3	–
Single, never married		5.1	59.0
Age at Interview			
Younger than 20		–	5.1
20–24		–	64.1
25–29		5.1	25.6
30–34		71.8	2.6
35 +		23.1	2.1
Age at Adoptee's Birth			
Younger than 13		–	2.6
13–15		10.3	5.1
16–18		51.3	48.7
19–23		28.2	41.0
24 +		10.3	2.6
Number of Children Given up for Adoption			
1		89.7	87.2
2		7.7	10.3
3		2.6	2.6
Number of Out-of-Wedlock Pregnancies Since Relinquishment			
0		87.2	78.4
1		5.1	13.5
2		5.1	–
3		–	5.4
4		2.6	2.7
Educational Status			
Eighth grade or less		30.8	20.5
Some high school or completed high school		51.3	51.3
Technical training after high school		10.3	23.1
Some university or university graduate		7.7	5.1

Catholic. The Protestants outnumbered Catholics in the 1968 group and the reverse was true in the 1978 group. It is possible that in the 1970s the influence of the church on Catholic girls began to attenuate, resulting in increased premarital sexual activity. It is also plausible that more Protestant girls began to use abortion services, which became relatively more accessible during that period. However, changes in the perceived control of religious values did not make differences in the age at which these women engaged in the premarital sexual activity that resulted in premarital pregnancies. Birth mothers in both groups experienced their first pregnancy before marriage, with the modal age being sixteen to eighteen years. These results are consistent with the profile of birth mothers reported in the literature (Bedger 1980; Joanes et al. 1986; MacDonnell 1981). However, the 1968 birth mothers were slightly younger than the 1978 mothers at birth of their first child. More than three-fifths (61.6 percent) of the former were between thirteen and eighteen years old, compared to a little over one-half (53.8 percent) of the 1978 mothers, who were in that age group at their firstborn.

In almost all cases, birth mothers who had multiple births gave the first child up for adoption. Significantly, the child more often surrendered was male, with almost equal proportion in both groups—54 males and 46 females. It is of interest to note that this proportion very closely resembles the gender distribution of infants adopted by the 1968 and 1978 adoptive parents in our study sample, as is shown in table 3–3.

It should be noted that there was a slight preference for boys for adoption, findings that parallel the results of the English and Scottish studies (Barth et al. 1988; Raynor 1980; Triseliotis 1984) but differ with those reported by the American national study (Fiegelman and Silverman 1983). The authors noted that girls were slightly preferred by their sample couples over boys for adoption.

Educationally, the two groups were remarkably similar. Judging from their educational achievements, the sample birth mothers were not highly educated. More than 90 percent had not gone beyond high school and a

Table 3–3
Percentage Distribution of Infants Available for Adoption by All Adoptive Parents and by Sample Parents

Year	Infants Available for Adoption		Infants Adopted by All Parents		Infants Adopted by Sample Parents	
	Male	*Female*	*Male*	*Female*	*Male*	*Female*
1968	53.8	46.2	54.5	45.5	52.0	48.0
1978	53.8	46.2	58.3	41.7	59.2	40.8

Table 3–4
Selected Demographic Characteristics of Adoptees
(percentages)

Characteristics	N =	Male (15)	Female (38)	All Adoptees (53)
Age at Interview				
20–22		53.3	31.6	37.8
23–25		40.0	44.7	43.4
26 +		6.7	23.7	18.9
Marital Status				
Married		33.3	47.4	43.4
Divorced		–	7.9	5.7
Separated		–	5.3	3.8
Single, never married		66.7	39.5	47.2
Educational Status				
Eighth grade or less		–	2.6	1.9
Some high school or completed high school		26.7	31.6	30.2
Technical training but not high school		–	2.6	1.9
Technical training after high school		33.3	26.4	28.3
Some university or university graduate		40.0	36.8	37.7

year in a trade college. Among marrieds, the level of educational attainment for husbands and wives was similar. Consistent with their low level of schooling, more than half of all birth mothers were currently or once employed as skilled or unskilled workers and one-third as sales or clerical workers. A higher proportion of husbands (60 to 75 percent) than the birth mothers held low-status jobs.

The birth mothers by and large belonged to low- to middle-income status, although the 1968 birth mothers were slightly better off economically because a greater proportion of them were married and therefore had a second income. For example, the 1968 birth mothers who had an income of $16,000 to $25,000 were twice as many as the 1978 birth mothers.

Adoptees

Adoptees ranged in age from twenty-two to twenty-six with an average age of 22.5. More than 60 percent of them lived away from home but described their relationship with their adoptive parents as close. They visited home quite frequently, distance permitting. Females far outnumbered male adoptees, with 71.7 percent and 28.3 percent, respectively. Almost half our adoptees were single and one-tenth were either divorced or separated at the time of the research interview. Among the married adoptees, one-third had up to four living children. Only three adoptees had adopted a child in addition to having their own.

The sample adoptees were not highly educated. Three-fifths had some high school or one year of technical education beyond high school. Only one-third had attended a university or completed an undergraduate degree. One-half were engaged in clerical or sales jobs; only one-quarter were placed in high-status jobs—professional or management. Being young, single females with low education made it highly likely that the adoptees in our study were financially disadvantaged. Less than one-quarter had an income of $20,000 to $34,000 and one-tenth had earned $35,000 or more during that year.

Summary and Conclusion

The 1958 parents were less homogeneous in sociodemographic characteristics than were the 1968 and 1978 parents. For example, the 1958 adoptive mothers had a wider age range (twenty-one to forty-nine years) at the time of adoption than did the 1968 or 1978, mothers, who were between twenty-one to thirty-nine at adoption. More than one-quarter each of the 1958 and 1978 couples and less than one-half of the 1968 were preferential adopters. All three groups had up to five living children and nearly half of them adopted at least two.

The 1958 adoptive parents were less educated than those in the 1968 and 1978 groups. More fathers in the 1968 and 1978 groups had higher-status occupations than those in the 1958 group. In terms of real income, the sample parents by and large belonged to lower-middle to middle income brackets.

The 1968 and 1978 birth mothers were remarkably similar in their educational attainment, which was mostly limited to high school. However, the groups differed in certain respects. More than four-fifths of the 1968 birth mothers were married and living with their husbands, compared to one-third of the 1978 birth mothers who were married. The younger birth mothers (1978) had experienced far more out-of-wedlock pregnancies (up to four) since the relinquishment of their firstborn than did their older counterparts. Both groups placed up to three children for adoption and more often the child relinquished was male.

In terms of religious affiliation, Protestants outnumbered Catholics in the 1968 group and the reverse was true in the 1978 group. The majority of birth mothers in both groups experienced their first pregnancy before marriage, when they were sixteen to eighteen years of age.

Adoptees ranged in age from twenty-two to twenty-six, with a mean age of 22.5. More than 60 percent of them lived away from home, but described their relationship with their parents as close. Females far outnumbered male adoptees in the sample. Almost half the adoptees were single and one-tenth were once married. Being young and not highly educated, the sample adoptees were financially disadvantaged.

4
Release of Identifying Information to Adoptees

This chapter provides views of our respondents on a policy permitting the release of identifying information about birth parents to their adopted children. It also explores the implications, conflicts, and fears of the members of the triangle arising as a result of such a policy.

As discussed in the literature review, three major types of information—identifying, nonidentifying, and medical—are the targets of the debate on greater openness in adoption. Because one may agree or disagree with the disclosure policy under certain conditions, three major criteria were identified: age of the adoptee, prior consent of the adoptive parents, and prior consent of the birth parent/birth relative whose information is being sought. But these conditions were not raised until the respondent had expressed his or her views fully on the issue. This approach was intended to enable respondents to offer an impromptu opinion without being influenced by the possible bias. Furthermore, it avoided the risk of restricting them from stating their own qualifications, if any, which several respondents did. An example of their responses to our general inquiry is represented by the statement of this 1978 adoptive mother: "I can't say yes or no because my philosophy or belief would be based on a number of things. If these factors are taken into consideration I would agree that identifying information should be given."

Each respondent was asked whether adopted persons should be given access to identifying information about their birth parents, should they request it. They were also asked to provide reasons for their position. Information such as name, address, age, ethnicity, place of birth, place of residence, date of birth, job title, or any other details that would lead to the identification of the birth parent were defined as identifying information. The responses of the three groups are provided in table 4–1.

The data reveal an overwhelming support among all groups for making identifying information available to adoptees. The level of support was considerably higher among birth mothers and adoptees, with close to 90

Table 4–1
Attitudes toward Release of Identifying Information to Adoptees
(*percentages*)

Degree of Agreement	N =	All Adoptive Parents (1958, 1968, 1978) (152)	All Birth Mothers (1968, 1978) (78)	All Adoptees (53)
Strongly agree to somewhat agree		69.7	88.5	81.1
Strongly disagree to somewhat disagree		30.3	11.5	18.9

percent (88.5 percent) and 80 percent (81.1 percent), respectively, endorsing such a measure, compared to almost 70 percent for adoptive parents. However, differences among groups were not highly visible in a simple for-and-against question. Probe questions revealed that the adoptive parents' support was more apparent than real. In other words, they acknowledged the rights of adopted people to information about and reunion with their birth parents when the issue was discussed on a theoretical, impersonal level and in the context of social justice. But they tended to manifest underlying apprehension and reservation when they were asked to view the policy in relation to their own adopted children. The discrepancy between attitude and behavior has been well documented in the literature on women seeking abortion. (Potts 1979; Sachdev 1981, 1985). For example, after parents answered the simple for-and-against question, they were asked how they would feel if their children wanted to seek identifying information about birth parents or possibly contact them. The following excerpts mirror anxiety and inadequacy experienced by several of these adoptive mothers.

[Whether adoptees should be given identifying information] If they want to know about their parents nobody should be allowed to keep that information from them. It's a natural desire and a part of growing up.

[If your daughter wants the information or desires to meet] I would probably end up being a little jealous and take tranquilizers. I raised her and she's always going to be mine. She can't look at a stranger and fall in love with her because someone says that's the person who gave birth to her.

[1978 Adoptive mother]

[Whether adoptees should be given identifying information] If adopted children are ready to trace their background and meet their real parents, I don't think that information should be denied.

[If your son wants the information or desires to meet]. I can't say to him how I feel deep down. I'd be a little upset inside and feel insecure and wonder if his birth parents could have given him a better life than we did.

[1978 Adoptive mother]

Adoptive Parents' Ways to Deal with Anxiety

Adoptive parents recognized that adopted people have natural curiosity about their biological heritage. But they hoped their children would not have such a desire because they provided them with a loving home, something perhaps not possible to attain from their birth parents. The following statements exemplify the fond hope of these parents:

I don't see any reason why Kevin[1] would ever want to go to his parents. If we were mistreating him then I could understand why he would think of his birth parents.

[1978 Adoptive mother]

I don't know why Mac would ever want to do it anyway; we are the only mother and father he has ever known.

[1968 Adoptive mother]

Some parents dealt with their anxiety by denying that their children would ever quest for their genetic origins or yearn to connect with their parentage. This 1968 mother typifies this phenomenon: "Knowing Lisa, I don't think she's ever going to do it"; or, as this 1978 mother expressed: "We have such a close relationship that I can't imagine that Linda will look for her real mother."

Closely related to denial was avoidance behavior. Some parents tried to suppress the issue and did not want to entertain the possibility that their child might one day want to seek contact with his biological parents. For them this question is largely presumptuous until their child takes such a step. Their attitude was, "Why worry about something that's too distant in the future and may never happen?" The following statements by a 1968 adoptive mother illustrates this point:

[Whether adoptees should be given identifying information] Every child has a right to know who his natural parents are and it's only right if they wish to meet them.

---

[1]All names are changed to protect anonymity.

[If your daughter wants to meet] I don't know how I would feel; I have never thought of this deeply; I'll cross that bridge if it happens.

Another 1968 adoptive mother replied in the affirmative to the question, but described her personal situation in these words: "Kevin hasn't started asking questions on this. I don't know how I would feel. This sort of thing doesn't come in your mind until you are faced with it."

Some parents felt that if their children did seek information about or contact with birth parents, they would not be able to forbid them once they were adults. Some parents saw changes in the current disclosure policy as inevitable and realized that any attempts on their part to restrain their children would only endanger their relationship with the child. They considered it wise, therefore, to swim with the current and not resist their child's efforts. In the event their child was reunited with his birth parents, their hope was that their bond of love was strong enough to keep their child loyal to them.

> The way I feel is that if the department had left the records sealed I would be satisfied with it. But the way things are it seems kids are going to ask for the information anyway when they are older and on their own. It would then be hard for me to stop them. I guess I would have to change too.
>
> [1968 Adoptive mother]

> It would be upsetting to us; but how can you say you can't look for your parents? He would do it anyway when he gets a certain age with or without our consent. It certainly would deteriorate our relationship if we went against him. However, if he does like his parents and wants to maintain a relationship, I hope by that time our love will be so strong that it won't make any difference between us.
>
> [1978 Adoptive mother]

> To be quite truthful, I would be devastated, but if it is something he has to do and he insists then I can't stop him.
>
> [1978 Adoptive mother]

Reasons for Release of Identifying Information

The most frequent reason given by respondents who favored disclosure of such information related to basic social and moral rights of adoptees to know their genealogy. They felt that denial of this information would be discriminatory. One-half of the adoptees and birth mothers and a little over one-third (37.4 percent) of adoptive parents considered access to identifying adoption information as adoptees' fundamental right. Adoptees and birth mothers were especially indignant at the practice that severs adoptees' ties to their genetic past, which, they said, inextricably belongs to them. This is how they expressed their sentiment:

These are basically your records and nobody should keep something that is strictly yours.

[Female adoptee]

I think it's a terrible thing to refuse to tell someone who their parents are.

[1968 Birth mother]

Nobody has the right to stop my daughter if she wanted information about me. If this society says that she is not entitled to know it's like saying she's some type of a black sheep.

[1978 Birth mother]

A large majority of adoptees (72.1 percent) and almost one-half of birth mothers felt that adoptees need identifying information to complete their sense of identity. They said it is natural for adoptees to desire linkage with their forbears because they share physical and personality traits with them. The adoptees said they are often reminded of their being different from the kin of the adoptive parents who have consanguineous relationships. A female adoptee who recently had a reunion with her birth mother said this:

The biggest thing about being adopted that bothered me was I did not feel a complete part of my adoptive family. At family gatherings you look and say, so-and-so looks like so-and-so and somebody behaves the way your grandmother does. I didn't have that sense of blood connection.

For some adoptees the completion of identity is a fundamental necessity for being able to relate to the external world. "You can't relate to people in the outside world unless you first know about yourself," said one female adoptee.

Grounds for Release of Identifying Information

The support of the respondents for the release of identifying information was not without equivocation, as they stipulated criteria for disclosure that included the age of the adoptee and consent of the adoptive and birth parents.

Age of Adoptee

The most frequent concern raised by the triad was the psychological and emotional maturity of the searching adoptees. This was required to make a well-considered dispassionate decision to seek information and to cope with revelations that might be damaging or traumatizing. They stressed that being mature would also enable them to deal with reunion, should they decide to meet, or rejection, in case of refusal by the birth parent. Since there is scant correlation between chronological age and emotional maturity, respondents varied in their specification of age at which adoptees should be given access.

Generally, a majority in all three groups felt that adoptees are likely to achieve maturity at least by legal age. As shown in table 4–2, adoptees and adoptive parents represent a much higher proportion (90.7 percent and 84.0 percent respectively) of those who thought this way, compared to 58 percent of the birth mothers. Adoptees and adoptive parents considered a higher age, preferably in the twenties, appropriate for providing identifying information to the adoptee. Sixty percent of adoptive parents and almost all adoptees were in favor of this requirement; they felt a person is not fully mature and able to make responsible and well-considered decisions until he has life experiences that normally do not occur at a younger age. A few adoptees and adoptive parents saw an added advantage for older adoptees because they are likely to be economically independent from their parents and, therefore, free to pursue search without interference. Only birth mothers had confidence in adoptees' ability to handle such information before they reach adulthood. An impressive 42 percent held this view, as opposed to only 16 percent of adoptive parents and less then one-tenth of adoptees who thought similarly.

Adoptive Parents' Consent

Parental consent for an adult adoptee is a contentious issue. It refers to the conflict between adoptive parents' desire to extend their control over adopted children even after they have reached adulthood, and adoptees' need to make independent choices, as adults, without interference. Table 4–3 reflects our sample respondents' tug and pull.

The table shows that more than one-third (36.8 percent) of the adoptive parents supported their prior consent as condition for releasing identifying information to the adoptee who has reached adulthood. Another one-quarter (23.6 percent) would like to impose parental consent on the adult adoptee but felt that such condition is unenforceable and potentially problematic. They also felt that mandatory imposition of their will could make the adult child rebel and thus could jeopardize their relationship.

Table 4–2
Age of Adoptees for Release of Identifying Information
(*percentages*)

Adoptee's Age N =	Adoptive Parents (1958, 1968, 1978) (106)*	Birth Mothers (1968, 1978) (69)*	Adoptees (43)*
At any age	–	4.3	–
Only when mature	16.0	37.7	9.3
Of legal age	84.0	58.0	90.7

*All those who agreed with release of identifying information in table 4–1

> Once he is adult and self supporting there is not much say we are going
> to have in this matter. I can't see Kevin listening to us.
>
> [1968 Adoptive mother]

> When she is nineteen and really wants this information I would have no
> right to stop her even if I disagreed with her. For me to say no you're
> not going to find this information will drive her apart.
>
> [1968 Adoptive mother]

These parents, however, would like the adoptee or the department to
inform them their child was seeking genealogical information. They said
that failure to inform and possibly consult with them would be regarded
as a discourteous and ungrateful act that would hurt their feelings.

> If you've had this child for twenty years and if the department is going
> to open his files the least they can do is to let us know. The department
> owes us this much for the contribution we have made to society. I do feel
> that we should be consulted and try to come to some sort of understand-
> ing. The department should not say to the adoptee, 'Here's the informa-
> tion and check with the adoptive parents.'
>
> [1978 Adoptive father]

Table 4–3
Prior Consent of Adoptive Parents
(*percentages*)

Agree or Disagree N =	Adoptive Parents (1958, 1968, 1978) (106)*	Birth Mothers (1968, 1978) (69)*	Adoptees (43)*
Agree in case of adult adoptees	36.8	27.5	9.3
Agree in case of minor adoptees	59.5	50.7	88.4
Consent not required	3.7	21.8	2.3

*All those who agreed with release of identifying information in table 4–1

> I would like my daughter to ask and talk things over with me and I
> suppose she would make her own decision. But I would feel hurt if she
> went behind my back and did it.
>
> [1968 Adoptive mother]

Contrasted with the adoptive parents' position, less than one-tenth
(9.3 percent) of adoptees found the requirement of parental consent acceptable when they are adults. However, they concurred with the adoptive
parents in supporting the requirement of parental consent when the adoptee is a minor. For example, if we assume that those who favored parental
consent for adult adoptees also favored this condition for minor adoptees,
96.3 percent of adoptive parents and an almost identical percentage of
adoptees (97.7 percent) held this position. A far more significant finding
was that among adoptees who were opposed to mandatory parental consent, more than one-third (35.3 percent) said that once ready to search
they would confide in their parents and seek their opinion, provided the
final decision was not made by the parents. They felt obligated to adoptive parents because of the role they played as real parents and thus
considered their participation in the decision as legitimate.

> I think adoptive parents are not just paper parents because they signed
> the adoptive form. They have a right to be involved in some way, but
> they should not have the final say.

> Their opinion is valid, but I don't like the word consent.

> Granted, they are part of my life. I'll get their opinion and find out how
> they feel. But I do have my own life now and will make my own
> decision.

These observations dismantle the misconception that adoptees are irrational, radical, and insensitive to the adoptive parents' feelings, or are ungrateful to them.

Birth mothers held a more liberal view on the parental consent than
did adoptive parents or adoptees. A considerably smaller proportion of
birth mothers, 78.2 percent compared to almost 97 percent for the other
two groups, were in favor of this requirement even when the adoptee is a
minor. Furthermore, a much higher percentage of them preferred granting
the right of access to adoptees at any age without mandatory parental
consent than did either of the other two parties. For instance, more than
one-fifth (21.8 percent) of the birth mothers showed their disapproval of
this requirement, compared to 3.7 percent and 2.3 percent, respectively,
for adoptive parents and adoptees who were opposed to parental consent.

However, a sizeable proportion of them (20.3 percent) would support the idea that the adoptee should not engage in search activity without the knowledge of the adoptive parents, although the final decision rests with the adoptee. Another one-quarter (27.5 percent) approved of parental consent as condition for access rights of adoptees who are adult. These findings are striking in the face of the prevailing myth that birth mothers are selfish and insensitive to adoptive parents' feelings.

The foregoing discussion applies to adoptive parents who were living at the time the adoptee seeks information. However, in the event of their death, respondents who were otherwise approving of parental veto thought this condition should be waived or consent of the relative or guardian be obtained, in case the adoptee is a minor.

Reasons for Adoptive Parents' Consent. Adoptive parents who supported parental veto were motivated mainly by the twin concerns for the well-being of the adoptee and for recognition as the child's real parents. They felt they knew the child's strengths and weaknesses and were therefore in a better position to counsel and prepare him or her for a reunion and provide emotional support in the event of a traumatic experience.

> The adoptive parents are the only ones who really understand the child's abilities and whether he's grown to the stage when he can fully appreci-ate and understand the situation and whether his decision was a spur-of-the-moment thing.
>
> [1978 Adoptive mother]

> The child is going to need an awful lot of support and especially if she is rejected by her birth mother she has to come back to the family. So if we are involved we can warn her about all possible problems that could present and gear ourselves to deal with them.
>
> [1968 Adoptive father]

Some parents felt they were given a pledge of confidentiality of adop-tion records. They said if the department decides unilaterally to change the ground rules it has the moral and legal obligation to grant them a definite say in the decision on disclosure of information to the child. They said any attempt on the part of the department to ignore them would undermine their status and disregard their contribution in raising the child. A 1978 adoptive father employed as a university professor made this point poignantly:

> It was hammered home that all records would be destroyed and our children would never find out information about their birth parents. It is especially important that we should have a say in the matter concerning the person who lived in our home and our hearts. To be honest, if I had

known that the department could violate its promise, I would probably not have adopted.

A 1958 adoptive mother emphasized a similar point:

> I adopted her when she was just a tiny little girl, and loved her as my own child. I think because of all I did for her she should get my permission.

Birth mothers in favor of mandatory parental consent for adult adoptees supported the adoptive parents' claim to being the child's true parents, who raised him and provided nurturing care. They contended it would not only be unfair to the adoptive parents, but could also cause them anguish if the adoptee was given access to this information without their concurrence. Typical of this view was expressed by this 1968 birth mother:

> Adoptive parents have a right to refuse permission because they adopted the child when it was a baby and reared it up. It is not who gave birth to the child but it's who raised it, that's the parents. Any woman can go out and have a child but that doesn't make her a mother.

> My daughter should get the permission of her adoptive parents who have brought her up all of her life. Otherwise it would only hurt them.

Some birth mothers empathized with adoptive parents, imagining their deep distress if an adoptee pursues the search clandestinely for his biological parents:

> If I had adopted a child I'd think it as my own. It would hurt me if he went looking for his other parents; I'd feel rejected.

> I think it would be distressing for the adoptive parents. These are the only parents an adoptee has ever known. I hope that's what my child thinks.

Some birth mothers agreed with adoptive parents and saw the value of their involvement in the decision so that they can provide support to the adoptee for coping with the search experience, should it prove calamitous.

The fear of causing hurt and anguish to adoptive parents was the major reason cited by seven adoptees who supported adoptive parents' veto. They felt their decision to seek identity of or contact with the birth parents without the concurrence of the adoptive parents would be ungrateful and insensitive to the significant role the adoptive parents played in their lives.

Reasons against Parental Consent. The most serious objection to the requirement of parental veto was voiced by adoptees who insisted that the decision to seek identifying information about or reunion with the birth parents is their personal matter, and should not warrant the involvement of adoptive parents, especially when they are adult. Typical of their statements were: "Birth parents are my own parents and it's my business if I want to find them or not." "It is between myself and my birth parents." "This information is mine, for my benefit and for my use." They said that as mature adults they can determine what is in their best interest and can handle the consequence of their decision. Their recurring statement was that, "At age twenty-one I should know what I want and should be able to accept consequences, good or bad."

Adoptees recognized that adoptive parents provided them with a secure and loving home; however, they viewed mandatory parental consent as an affront to their dignity. A twenty-four-year-old female adoptee said:

> It's ridiculous to ask for your mother and father's consent for a thing like this. It's like asking them if you can go to bed with your husband tonight.

Some adoptees were afraid that, given veto power, adoptive parents might never allow them to gain access to the adoption information, which would make adoptees bitter and resentful. In such situations, adoptees might react defiantly and pursue the search using any means available. These adoptees underlined the inability of the adoptive parents to enforce mandatory consent: "If you really want to search, the requirement of parents' signatures won't stop you." "If I'm interested in finding out about my biological parents there is not a hell of a lot they can do." Some adoptees lamented that they might have to defer the search until after the adoptive parents are deceased and run the risk of forever losing vital information on genealogy and hereditary diseases if birth parents were no longer living. Their fear is illustrated by these telling statements:

> In my case I know I'll never get the consent of my adoptive parents and then I would never have a chance of finding out until they are dead. By then I could have my own children and it could be too late to know my health history.

> My parents could refuse their permission and then for the rest of my life I'm going to resent them. That would certainly not make a good relationship between us.

> It is my feeling that because of their paranoia that they might lose the child, the parents will not give the signature, which will put the adoptee in a bad spot.

Birth Mothers' Consent

One can argue in favor of the adoptee's right to contact only if the birth parent is willing to meet. Like adoptive parents, the department pledged permanent anonymity to birth mothers, who are likely to suffer the greatest harm among the three principals from unscrupulous disclosure of her identity. Thus, the act of finding a fulcrum between the adoptee's right to seek identifying information and the birth parent's historic right of privacy contributes to the controversy. Mindful of this dilemma, we asked each respondent who was supportive of disclosure whether an adoptee should be provided identifying details with consent of the birth mother. The responses of the adoptive parents, birth mothers, and adoptees are depicted in table 4–4.

There was overwhelming support among the three groups for the requirement of the birth mother's consent. The support was strongest among adoptive parents, with 84 percent, followed by birth mothers and adoptees, who constituted 75 percent and 69.8 percent, respectively. The high degree of concurrence among the adoption triad for requiring the birth mother's consent contrasts with the lack of consensus on giving adoptive parents a veto power.

Reasons for Birth Mothers' Consent. All respondents were concerned about protection of the birth mother from an indiscreet and unwanted intrusion by the adoptee in her newly formed life. They said the birth mother might have married since the relinquishment of the child and might have kept the premarital pregnancy a secret from her husband and children.

> She has got her own life now and no one should have the right to disrupt it. She could be married and not have told her husband. So if one day a young man turns up on her doorstep and says he was her son it could turn her world upside down.
>
> [Male adoptee]

Table 4–4
Prior Consent of Birth Mothers
(*percentages*)

Degree of Agreement	N =	Adoptive Parents (1958, 1968, 1978) (106)*	Birth Mothers (1968, 1978) (69)*	Adoptees (43)*
Strongly agree to somewhat agree		84.0	75.4	69.8
Strongly disagree to somewhat disagree		16.0	24.6	30.2

*All those who agreed with release of identifying information in table 4–1

> She could be married and might not have told her husband that she had
> a baby before marriage. The adoptee's sudden appearance in her life
> might open a can of worms and probably destroy her marriage.
>
> [1968 Adoptive mother]

Adoptive parents advocated prior consent of the birth mother because
it could protect the adoptee from the trauma of possible rejection by the
birth mother. They felt strongly that the department should prevail upon
the unwilling birth mother to agree to the disclosure of her identity to the
searching adoptee. Adoptees, however, did not share the adoptive parents'
concern that they would feel dejected and hurt. Instead, they displayed
understanding and appreciation of the birth mother's reasons for her lack
of interest in them. They thought it legitimate that her new circumstances
might not permit her to admit their existence and accept them in her life.
They realized that the appearance of the adoptee might exacerbate the
feelings of the birth mother, who may be troubled with guilt. Adoptees
would not like to force themselves on a reluctant or unwilling birth
mother, however much they might desire to meet. These male and female
adoptees demonstrate their understanding of birth mothers' predicaments
and their need for privacy:

> The whole exercise of this thing is not to hurt people. If I barge right
> into her life after twenty-five years without her permission and knowing
> her circumstances I could do irreparable damage.
>
> [Male adoptee]

> I think birth mothers deserve protection. If this is the course they have
> chosen, they should not be in fear of having someone show up at the
> doorstep. That's not what they are prepared for.
>
> [Female adoptee]

Adoptive parents and adoptees contended that the birth mother might
want to keep her past permanently behind her; she might not like to meet
the adopted child, now an adult, for fear of dredging up painful memories
or revealing information that could be incriminating to her and to the
adoptee.

> The birth mother signed away all her rights to that child so that she
> could go on with her life. For her it was a permanent arrangement and
> all of a sudden it's not permanent anymore. It could be a terrible shock
> because there may be something in that lady's past that she may not
> want reopened.
>
> [1968 Adoptive mother]

Maybe she won't feel comfortable meeting the adopted child after so long, because the reasons for the adoption are still troublesome to the biological mother and she'd prefer not to get involved.

[Female adoptee]

However, a large majority of the birth mothers rejected the myth about a need for permanent anonymity. They said they would like to see the relinquished child and would give their consent if requested. However, they would like to be informed so they can prepare themselves and their husbands or children for the adoptee's arrival.

If my boy was coming to see me I wouldn't just want him to walk in, because I don't want to put on a fake pretense or act like somebody I'm not. But if I knew he was coming I'd be all prepared to meet him. Also, I can let my children know, explain to them so that they wouldn't get a big shock.

[1968 Birth mother]

I don't know how it would affect me to open up the front door and have him say, 'I'm your son.' I think the initial shock alone would take a while to sink in. I would give permission anyway, but if I was told beforehand that he was coming, I could more or less prepare myself for the shock.

[1968 Birth mother]

Some birth mothers who said they would provide consent cautioned that, despite their desire to meet, they would tend to give a negative response to the initial request. This might be caused by their fear of an adverse reaction by their husbands and children or some extenuating circumstances, and therefore it should not be treated as their final decision. They emphasized that, given time, they would assess their circumstances and after mobilizing courage and a discussion with their husbands and children, they would likely change their minds.

I definitely would like to see my child, but it is not something you can come right out and say, 'yes, it's all right.' You have to talk this over with your husband and children. A lot depends on their reaction.

[1968 Birth mother]

There are probably some birth mothers who want to see their child but might back out at first when they are asked their permission because of the family situation.

[1978 Birth mother]

Some birth mothers gave an additional reason why they needed time to ponder the request and prepare themselves for a possible contact before giving their approval. They said that normally birth mothers do not dwell on the child because they have been conditioned by social workers to believe they renounced all their rights once they relinquished it. With no hope of learning about or reuniting with the child, they are forced to repress their memories. For some birth mothers, the experience of birth and relinquishment is too painful to keep alive. Consequently, they are likely to react to the initial contact with surprise and confusion. This thirty-three-year-old married birth mother and also an adoptee said:

> In lots of cases, birth mothers have been told for years that they have no right to the child anymore. Therefore, most do not think of the possibility of ever seeing the child again. For some it is a painful experience which they had put at the back of their mind.

Reasons against Birth Mothers' Consent. Adoptive parents and birth mothers who were opposed to this condition believed interested adoptees should by rights have unrestricted access to identifying information. They said that refusal by the birth parent would unjustly cutoff adoptees from their genealogical past. Adoptees who rejected this requirement viewed such a step discriminatory, unfair, and unidirectional because it takes into account the interest of only one party, the birth mother. They stressed that while this policy assures the privacy of the birth mother it unfairly denies the adoptee the information of which he or she is co-owner. They found it ironic that a mother would require anonymity from the child to whom she gave birth and would not regard it natural for the estranged child to have desire to eventually know and possibly meet his or her mother. In respect for the birth mother, they support the idea of requiring the department to notify her that her adult child has been given identifying information.

> My opinion is that birth mothers should know from day one that the children they gave up are eventually going to find out who they are. My birth mother's name is just as much my information as it is hers. She's a part of me and I don't think she has a right to anonymity from me. Probably she should be contacted and let her know that her adopted child is going to get the identifying information so she can be prepared.
> [Female adoptee]

Adoptees' fear of denial of birth mothers' permission stems partly from the fact that she did not follow through on them since relinquishment. They interpreted this as an indication of her lack of interest in them. They were afraid that given the opportunity the veto right would afford, the birth mother would refuse permission for the release of identifying information. Should that happen, their questions concerning their origins would remain unresolved. A few adoptees suspected that the requirement of birth mothers' consent would cause a serious blow to the adoptees' rights movement for open adoption. "If birth mothers do not give permission then we're back to where we started from," they say, or "They could stop the movement so easily and we would just be stuck again."

Some adoptees felt that if the birth mother's right of choice to give up the child is acknowledged because of her unwarranted circumstances, then the child, now adult, should be entitled to find out the circumstances that prompted his mother's decision. A male adoptee asked: "If she made her choice to give me up why shouldn't I have the right to find out why?"

A few adoptees, mostly males, were highly indignant and bitter at being an unwitting victim of what they viewed as the birth mother's irresponsible acts, first by becoming pregnant and then by abandoning them. They argued that the birth mother's right of approval for release of identifying information was lost once she renounced her responsibility as parent toward that child. Their emotional catharsis is evident in these statements:

> I don't think birth mothers should be given the right to decide at all for the simple reason that you don't go around lighting a fire if you can't put it out. The way I look at it is if you are going to be out screwing around without any precaution and you do have a child and you put it up for adoption, you have the responsibility to that child. I think you do morally, not maternally, even to just check to see if he's doing all right.

> The birth mother gave up her right to that child when she left it in the hospital or as soon as somebody else adopted it. I don't think she should have too much to say whether I can get any information.

Time Period for Seeking Birth Mothers' Consent. If an impressive majority of respondents in all groups were committed to requiring birth mothers' consent, it is obvious that the first and foremost task of the department would be to trace her to obtain her consent. The question that seems vital is how long the department should search—as long as it takes; up to a certain time period; or if she cannot be found the department should release her identity to the adoptee (or should not undertake a search or release her identity until the birth mother registers her consent voluntarily). The three options were presented to the respondents, who favored birth mothers' consent as condition for disclosing their identity. Their responses are portrayed in table 4–5.

It is noteworthy that consistently a small majority of respondents in all groups (56 to 59 percent) supported the option involving indefinite search. This finding presents a queer paradox in the face of robust support for the condition of birth mothers' consent. A little over one-third

Table 4–5
Time Required for Seeking Birth Mothers' Consent
(*percentages*)

Time Required	N =	Adoptive Parents (1958, 1968, 1978) (89)*	Birth Mothers (1968, 1978) (52)*	Adoptees (30)*
As long as it takes to locate		56.2	53.9	58.8
Locate up to a certain time period		37.1	36.5	38.2
Wait until she contacts the department		6.7	9.6	2.9

*All those who agreed with consent requirement in table 4–4

(37 to 38 percent) in each group preferred a time-limited search for the birth mother not exceeding one year.

Three aspects of this data are noteworthy. First, an overwhelming majority of respondents in each group (more than nine out of ten) favored an active search of the unregistered birth mother at the behest of the adoptee. Their meager support for an indefinite search is not tantamount to abridgement of privacy rights of the birth mother, but underscores their desire to suppress permanent barriers to adoptees' need to know. In other words, judging from the detailed reasons for their less-than-enthusiastic preference for the indefinite option it seems they sought to balance the birth mother's right to anonymity and the adoptee's right to information. They were concerned that the option of unlimited time would reduce the department's search activity to a low priority. They feared that an unsympathetic and uncaring social worker could prolong the process, which could discourage the adoptee from continuing his interest. The interminable search can be detrimental to the adoptee, whose need for this information is psychologically compelling. They also suspected a protracted search would be costly particularly if the birth mother had moved out of the province and the department would not commit sufficient resources to meet increasing demands of searching adoptees. However, they uniformly stressed that the search should be as thorough and exhaustive as possible before the birth mother's identity is disclosed without her consent. They also emphasized that the department should not limit its search efforts to the provincial boundaries, but should expand them to the entire mainland country if it is believed that the mother left the province.

Second, the birth mothers, too, favored an indeterminate search for them only marginally (53.9 percent), which signifies that they did not want to make access to their identity too restrictive for the adoptee.

Third, those who supported a no-search/no-release option accounted for a mere 3 percent (adoptees) to a maximum of 10 percent (birth mothers). Both the adoptive parents and adoptees rejected the passive approach because they were afraid the birth mother might never register her consent on her own, thus making it impossible for adoptees to gain access to the information. The adoptees' doubts about whether the birth mother would make voluntary contact with the department was reflected in these statements: "God only knows when she would come forward." "I could be waiting for a lifetime and that may never happen because she might have forgotten all about me."

Significantly, birth mothers agreed that they generally would not make the initial contact but disagreed on perception of the reasons. Contrary to what adoptees thought, birth mothers stressed that they did not forget the child they relinquished, but they were fettered by the belief that they had renounced all their rights to the child because his real parents were the people who adopted and raised him. Furthermore, they were afraid their initiative might upset the adopted child or disrupt his life. The fact that an overwhelming proportion (90.4 percent) of them favored an active search policy indicates that birth mothers would prefer to be met by the relinquished child.

> To expect that a birth mother will voluntarily contact the department may never happen, especially if a lot of mothers feel the way I do, that I have no right to find out anything about him or his adoptive parent. At least this is the way I was told since I signed the papers.
> [1968 Birth mother]

> The birth mother may never come to the department voluntarily even if she wanted to meet the child, feeling that she should not interfere with the adoptee's life or cause trouble in the adoptive family.
> [1978 Birth mother]

> Some birth mothers may want to see their child but haven't got the nerve. It's a lot easier if their child came to them.
> [1968 Birth mother]

One birth mother made a very cogent comment on the third option of voluntary consent presented to her:

> If there is an option of making a voluntary contact with the department of social services, I don't think any birth mother would ever contact and the adoptee could be waiting indefinitely.

Birth Mothers' Refusal of Consent after Identification. Despite optimism raised by birth mothers about their continued interest in the relinquished child and their willingness to be contacted, it is possible that some birth mothers may find themselves in circumstances that do not permit the reentry of the child, now adult, in their lives. Thus, after the birth mother has been located and identified, the department may face her refusal to consent. This leaves the department with one of three policy options: it should use its judgment and release the information requested; it should advise the adoptee to petition the court or any such body empowered to hear appeal; or it should not release the identifying information.

As shown in table 4–6, a majority in each group (68 to 74 percent) upheld the absolute rights of the birth mother to privacy if she refuses her consent to the information or possible contact. The appeal option was recommended by a minority, a little over one-tenth (12.8 percent) each of the adoptive parents and birth mothers. Adoptees felt more strongly, with over one-fifth (20.7 percent) preferring to appeal the negative decision of the birth mother.

Those who supported the birth mother's privacy right believed identifying information is a personal and private matter of the birth mother and her decision should be respected. They thought it would cause pain and agony to both parties if the adoptee pursued the information through the appeal procedure or forced personal contact with the birth mother. Adoptees felt strongly that they did not see any value or satisfaction in seeking information or contact with a birth mother who is equivocal about her interest in them.

Several respondents, however, felt that it would make it easier for the adoptee to accept the birth mother's refusal if given the reasons for it.

Table 4–6
Policy Options for Disclosure in Case of Birth Mothers' Refusal to Consent
(percentages)

Department's Policy Option	N =	Adoptive Parents (1958, 1968, 1978) (83)*	Birth Mothers (1968, 1978) (47)*	Adoptees (29)*
Act on its judgment and release identifying information		12.1	19.1	10.3
Advise adoptee to petition to court		14.5	12.8	20.7
Do not release information		73.5	68.1	69.0

*All those who agreed with search in table 4–5

They said the knowledge of the circumstances that prompted her negative decision would assure the adoptee the birth mother was alive and well and that if she did not wish to meet it was because of her forbidding circumstances.

> If she refuses to give consent I think the child should forget about it and learn to accept that it's her decision and the child should understand it and no way should he or she try to trace her. Digging up her past could probably hurt the child and the birth mother.
>
> [1978 Adoptive mother]

> It is her personal decision and her private information and if she doesn't want to give out she doesn't have to. But the department could give the child as much as possible the reasons for her decision.
>
> [1958 Adoptive father]

> If the birth mother says, 'no,' that information is no good to the child anyway. Pursuing the mother would only hurt the child by her further rejection.
>
> [1968 Adoptive mother]

Absence of Birth Mothers' Consent Because of Death. The department will be unable to get the birth mother's consent if she is dead or believed dead. In that case the department could undertake one of three policy considerations: It could use its own judgment and release the identifying information to the adoptee; it could ask the court to appoint a guardian to represent the absent birth mother's interest; or it should not release the information. The resulting data are presented in table 4–7.

Table 4–7
Policy Options for Disclosure of Identifying Information on Birth Mothers In Case of Their Death
(*percentages*)

Department's Policy Options N =	Adoptive Parents (1958, 1968, 1978) (83)*	Birth Mothers (1968, 1978) (47)*	Adoptees (29)*
Act on its judgment and release identifying information	64.8	72.3	66.7
Ask court to appoint guardian to represent birth mother's interest	22.7	25.5	20.0
Do not release identifying information	12.5	2.1	13.3

*All those who agreed with search in table 4–5

As is clear from the table, a large majority of respondents in all groups (two-thirds to seven-tenths) favored the release of identifying information to the adoptee in the event of the birth mother's death. But they preferred to leave the final decision to the department, which they felt was in a better position to assess factors such as the circumstances of the deceased birth mother, the nature of the information, and the motives and emotional maturity of the adoptee. Adoptive parents added that the department should make sure that the adoptee does not abuse the information.

> If for some reason the information is still necessary for the child it should be given to him. I have confidence in the department that it will make a proper decision while taking into consideration the circumstances of the birth mother. It would probably talk to her family members before finally deciding what was good for the birth mother.
>
> [1978 Adoptive mother]

> It should be the judgment of the department as to how the adopted person has been coping and what he/she is really like and how he/she can handle the information.
>
> [Male adoptee]

It is significant to note that a higher proportion of birth mothers (72.3 percent) than adoptive parents and adoptees endorsed this measure. Also, unlike the adoptive parents and adoptees, birth mothers' endorsement was without equivocation.

Respondents were unanimous in their reasons for supporting this option. They felt the disclosure of a birth mother's identity is least likely to cause any harm if she's dead. At the same time, the information can at least provide the adoptee with some background knowledge of genealogical roots and thus help satisfy his or her sense of identity.

> If the birth mother is dead, I doubt the child can find her. So it won't do any harm in giving him the information. The child would know where he stands. At least he won't always be going through life wondering about the whereabouts of his birth parents.
>
> [1968 Birth mother]

> I would say the department should give the adoptee the information, because it poses no threat to the birth mother. At least his curiosity will be satisfied that he has found what he wanted to know.
>
> [Male adoptee]

The respondents saw another advantage in releasing identifying information to the adopted person; it might provide important clues to locating other members of the genetic family with whom he or she might want to meet. This should satisfy the adoptee's psychological need for connectedness.

> The adopted child might try to find her father or other blood relatives who could tell her who she was and what type of family she came from.
>
> [1978 Adoptive mother]

> If there are brothers and sisters I'll continue my search and this information can be quite helpful.
>
> [Female adoptee]

> An adoptee can feel better inside because he would know who his mother was and where she came from.
>
> [1978 Adoptive mother]

> If my daughter came back looking for me and I'm dead at that time, maybe she'd like to see her brother and sister. At least she has got someone there to understand her.
>
> [1978 Birth mother]

One-fifth (adoptees) to one-quarter (birth mothers) of respondents thought the department should decide to release information only after consultation with a court-appointed representative of the absent birth mother.

Among the respondents favoring a total ban on the release of identifying information under any circumstances, birth mothers offered the least opposition with 2.1 percent, compared to a little over one-tenth (12.5 to 13.3 percent) for the adoptive parents and adoptees. The most common reason cited by these respondents was that the birth mother's husband and children might not know about the relinquished child. The appearance of the adopted child, now an adult, might prove traumatic for them as well as engender embittered feelings toward the deceased birth mother.

> I have no right to barge into the life of my birth mother's children and to say to them, 'By the way, you may not know, I'm your brother.' The kids may be completely devastated to know that their mother had an illegitimate child.

Procedures for Assessing Adoptee's Request

Almost all respondents, except birth mothers, suggested that the adoptee may meet the criteria regarding age, consent of the adoptive parents, and consent of the birth mother, but that may not ensure that the information, as sensitive as identifying details, will be handled with responsibility and canny judgment. They said it is important that the department define procedures to screen requests from adoptees to determine their attitudes and motives for receiving this information. Specifically, they felt the department should follow three important criteria:

First, the adoptee's desire for the information should stem from a genuine need for identity information and not reflect idle curiosity or a precipitous decision. Furthermore, the interest shouldn't be an evanescent phase or a developmental crisis but should represent sustained psychological and emotional distress that is likely to interfere with normal functioning. This is how a female adoptee expressed her view:

> I don't agree that this information should be released just to satisfy curiosity. It should be given to adult adoptees who are having some problem in their lives because they don't know about their parents. Sometimes, people get so obsessed that they cannot get on with their day-to-day lives and these cases deserve the information.

A 1968 adoptive mother said:

> Make sure the adoptee wants it really badly enough and is able to put his finger on the reason. I don't think the department should pass this information left and right.

Second, the adoptee's motives should be positive, not a need to express vengeance or to cause harm to the birth parent.

> I don't think it should be given to people who could be vindictive or resentful or could hurt the people who gave them up. The department should assess that the person wants to know for genuine reasons and is not going to harass his birth parents.
>
> [Female adoptee]

> I would like to see that the child brought no harm to one side or the other or did not inflict pain on the real mother.
>
> [1978 Adoptive mother]

Third, the adoptee should be emotionally mature and able to cope with a revelation that might prove embarrassing or hurtful. Also, he or she should be able to deal with an unanticipated reaction of the birth parent or with the new relationship if a reunion is intended. A male adoptee highlighted this point:

> Adoptees should be screened to see if they can handle the identifying information and the kind of situation that arises out of having two parents. If that opens a whole new can of beans they should be able to handle it.

One concern that was raised by adoptees had to do with the process for dealing with the inquiries. Adoptees stressed that the sharing of sensitive information such as identity of birth parents should be handled with discretion and circumspection. They were unanimous that the disclosure procedure should be streamlined, properly monitored, and should adhere to the principles governing confidentiality.

> Don't give the whole file wide open, and say here you go and read all about the incest case and about the illegitimate child and the wife beating by the birth father. Also, I should not be able to call up the department and get the information on phone. I think there should be set procedures laid down.
>
> [Male adoptee]

> I think there should be a lot of red tape involved before you can get this information. I don't think the files should be just sitting there and anybody could come in the office, off the street, and pick them up.
>
> [Female adoptee]

Differences within Groups

Adoptive Parents

The 1958 parents seemed less supportive, with a little over three-fifths, compared to almost equal seven-tenths for the 1968 and 1978 parents, who agreed with the disclosure of identifying information as depicted in table 4–8.

However, contrary to our expectations, the support of the 1958 parents was less equivocal and prescriptive. They displayed far less apprehension on the prospect of losing their children should they decide to seek the

Table 4–8
Attitudes of Adoptive Parents toward Release of Identifying Information to Adoptees
(*percentages*)

	Adoptive Parents by Year of Adoption			
Degree of *Agreement* N =	*1958* *(48)*	*1968* *(50)*	*1978* *(54)*	*All* *Adoptive Parents* *(152)*
Strongly agree to somewhat agree	62.6	72.0	74.0	69.7
Strongly disagree to somewhat disagree	37.5	28.0	25.9	30.3

identity of their birth parents. They were more likely to feel confident about the adoptees' ability to handle identifying information, even as minors, than did the 1968 and 1978 parents. For example, one-third (33.3 percent) of the 1958 parents endorsed the release of such information to minor adoptees, compared with only 5 to 12 percent of the 1968 and 1978 parents who felt this way. The 1958 parents seemed less threatened by the prospect of discovery of birth parents by their adopted adults, and were, therefore, less favorable toward the requirement of older age than were the 1968 and 1978 parents. For instance, 80 percent each of the 1968 and 1978 parents felt the adoptee should be in his twenties to be eligible for identifying information, contrasted with 30 percent for the 1958 parents. The requirement of a higher age may symbolize the attempt of the 1968 and 1978 parents to suppress efforts of their children to search.

The 1958 parents also felt more secure in their relationship and therefore had less need to exercise control over the decision of the adult adoptees to seek information or reunion. While 42 to 45 percent of the 1968 and 1978 parents were in favor of mandatory parental consent for adult adoptees, only about 20 percent of the 1958 parents supported this requirement.

It is reasonable to assume that feelings of security among the 1958 parents was attributed to their relationship with the adult adoptee, which had endured the test of allegiance over the years. They were confident their child would not betray their love and accept the birth parents as real parents. The following statement by a 1958 adoptive mother exemplifies these parents' supreme confidence in their adoptive relationship.

> If he came to me and asked me if his parents were really dead or alive, I would tell him the truth now. I think our love has been tested and established. His natural mother is a total stranger and he cannot, all of a sudden, fall in love with this person.

Another 1958 adoptive mother was reluctant to know background information on her child's birth parents when it was offered to her at the time of adoption. But twenty-five years later she had a different perspective:

> I didn't want the information at the time because I was afraid that if my children found out they might be able to locate their mother. Now that my daughter has gotten older and I know she loves me more than anybody else, I wish I had that information so that I could give it to her. It doesn't upset me now when I know she's sometimes thinking about her parents. I'm sorry I did not tell my daughter earlier that she was adopted. I'm very happy I can accept things now and tell her the truth.

Birth Mothers

The two subgroups of birth mothers also differed in the degree of support for the release of identifying information. As shown in table 4–9, the 1978 birth mothers were more favorable, with 95 percent supporting this policy, compared with 82 percent for the 1968 cohort.

The higher support among 1978 birth mothers may be due to a high preponderance of single, unmarried woman in that group (59 percent), compared to merely 5 percent of the 1968 birth mothers who had not married at the interview. It stands to reason that a married birth mother living with her husband and children, compared to a single birth mother, is more vulnerable to embarrassment and disruption in her life, especially if she kept her premarital pregnancy secret. The married birth mother also faces greater difficulties incorporating the adopted child, the familiar stranger, in her new family than might the unmarried birth mother, who does not have the same considerations to reckon with. This is how currently married birth mothers described their predicament:

> I would definitely like to see my child but it's not something I can come out and say, "Yes, it's all right." I have to talk this over with my husband and with my children.

> I honestly don't think my husband would be able to accept it and understand it. There are so many lives involved and an awful lot of unanswered questions. It could really destroy a lot of people.

Because of the greater need of the 1968 birth mothers for privacy, they were less approving of the department's right to override their veto or release identifying information in the event of their death than were the 1978 birth mothers. For instance, almost 80 percent (79.2 percent) of the 1968 group said the department should accept their refusal as irrevocable

Table 4–9
Attitudes of Birth Mothers toward Release of Identifying Information to Adoptees
(*percentages*)

		Birth Mothers by Year of Relinquishment		
Degree of *Agreement*	*N =*	*1968* *(39)*	*1978* *(39)*	*All* *Birth Mothers* *(78)*
Strongly agree to somewhat agree		82.0	94.8	88.5
Strongly disagree to somewhat disagree		18.0	5.2	11.5

and almost 40 percent (37.5 percent) would favor the appointment of a guardian to prevent unilateral decision by the department to release their identity after their death. The corresponding proportion for the 1978 cohort was 64.3 and 13 percent.

Adoptees

The degree of support for disclosing identifying information varied among adoptees by gender. Females were more approving, with 84.2 percent, than male adoptees, at 73.3 percent. It is possible that females are more sensitive to issues involving social justice than males. Also, female adoptees tended to experience a greater desire for information or contact someday with their birth parents than did males. However, there was no relationship between adoptees' support for disclosure and their desire (p>.05). In other words, of those who favored disclosure of identifying information, almost equal proportions (53.5 percent) of them had moderate to great desire, or little or no desire (46.5 percent) to meet.

Females were more equivocal to the release of identifying information to minor adoptees who may not be emotionally mature and were more protective of the privacy rights of the birth mother than their male counterparts. A higher proportion of them (94 percent) favored the legal age of the adoptee than did male adoptees, who constituted 82 percent. Significantly, a much higher percentage (three-fourths) endorsed the requirement of the birth mother's consent compared to a little over one-half (54.5 percent) for male adoptees. Similarly, female adoptees outnumbered males, who were in favor of an indefinite search for the birth mother to obtain her consent. Their respective proportions were 61.5 percent and 50 percent. It appears that female adoptees more than male adoptees can tune in to the problems of another female and appreciate her dilemma. Their understanding of the birth mothers' predicament and occasional empathy with them are reflected in these statements:

> I know if I gave my child up, I'd want to know about him.

> As an adoptee I like the idea of receiving identifying information with my birth mother's consent, even though I face the possibility of being turned down. As a mother I realize why she is having problems. I like to see both sides of it; this is doctrine of fairness.

Contrast that with these male adoptees' statements, which manifested their resentment and indignation toward birth mothers:

> I would say it should be made a bit harder for the birth mother to contact the adoptee than it's for the adoptee to contact her. Throw more red tape for the birth mother (laugh).

> You might not want this woman chasing after you all over the place.
> You never know, she could be an emotionally unstable and unfit person.

Interestingly, none of the female adoptees felt bitter or passed harsh judgment on birth mothers' conduct, as this male adoptee did, "You don't go around lighting a fire if you can't put it out." Another single male adoptee attending vocational school was also highly judgmental:

> At age fourteen I had another realization when the sex part of this age
> came into it. I realized how boys meet girls and all that stuff and began
> to feel that my mother had loose morals.

Adoptees' Desire and Support for Disclosure. Earlier, it was noted that adoptees' endorsement of disclosure policy was not related to their desire for information or contact with birth parents, at least for now. Our data, however, show that curiosity about birth parents and heredity was widespread among the sample adoptees. For example, one-half (49.1 percent) of all adoptees experienced moderate to great desire and the other half (50.9 percent) reported a little or slight desire. It stands to reason that desire to know manifests in varying magnitudes, ranging from fleeting interest or curiosity to compulsive yearning. "My brother is occasionally curious but largely for him it doesn't mean more than a can of beans," said a male adoptee." "But for me it's the most important thing in my life because I have a great desire to know." Furthermore, as noted in the literature review (see chapter 1), desire in some adoptees is limited to learning about genealogical background, while others are not content until they have met their parents. Yet, some would be satisfied by a glimpse of their birth parents, rather than a face-to-face encounter with them. This single twenty-one-year-old male adoptee said:

> I wouldn't want to meet my birth mother but would like to see her at a
> distance.

A twenty-three-year-old registered nurse said:

> I would just walk past my mother's house or meet her on the street and
> would like to look at her and see what she looked like. I'm not sure if I
> would like to talk to her or not.

Factors Inhibiting Curiosity. To be sure, the capacity to be inquisitive is innate; some children are naturally inquisitive and others are simply indifferent to their surroundings. However, development and expression of curiosity is mediated by a number of factors, both inhibiting and promoting. First, some adoptees in our sample reported an intense curiosity about their birth parents during their growing-up period, but they learned to suppress it, fearing disapproval of their adoptive parents. Every time curiosity or desire for genealogy surfaced in their awareness they felt guilty and regarded their interest an act of betrayal. They felt eternally indebted to their adoptive parents for giving them love and care and didn't want to hurt their feelings by raising the subject. The following excerpts typify these adoptees' predicament.

> My adoptive mother didn't encourage me to talk about it. I think what she wanted was that I was hers, and that's it. I used to feel I would upset her if I asked any question or expressed my curiosity. So I didn't like to ask her too much.

> The only thing that kept me from asking about my biological mother was my adoptive parents' feelings. They have been so caring and good and I was afraid it wouldn't be fair to them to ask.

> I remember asking Mom one time about my birth mother. She got such a look in her eyes that I never asked her anything else. It was a look of hurt and anger.

Second, some adoptees did not raise the subject or admit their interest to the adoptive parents. It was because they were afraid their motives, however sincere, might be misconstrued and their interest might be interpreted as an indication of dis-satisfaction with their adoptive home.

> She has been a wonderful mother and I wouldn't want her to feel that I was not satisfied with her and that my desire to look for my birth mother meant that I want to grow away from her. I just as well not mention it.

> I didn't feel like asking my adoptive parents questions about my background. I thought they might take my questions and read them their way and think, 'Gee, she is not happy, what have we done wrong?' So I figured the simplest thing to do was to let it pass.

Third, the fear of facing embarrassing information or rejection by the birth mother inhibited curiosity among some adoptees. Consequently, they rationalized or denied their feelings.

> I wouldn't like to meet my birth parents; maybe they wouldn't want me. Well, it doesn't bother me if I met them or not.

> I don't want to know about them. I'm happy as it is. [I'm afraid] I might find out something I wouldn't want to know. So it would be just as well not to know.

Fourth, some adoptees were indifferent to genealogical concerns because they resented their birth mothers for getting pregnant illegitimately and then giving them up. They regarded their genealogical past as tainted. Identification with it meant resurrection of painful and embarrassing circumstances of their birth and adoption. A single twenty-four-year-old male adoptee told us:

> At age fourteen I began to realize the full weight of adoption and the thing about being an unwanted child. I often wondered why my mother got rid of me. At this age I had another realization. I visualized how boys meet girls and all this stuff and felt that my mother was of loose morals. Then I didn't want to think about her anymore.

Another single male adoptee working as a skilled manual worker at an oil industry said:

> Whenever the subject is brought up I feel resentment toward my birth parents for not knowing why I was given up.

Factors Promoting Curiosity. We discussed factors that inhibited desire in our adoptees for wanting to know and discouraged them from recognizing and expressing it to themselves and to their parents. However, we also noted certain factors that served to foment latent desire among some adoptees. The most important among them were exposure to adoptees activist groups such as Parent Finders, discussion on the subject, and publicity in the media advocating the rights of adoptees. This twenty-five-year-old married woman with two children explained the profound effect the movie "Roots" had on her desire to search:

> I think curious was merely the word until I saw the movie "Roots"and that was such an overwhelming feeling. Every time it would come on I'd sit there and cry. This man could trace his roots back generations after generations and here I was that my generation started with me. That made me realize if he could do it, I was going to do it.

Another woman aged twenty-three, separated and working as a credit manager, said:

> My curiosity wasn't really strong until I read a few articles or we talked about adoption in school. I used to wonder about adoption. Sometimes when some people asked me if I ever wonder what my birth parents were like, then I started to think about it.

> When I was about sixteen or seventeen, I was curious as to who she is, what she does, what she looks like, what makes her tick, why she gave me up etc. Then at age twenty or twenty-one I saw on T.V. news about a long-lost daughter for forty years who met her birth mother. Those kinds of stories got me more into thinking that I should also find out my birth parents.

Certain major life events such as marriage, pregnancy, or the birth of a child triggered dormant desire in our adoptees, mostly females. They started to experience serious concern regarding continuity, ancestry, heritage, and most frequently, hereditary diseases, when they decided to have a child. This twenty-four-year-old woman had curiosity about her birth parents that grew stronger around the time of her marriage. It developed into a compelling quest as she was planning to have her first child:

> At twenty-one it was a strong enough curiosity for one to go to the Department of Social Services. I was married then and we were considering having a child. The most I wanted to know was if there was anything in my medical background that indicated that I shouldn't have children.

Another factor that contributed to deepening curiosity in some adoptees was economic and psychological independence from adoptive parents, which usually occurred later in life. They had met other life tasks, such as education, marriage, and career and could turn their attention to their identity concerns. Also, when employed they had better means to finance the lengthy search activity. Until their late teens and early adulthood, these adoptees were preoccupied with achieving educational and career goals, which assumed greater priority than the concerns regarding identity and heritage.[2] This single male, twenty-one, a geology student, had a slight curiosity about his birth parents until he was eighteen. It began to intensify after he was employed, which motivated him to search:

> I used to wonder, more or less, during my adolescence whether I was the same as my birth father. But I had hardly a desire to meet him. I was just too busy to think about anything like that. When I started making some money I started to think I might dig up as to where my birth parents live.

For some adoptees, being older also meant being emotionally more mature, more self-confident, so that they could handle the impact of the information and/or the reunion, as this married housewife said:

> I was curious about my birth parents but I never thought of meeting them when I was young. Now I have an awful lot of desire. In a way I'm glad that the possibility didn't arise when I was young because I don't know if I would have been able to handle it or not. Now I feel I can

---

[2]Having analyzed the characteristics of 732 searchers who applied for help from a Chicago search and support group, Truth Seekers in Adoption, Gonyo and Watson (1988) observed that many adoptees decided to embark on a search after they "attained a more independent adult identity" (p. 19).

handle it no matter what circumstances are surrounding her. Maybe she is what I dreamed of or maybe she is the other way. But I can really handle her now.

In some cases, death of the adoptive parents kindled dormant desire and served as an added impetus for their decision to initiate search. The death of a parent created a void they wanted to fill. At the same time, it removed a source of guilt that had forced them to suppress or deny their desire.

> I have always said that until my mother died I would never physically want to see my natural parents. This was the commitment I made to myself but I didn't want to hurt my adoptive mother. Now that she has passed away, I feel a strong desire to search, no matter what.

Another male adoptee told us:

> I have no desire to meet. Right now I'm pretty content. Both my parents have to be dead before I ever think about something like that.

Studies on searching show that adoptees are generally in their middle thirties when they embark upon search (Day 1979; Gonyo and Watson 1988; Lamski 1980; Triseliotis 1984; Yellin et al. 1983; Weidell 1980). In view of our study findings, it may be argued that age per se seems to be spuriously related to adoptees' decisions to search. It is possible that factors such as marriage, pregnancy, children, maturity, financial resources, independence from adoptive parents, and priority for identity concerns kindle adoptees' interest and motivate them to seek information or contact with birth parents. And these events generally occur at a later age. Given the demographic profile of our adoptees—mostly young, unmarried, dependent on adoptive parents for maintenance and education—it can be understood why there is a low interest among our adoptees and why very few of them had experienced a compelling desire. All adoptees, except five, had no immediate plans to search.

The foregoing discussion also underlines the difficulty in interpreting adoptees' avowed lack of desire for knowledge or contact. As we noted, the development and expression of quest for origins are largely reflective of temperamental and environmental factors. An adoptee's indifference toward genealogy may be real or desire may be repressed or denied.

Summary and Conclusion

There was strong support among birth mothers and adoptees for release of identifying information to the adult adoptee. Female adoptees and the 1978 birth mothers expressed stronger approval than did male adoptees and the 1968 birth mothers. A strong majority of adoptive parents also endorsed this measure but their support was more apparent than real—it was filled with reservations and conditions. This was more true for the 1968 and 1978 parents, who favored the disclosure policy because they saw no choice if the adoptee was an adult and determined to seek information or contact. However, they feared the loss of their children's love should adoption records become available. To deal with their anxiety, some adoptive parents denied their children's interest in birth parents or avoided the issue. The 1958 adoptive parents, on the other hand, were less apprehensive and their support was less equivocal. The reason was that they felt more secure in their relationship and more confident about the adoptee's ability to handle the information even as a minor than did the 1968 and 1978 parents.

Adoptive parents and adoptees preferred the adoptee to be in his twenties to be eligible for identifying information. Older adoptees, they thought, would likely be emotionally mature to make a well-considered decision. Female adoptees were more concerned than male adoptees with the possibility of information getting into the hands of a minor adoptee who is emotionally immature.

In addition to the requirement of legal age of the adoptee, respondents in all groups overwhelmingly approved consent of the birth mother as a condition for permitting adoptees access to this information. Support for this requirement was strongest among adoptive parents, birth mothers, and adoptees, in that order. The 1968 birth mothers and female adoptees were more supportive of birth mothers' consent than were the 1978 birth mothers and male adoptees. A large majority of birth mothers rejected the myth about their need for permanent anonymity. They were receptive to providing consent, if requested, but would like to be alerted before the adoptee's appearance so that they could prepare themselves and members of their family.

Interestingly, despite their robust support for the birth mother's consent, a small majority in all groups favored an indefinite search for the birth mother whose consent is being sought. Far more female adoptees than males were in favor of an indefinite search. A passive involvement of the department in seeking the birth mother's consent was overwhelmingly rejected by respondents in all groups.

A large majority in all three groups thought it desirable for the adoptee to accept a birth mother's refusal to divulge her identity. However, these respondents supported a policy permitting the release of the birth mother's identity without her consent if she is dead or believed dead. The 1968 birth mothers were more approving of this policy option.

Consent of adoptive parents as requirement for adopted adults was mostly opposed by adoptees. Least opposition to this requirement came from adoptive parents, followed by birth mothers. A sizeable majority among adoptive parents wanted to impose their consent or be informed voluntarily by the adopted adult that he or she was seeking information about or contact with birth parents. The 1958 adoptive parents were far less favorable toward this requirement than the 1968 or the 1978 parents. Regardless of their degree of support for parental veto for adult adoptees, adoptive parents, birth mothers, and adoptees were unanimous in their support for parental consent when the adoptee is a minor.

Although curiosity to know about birth parents was widespread among adoptees, there was no relationship between adoptees' supports for disclosure and their desire to search. The data point to several factors that promote or inhibit desire among adoptees.

The findings unequivocally reject several myths regarding birth mothers—principally, that they forget the relinquished child and wish to remain permanently anonymous. More significantly, birth mothers who were opposed to disclosure of identifying information continued to experience feelings of pain, loss, and guilt even fourteen years after relinquishment. A large majority wished to meet the child, preferably if the adoptee took the initiative. The data do not substantiate adoptive parents' fear that a birth mother would be insensitive to their role and contribution in raising the adopted child and would intrude in the lives of adoptees. There is ample evidence that birth mothers accept the forfeiture of their rights and regard adoptive parents as real parents.

The data also categorically dismiss long-held beliefs that adoptees are inconsiderate and ungrateful toward the parents who raised them and provided them with a secure and loving home. It demonstrates that adoptees regard their allegiance to adoptive parents as irrevocable and do not seek their substitution by birth parents. Furthermore, they do not want to hurt their feelings by surreptitiously pursuing search.

The findings do not offer any basis for birth mothers' fear that adoptees are self-centered, resentful, and willing to wreak havoc with their lives by capricious appearance. On the contrary, adoptees by and large feel that the birth mother's right to remain anonymous outweighs their need to know.

5

Release of Nonidentifying Information to Adoptees and Adoptive Parents

Nonidentifying information is defined as background material that would not lead to identification of the birth parent, including personal history (that is, physical description, education, marital status, number of siblings, and so on) and social history (that is, occupation, hobbies, interests, talents and so on). Medical information is that pertaining to hereditary characteristics, diseases, and disabilities, including those of the parents of the birth parents. It is noteworthy that in small communities certain types or combinations of nonidentifying information are potentially identifying. Thus the definition of nonidentifying information is relative to the size of a given community and subject to the judgment of the department.

Nonidentifying Information to Adoptees

Our data show that releasing nonidentifying information to adoptees is not as controversial as releasing identifying information. Support for its release was not only consistently high among members of the triad, but was also less prescriptive. As depicted in table 5–1, an overwhelming majority in all groups (83 to 94 percent) approved the availability of this information to adoptees who request it. Interestingly, the strongest support came from birth mothers, with 93.5 percent approving its release, compared to 86.8 percent and 83 percent of adoptees and adoptive parents, respectively. The difference between birth mothers and adoptees was, however, not significant. Also, differences within each group were minor except among adoptees. Female adoptees were more supportive of such a policy, with 92.1 percent, than were males, who constituted 73.3 percent. A higher level of support among females may be attributed to their stronger interest in genealogy, as noted in the previous chapter.

Table 5–1
Attitudes toward Release of Nonidentifying Information to Adoptees
(*percentages*)

Degree of Agreement	N=	All Adoptive Parents (1958, 1968, 1978) (152)	All Birth Parents (1968, 1978) (78)	All Adoptees (53)
Strongly agree to somewhat agree		82.9	93.5	86.8
Strongly disagree to somewhat disagree		17.1	6.5	13.2

Reasons for Release of Nonidentifying Information

The dominant reason favoring release of this type of information was that it helps adoptees satisfy their curiosity about genealogy without being injurious to the interest and rights of any party. Since the information does not disclose the identity of the birth parent, it obviates the likelihood of an actual contact, which is usually threatening to adoptive parents. A 1978 adoptive mother said:

> If the child wants to know what his parents look like and stuff like that, I don't think that could harm anybody, except to satisfy his curiosity.

Adoptees felt that background information may be all that is needed for some searchers to satisfy their identity concerns, since they may not have the desire to seek contact with birth parents:

> In lots of cases nonidentifying information may be enough that any adoptee might need and he or she may not want to search out the birth parents.

> Adoptees do not always want to meet their parents; they want to find their identity. If they just know what color their birth parent's hair is, what kind of work they do, what type of persons they are, they will feel satisfied.

For some adoptees the original birth certificate is enough to feel connected with their past and to discover their identity:

> When I found just my birth certificate with my name on it I felt great. This was the beginning link of the chain that led me to realize who I was, what made me tick and do the things I do.

Adoptive parents felt a sense of relief in the possibility that adoptees could resolve their identity concerns without kindling their desire to reunite. This 1958 adoptive mother said:

> Maybe the background information will make them less curious; their mind will settle down a bit and they may not want to look for their real mom.

Both adoptees and birth mothers thought nonidentifying information could serve as a preliminary basis to determine whether it would be desirable for the adoptee to pursue contact with his parent. Adoptees feared that the nature of the background information could be such that an actual encounter with the birth parent might be hurtful. Birth mothers were afraid that certain information in their background might be embarrassing and stigmatizing and were uncertain how their child might react to them if they ever met.

> The nonidentifying information would help adoptees to realize whether or not they want to continue. When I was given this information I sat down and took a hard look at my feelings before I made up my mind.
>
> [Male adoptee]

> I don't think I did anything to be ashamed of other than getting pregnant outside of marriage. I hope this wouldn't be viewed by my son as a shameful act.
>
> [1978 Birth mother]

> I was on welfare then and I was finding it hard being alone with two kids. I hope my daughter will understand that.
>
> [1968 Birth mother]

Some birth mothers favored the release of nonidentifying information because they viewed it as an opportunity to present to the relinquished child the facts of the circumstances that forced them to give him up. They hoped the adoptee's misgivings would give way to appreciation and understanding of their decision. Their recurring comments were: "Even if my child doesn't have a chance to see me, I would like her to know that giving her up for adoption was giving her a break in life." "I'm sure she'll probably understand more about me and why I gave her up, so she can understand that her mother was good to her when I placed her in a good home."

Some birth mothers thought their child's request for background information would be an unequivocal indication of his or her interest in them. This knowledge would be reassuring and would provide them with considerable relief from feelings of self-incrimination.

> I would like to know that my child is trying to find out something about me, which would make me feel better. I think that would be a boost for me because right now I don't know if she is going to hold it against me.
>
> [1978 Birth mother]

> I would be interested to see if my son was interested enough to know what his parents' background was.
>
> [1968 Birth mother]

Suggestions for Release of Nonidentifying Information. Respondents offered some suggestions and caveats that may guide policy implementation on release of nonidentifying information to adoptees.

First, adoptive parents strongly felt that nonidentifying information should be given to them, preferably at the time of adoption. They contended that as their children began to understand the meaning of adoption, they raised questions concerning their genealogy that parents found hard to answer adequately. Many parents found their inability to satisfy their child's queries embarrassingly uncomfortable, while others felt they had to concoct an explanation. Adoptive parents say they have better knowledge of the child, his or her abilities, and the level of maturity required to handle the nonidentifying information, and are therefore in a better position than the department to determine the manner in which the information should be provided to the child. They also felt that sharing information with their child was a personal matter that should be handled within the adoptive-family. Typical of this viewpoint was expressed in the following statement by a 1978 adoptive mother:

> I'm convinced that my husband and I can present the information in a better manner to our child than anybody else. I would like to know more about his parents so that I can answer a little more honestly some of the questions he has been asking, instead of saying that I really don't know.

Some adoptive parents recognized that there are certain traits, talents, and interests the child inherits from his genetic parents. They said they could provide the child with the opportunities and encouragement for the development of these talents, such as music or art, if they had knowledge of the background and personality characteristics of the child's parents. This 1968 adoptive mother said:

> Kevin is a musical nut and he wanted to know what kind of music his parents played. This information could encourage him to develop his talent in that kind of music.

Adoptees, however, were divided on the question of providing nonidentifying information to adoption parents. Those who supported this measure were of the opinion that adoptive parents could use their best judgment about the appropriateness of time, situation, and the kind of information relevant to the child's maturity level and needs. Besides, they could be sensitive of the child's feelings and reactions. This female adoptee typified this viewpoint:

> If the adoptive parents received this information ahead of time, they could provide it to the child, instead of an outside agency, which could be indifferent toward the feelings and concerns of the child.

Adoptees who were opposed to such a move suspected that the adoptive parents might not maintain objectivity, candor, and dispassion in sharing the information with the child because of an inherent fear of losing the child's love and allegiance. Some adoptees felt they might not feel free to raise questions for fear their expression of interest might upset the adoptive parents. This twenty-three-year-old single male student expressed his abiding faith in the professional judgment of the department:

> The department is a sacred institution; it is holding all the trump cards and it knows how to play them. On the other hand, adoptive parents are a little too emotional and you don't get information straight from them. They are too involved to be able to give you the information without being biased.

This twenty-five-year-old married female adoptee, working as a waitress, recalled having strong interest in her origins when she was a teenager, but was reluctant to admit it to her adoptive parents because she was afraid she might hurt their feelings:

> I know what it was like when I was a teenager and I couldn't bring the subject up with my adoptive mother. I was always afraid I was going to hurt her by showing too much interest in my birth parents and possibly to make her afraid that I didn't love her.

Second, adoptees said that certain background information on birth parents could be emotionally damaging and extremely embarrassing and suggested that the social worker use discretion in screening the contents before making it available to the adoptee. Birth mothers also felt that the department should not provide the information to adoptees in a cavalier manner but instead should assist them in understanding the rationale and meaning of the items that are especially distressing. A male adoptee commented:

> I wouldn't want to find out that my birth mother was a whore and that my father was in a penitentiary for committing incest. I don't think such information can do me a bit of good.

Reasons against Release of Nonidentifying Information

A very small percentage of respondents (6 to 17 percent) who were opposed to the release of nonidentifying information to adoptees were unanimous in their view that it would not appease adoptees' curiosity and pacify their interest in genealogy. It might, instead, serve to ignite their desire for more information and possibly actual contact with their birth parents. They said the resultant continual interest in biological roots could interfere with integration of the adoptee into the adoptive family and cause distress to the adoptive parents. These respondents, therefore, would like the status quo maintained in the department policy:

> Giving him that information is not going to do him all that much good because it will only whet his appetite for more information. The only way to satisfy the child is to stop him now.
>
> [1968 Adoptive father]

> If you are given some information about your birth parents it would make you more curious to get identifying information and to go still further, so you would like this wheel going.
>
> [Male adoptee]

> The child might be thinking about the information all the time and might ask the adoptive parents more about it, making them feel bad.
>
> [1968 Birth mother]

A few birth mothers and adoptees were of the view that the background information contained in the department files was far from being adequate, accurate, and complete. They said the only way an adoptee can receive such information that is meaningful, satisfying, and free from bias is through a direct encounter with his birth parents.

> If the adopted child wants to know his birth mother's hair color or education I don't think it'll make much difference to him. He should meet his birth mother if he is really interested to know his background.
>
> [1978 Birth mother]

> The nonidentifying information with the department is so little that you can't make much of it. If you want to know what your birth mother really looks like, you should go and look for her. Besides, what the department provides you may not be wholly true.
>
> [Male adoptee]

Some adoptive parents felt that because the department would screen and sift items in the background information and provide its own interpretation of it, the resultant information could create a profile of the birth parents that might be unrealistic, exaggerated, or distorted. They said if the adoptee ever met his birth parent he would likely feel disillusioned and disappointed if his fantasized picture failed to match the reality.

> I see that sort of information as being placebo; it would quell certain feelings for a while but it could have the opposite effect. When you give this sort of information, it is going to create an image in that child's mind. The child will naturally fantasize someone who is almost perfect. When this child meets the real biological father or mother, they are obviously going to be less than perfect and this can cause disappointment or disillusionment to the child.
>
> [1978 Adoptive mother]

A couple of adoptees were opposed to the release of background information because they feared that knowledge of outstanding abilities and high achievements of their birth parents could raise their own expectations and make them feel pressured to perform at a level equal to their parents. A male adoptee said, "I would be worried whether or not I was able to uphold the image of my biological father, who could be a real brain; that could be a bit detrimental."

Grounds for Release of Nonidentifying Information

As in the case of identifying information, respondents' approval or disapproval for release of nonidentifying information was contingent upon the age of the adoptee and consent of the adoptive parents and birth parent.

Age of Adoptee

As stated in chapter 4, age of the adoptee was viewed by respondents as a highly critical, though crude, indicator for assessing emotional maturity of the adoptee requesting this information. Age was also considered a legal and/or psychological base for determining whether the consent of adoptive and birth parents is desirable. The resulting data on the age requirement is depicted in table 5–2.

As is evident from the table, adulthood was not considered a necessary condition by the triad, and particularly by birth mothers and adoptees, to obtain background information. This contrasts with their position identifying information. An almost equal proportion of birth mothers (68.5 percent) and adoptees (63 percent) thought the information should be provided to adoptees who are minors but mature enough to handle it. Only about one-third each (31.5 percent and 37 percent) said the adoptee

Table 5–2
Age of Adoptees for Release of Nonidentifying Information
(*percentages*)

Adoptee's Age	N =	Adoptive Parents (1958, 1968, 1978) (127)*	Birth Mothers (1968, 1978) (73)*	Adoptees (46)*
At any age		13.4	21.9	23.9
Only when mature		37.0	46.6	39.1
Of legal age		49.6	31.5	37.0

*All those who agreed with the release of nonidentifying information in table 5–1

should be an adult. Adoptive parents were almost evenly divided, with 50.4 percent supporting the minor age and 49.6 percent favoring the age of majority.

It is worth noting that birth mothers held the most liberal views on the requirement of age, while adoptive parents were the most conservative.

Adoptive Parents' Consent

Adoptive parents showed more relaxed attitudes toward disclosure of non-identifying information than they did toward identifying details. Only one-tenth (10.3 percent) favored releasing this information to an adult adoptee with their consent. (See table 5-3.)

Birth mothers followed suit, with less than one-tenth (8.2 percent) supporting this requirement for adult adoptees. Once again they gave evidence of their consideration toward adoptive parents. None of the adoptees favored parental consent for an adoptee who has achieved adult-hood. However, respondents in all groups considered parental consent desirable when the adoptee is a minor, with 65.2 percent (adoptees), 61.9 percent (adoptive parents), and 41.1 percent (birth mothers) supporting

Table 5–3
Prior Consent of Adoptive Parents
(*percentages*)

Degree of Agreement	N =	Adoptive Parents (1958, 1968, 1978) (127)*	Birth Mothers (1968, 1978) (73)*	Adoptees (46)*
Agree in case of adult adoptees		10.3	8.2	–
Agree in case of minor adoptees		61.9	41.1	65.2
Consent not required		27.8	50.7	34.8

*All those who agreed with release of nonidentifying information in table 5–1

this measure, in that order. These respondents were unanimous in their concern that a child is most likely immature and is not capable of making decisions that serve his best interest. They said the adoptive parents are the best judges of his emotional strength and ability and have legal responsibilities to ensure that the information will prove beneficial to him. Typical of their concern is reflected in these statements:

> I raised the child and know every move and reaction he had. I would, therefore, know if there is anything that could affect his life.
>
> [1958 Adoptive mother]

> If the child is a minor, he is not supposedly capable of making decisions that would be in his best interest. That's why the parents are supposed to help the child up to a certain age. I couldn't have handled this information when I was 14 or 15 or even 17.
>
> [1968 Birth mother]

Reasons for Adoptive Parents' Consent for Adult Adoptees. The adoptive parents and birth mothers who advocated parental consent for release of nonidentifying information to adult adoptees offered two reasons. First, they felt the adoptive parents' involvement would ensure that the department did not undermine their status. They contended that the department would cause strain on the adoptive-parents—adoptee relationship if it provided the adoptee with nonidentifying information without their knowledge:

> In the interest of a good relationship between adoptive parents and adoptee the department should let them know the child is looking for this information. I don't think it's healthy to go behind their back.
>
> [1978 Adoptive father]

> Adoptive parents are the adoptee's real parents who raised him. It would hurt their feelings if their child had been told this information and they didn't even know about it.
>
> [1968 Birth mother]

Second, they were concerned there might be certain aspects of the adoptee's genealogical information that could be traumatizing. In that case, the adoptee would need adoptive parents with whom to discuss his feelings. Adoptive parents said they would like to be involved so they could help their children and provide them with the necessary support and guidance to cope with any distressing information. They assured they would not prevent or discourage, in any way, their adult children from learning about their birth parents. Typical comments were:

I would like to help my daughter, to share my love, to show that I'm not against her so she wouldn't go through it alone. I'd like to keep my son and prepare him for it and tell him what to expect.

[1978 Adoptive mother]

I do think adoptive parents' consent should be required because that way the child has got someone he can talk to about it. If he finds out certain things he is puzzled about or he has got something on his mind, he can discuss it with his adoptive mother, who may help him out a bit.

[1978 Birth mother]

Some adoptive parents fear that nonidentifying information carries with it a high risk of actual reunion, either because adoptees would discover clues to their birth parents' identity or they would be tempted to seek further information regarding their whereabouts. They said the reunion, should it occur, is most likely to present stress and strain on the adoptee's life. In that situation the adoptive parents felt they could offer guidance and support to enable the adoptee to cope with the impact of profound changes. This 1978 adoptive mother noted:

In some cases, the child starts looking for nonidentifying information, but it could lead to more specific search and in that situation the parents would be able to help the child prepare for the unexpected.

Reasons against Adoptive Parents' Consent for Adult Adoptees. The reason advanced in a rhythm-like manner by triad members pertained to the nature of information. They said that since adoptees are not likely to identify birth parents, the status of the adoptive arrangement will remain undisturbed. Such a possibility removes the fears on the part of the adoptive and birth parents, while serving adoptees' curiosity. Typical comments were:

If the child is not going to look for the birth parent, why, you should keep that stuff away from him. All the child wants to know is what his mother looks like, where she grew up, and what kind of family she came from; that kind of stuff shouldn't hurt anybody.

[1968 Birth mother]

The knowledge about the background of one's natural parent can't do any harm. Sometimes it does good to some people to know a little about their heritage.

[1978 Adoptive mother]

The nonidentifying information is not going to do any harm. The adoptive parents still have their adopted child and the kid still loves them and they are still his mom and dad.

[Female adoptee]

Some adoptive parents disagreed with this requirement because they felt they would not be able to deflect a determined child's desire to seek information. This 1968 adoptive mother explained her helplessness:

> Anything he wants to find out about his birth mother he is going to find out anyway whether I like it or not. If he wants the information bad enough he'll nag us until I agree with him. There's nothing I can do to stop him.

Some adoptive parents considered this condition inappropriate and unjust for the adoptee who is an adult. They felt it would be an affront to the adoptee's dignity if the release of nonidentifying information was made conditional upon their consent. They would, however, like to be informed (preferably by the adoptee) as a matter of courtesy about a decision to seek such information. Illustrative of this point is the statement by a 1968 adoptive mother:

> Our consent is not required when the adoptee is adult, but we should be notified that the department is going to give our daughter this information. Again, we are asking out of courtesy and in the spirit of sharing things between the child and her parents. I don't mean the department should write us secretly. Perhaps it's better if our daughter would tell us.

Surreptitious sharing of information with the adoptee by the department was also opposed by birth mothers. They rejected mandatory parental consent because they were afraid the adoptive parents might not grant permission out of apprehension or jealousy. However, they strongly felt that adoptees should confide in their parents to avoid their feeling hurt or slighted. They recognized the significant role of the adoptive parents who deserve to be kept informed about the adoptee's interest in his genealogical background.

> I think the adoptive parents should be taken into consideration, because, all in all, they are the adoptee's real parents. They took the child probably from day one and it's their child. Adoptive parents, therefore, have a right to know what's going on.
>
> [1968 Birth mother]

> I think it's up to the adopted child to be open and honest with the adoptive parents. Generally, such information could do no harm because it's only general information. But it might hurt the adoptive parents' feelings if the child goes behind their back to get it.
>
> [1968 Birth mother]

It is of interest to note that contrary to the prevailing belief, birth mothers gave evidence of their sensitivity to adoptive parents' feelings, and regarded their contribution to raising their birth child as highly significant.

Birth Parent's Consent

An overwhelming majority of all three groups (81 to 83 percent) rejected birth parent's consent as a requirement for providing nonidentifying information to adoptees, a reversal of the position presented by them in the case of identifying information. Adoptees posted the highest proportion, with 91.3 percent, who disapproved of this requirement, followed by adoptive parents (82.7 percent) and birth mothers (80.8 percent) (see table 5–4).

Of those who stipulated the birth parent's consent for release of nonidentifying information, birth mothers and adoptive parents represented almost equal proportions, with 19.2 percent and 17.3 percent respectively. Only four adoptees agreed with this position.

Reasons against Birth Parent's Consent. The predominant reason given by all respondents was that such information does not disclose the identity of the birth parents, a major concern associated with the disclosure of identifying information. They said the department is able to maintain its pledge of secrecy and anonymity, while at the same time satisfies adoptees' need for connectedness with their genealogy. Their typical comments are illustrated by this male adoptee.

> It is not going to identify the birth parent. If she still wants to play a mystery person this information is not going to hurt her because all the child wants to know is general information, such as her hair color, hobbies, her looks, etc.

Table 5–4
Prior Consent of Birth Parent
(*percentages*)

Degree of Agreement	N=	Adoptive Parents (1958, 1968, 1978) (127)*	Birth Mothers (1968, 1978) (73)*	Adoptees (46)*
Strongly agree to somewhat agree		17.3	19.2	8.7
Strongly disagree to somewhat disagree		82.7	80.8	91.3

*All those who agreed with release of nonidentifying information in table 5–1

A sizable number of adoptive parents found this requirement daunting. They said the birth mother supplied background information to the department at placement with the understanding that it would be shared with the parents who adopted her child. They argued that the department expected them to tell the child and discuss his or her genealogical background so as to help him or her come to terms with the adoption. A few adoptees echoed a similar point, that the birth mother should regard it as a natural occurrence when the relinquished child raises questions about genealogy. This male adoptee asked:

> Why did she ever go through the pregnancy and give it up if she didn't figure out then that the child can have curiosity about the people who gave birth to him?

Adoptive parents also argued that since the birth mother has no knowledge of the child's needs and strengths, it makes the requirement of her consent pointless. The department should take the adoptive parents, if anybody, into confidence in making decisions on how the child's interest can be best served. They stressed that they raised the child and are therefore, familiar with the child's abilities, and psychological needs and thus are the most logical participant in such decisions. These beliefs were reflected by this 1958 adoptive mother:

> Birth mothers gave the child up as an infant and thus they don't know anything about him now. I don't see why they should be consulted.
>
> [1958 Adoptive mother]

Reasons for Birth Parent's Consent. The main reason the triad cited in support of this requirement was that the background information might contain incriminating or embarrassing items the birth parent would not like to share with the relinquished child. It is, therefore, fair that the birth parent be given an opportunity to assess the nature of the background details supplied at the time of placement and determine whether the department should release the information in its entirety, delete certain items, or not disclose it all.

> I think I should know that my daughter wants information about me. There are probably things that make me feel uneasy that I don't want her to know. If there is anything necessary for her to know, she should know. But I should be able to decide.
>
> [1978 Birth mother]

> There might be a deep dark secret she has kept all these years that she doesn't want found out by her child.
>
> [1978 Adoptive mother]

Adoptive parents and birth mothers who favored requiring birth parent's consent were afraid that nonidentifying information could give important clues to the identity of the birth parent, despite careful screening by the department. They felt the birth parent was the best judge to determine if the details were truly nonidentifying:

> There could be some information in the file that only I could say that it's identifying and is cutting it pretty fine.
>
> [1978 Birth mother]

> Although it is nonidentifying information it could lead to a situation with the potential to devastate the birth mother's life.
>
> [1968 Adoptive mother]

A few birth mothers and adoptees supported this condition because it goes against the fundamental principles of morality and ethics to share information that pertains to another person, in this case the birth parent, without her or his knowledge. A female adoptee echoed this sentiment:

> To just go ahead and give out information about the birth mother without her consent would be an infringement on her privacy. You are peeking into a part of her life that she probably has not told to too many people. I think it is just good manners to get her permission.

Differences within Groups

There were remarkable similarities within each subgroup of adoptive parents and birth mothers in their attitudes toward the release of nonidentifying information and the accompanying criteria. Male and female adoptees, however, differed markedly on these dimensions. Because of the small number of males in the sample, these findings should be treated only as speculations.

As shown in table 5–5, female adoptees were more approving of disclosing nonidentifying information to adoptees than males, with respective proportions of 92.1 percent and 73.3 percent. Since women are assumed to have greater interest in genealogy, it is believed they tend to support a more liberal policy. It is interesting to note that unlike female adoptees, males did not differentiate between the significance and implications of identifying and nonidentifying information. The proportion supporting the disclosure measure on identifying and nonidentifying information was exactly identical among male adoptees, while a higher percentage (8 percent) of females were in favor of releasing nonidentifying information than identifying information (see table 5–5).

Female adoptees also held a more liberal position than did their male

Table 5–5
Adoptees' Attitudes toward Release of Nonidentifying Information on Birth Mothers, by Gender

Degree of Agreement	Release of Nonidentifying Information to Adult Adoptees		Release of Nonidentifying Information to Minor Adoptees		Adoptive Parents' Consent for Minors		Birth Mothers' Consent	
N=	Male (15)	Female (38)	Male (11)	Female (35)	Male (11)	Female (35)	Male (11)	Female (35)
Strongly agree to somewhat agree	73.3 [73.3]*	92.1 [84.2]	45.5	68.6	54.5	68.6	—	11.4
Strongly disagree to somewhat disagree	26.6 [26.7]	7.9 [15.8]	54.5	31.4	45.5	31.3	100.0	88.6

*Figures in brackets represent adoptees' agreement or disagreement with release of identifying information to adoptees

counterparts on the age requirement. More than two-thirds (68.6 percent) endorsed the release of this information to the teenage adoptee, compared with less than one-half (45.5 percent) of male adoptees who thought similarly. Female adoptees supported the younger age because they believed a minor has the maturity and ability to handle nonidentifying information. In contrast, male adoptees contended that maturity and a sense of responsibility dawns quite late in one's life, at least not before adulthood. This is how they expressed their respective convictions as to when a child experiences maturity.

> Nowadays kids in their teens, fourteen or fifteen, are a lot more mature than they were some years ago. I think a child aged eleven years or older can handle this information.
>
> [Female adoptee]

> I think nineteen or twenty is the appropriate age to make sure the child is mature to understand completely An awful lot of young people don't have their minds made up as to what they want to do until they are much older.
>
> [Male adoptee]

Female adoptees also differed with their male counterparts on consent of the adoptive parents and the birth parents as conditions for release of nonidentifying information. They tended to be more guarded than male adoptees in permitting access. While all adoptees rejected the condition of adoptive parents' consent when the adoptee is an adult, female adoptees were, however, more supportive of this condition in the case of a minor than were males. They represented more than two-thirds (68.6 percent) and a little over one-half (54.5 percent) respectively. Likewise, all male adoptees were opposed to the birth mother's consent as stipulation for receiving nonidentifying information, whereas more than one-tenth (11.4 percent) of females showed their approval for this requirement. The differential level of agreement/disagreement with the consent requirement may be due to females' inherent ability to identify with the situation of another female, illustrated by these statements: "I can put myself in the adoptive parents' shoes." "If it were my child looking for information about me, I would want her to let me know." The empathic attitude of females contrasts with male adoptees' more cavalier, insensitive attitudes, as reflected in these statements: "It's none of their business." "A lot of adoptive parents don't make the right decision for their child."

Medical Information to Adoptees

While the influence of psychological environment in the adoptee's development has long been recognized in the literature, it is only recently that the role of genetic inheritance in the nature-nurture configuration has received prominence in the search movement. With increased recognition in the medical field of genetic links for cause and treatment of many life-threatening diseases, adoptive parents and adoptees have become more interested in the biological family for medical history and hereditary factors. Recent publicity regarding a few adoptees' unsuccessful attempts to receive bone marrow transplants from their birth relatives has further heightened the interest in medical information on birth relatives.

Not surprisingly, as shown in table 5–6 our respondents were almost unanimous in their support for the release of information to requesting adoptees on medical history and hereditary diseases.

Their main reason was that such information can be critical in the early detection, prevention, and treatment of fatal diseases. They said information concerning hereditary diseases can be vitally important in making decisions about childbearing. The respondents considered medical information a basic right. This twenty-five-year-old single adoptee and university student was in tears when she told us why she would like medical information on her birth family:

> I do not have a medical history and when people ask my medical background I put down whatever information I have about the family I have now. If I think about having children I'm afraid of the chances that there could be some dreadful genetic things that could affect my children.

This twenty-four-year-old married adoptee experiences anxiety because of a constant fear of disabling diseases in her children:

> How do I know whether I'm a carrier of some hereditary diseases I might have passed on to my children? What would happen when my child came down with this disease? I'd say, 'Where the hell did it come from?'

Table 5–6
Attitudes toward Release of Medical History on Birth Parents to Adoptees
(*percentages*)

Degree of Agreement	N =	All Adoptive Parents (1958, 1968, 1978) (152)	All Birth Mothers (1968, 1978) (78)	All Adoptees (53)
Strongly agree to somewhat agree		93.4	98.7	96.2
Strongly disagree to somewhat disagree		6.6	1.3	3.8

Like female adoptees, adoptive parents were highly concerned about the possibility of deformity in their grandchildren and said they would like to have full disclosure of medical history of the birth family.

> When my daughter gets married she may want to know if there is something in her blood so that she can decide whether to have her own children.
>
> [1958 Adoptive mother]

Birth mothers were motivated by concerns for health and well-being of the child they relinquished. Since medical history can be crucial to a child's life, some birth mothers considered this information more important than any other. Others maintained that access to such information is the adoptee's basic human right:

> He should have this information more so than the two other types of information. There could be a hereditary disease, the information of which could save his life.
>
> [1968 Birth mother]

> If the child has a hereditary disease and it's passed down, the child has a right to know, especially if she is going to get married. It is her right to know.
>
> [1978 Birth mother]

Some birth mothers had genetic diseases, such as diabetes or coronary conditions, present in their family members or themselves. Thus, they worried about the possibility of having passed them on to the relinquished child:

> Heart trouble runs in our family. Both my parents died of heart problems. I think my child should know about this.
>
> [1968 Birth mothers]

> I think this child I had will have diabetes, because I have this condition. I would like to give this information to his adoptive parents.
>
> [1978 Birth mothers]

Only one birth mother (1978), two adoptees (male and female), and ten adoptive parents disagreed with release of medical information to adoptees. The birth mother thought that certain health-related information such as AIDS, alcoholism, and mental illness is stigmatizing, and genetic diseases such as cancer, diabetes, and heart disease could cause the adoptee lifelong anxiety. The two adoptees and five adoptive parents concurred with the birth mother's 'ignorance is bliss' attitude. Adoptees argued that they would be constantly worried about debilitating diseases if they knew these afflictions existed in their biological parents. They also felt that even with advance information, there is not much current medical knowledge can do to prevent these diseases. Furthermore, they might not suffer from these diseases, and even if they did contract them, they would have, until then, enjoyed life free from anxiety.

> I don't want to know that I'm going to die of this or that. It would be pretty scary if I found out that my birth parents had both died at twenty-five or thirty of a heart disease. I'll probably worry to death until I am past that point. If it's visible in my health then I'm in trouble anyway and the information about my parents' health is not going to help me.
>
> [Male adoptee]

Five adoptive parents were against the release of medical information to adoptees because they did not want the adoption records opened for any reasons. This 1958 adoptive mother said. "I should like to think that my file is closed and sealed forever."

Medical Information to Adoptive Parents

Respondents were unanimous in suggesting that medical history should be provided to adoptive parents at the time of adoption. They said adoptive parents are responsible for the care and well-being of the child and would need the information in the event of sickness. A male adoptee said, "Medical history should be a part of the adoption package that should go to the parents adopting the child. Then it's up to them to inform the child's doctor and how to tell the child."

Some adoptive parents encountered embarrassing moments during their child's sickness because they could not supply genetic history to the doctor who needed it. This 1968 adoptive mother described her predicament and anguish:

> When I got Kevin he was sick and had deformity of the ankle and every couple of days I'd take him to hospital. The first thing the doctors asked me, "Where was your baby born? What was wrong with him then? Did he have asthma? Were his feet turned out at birth?" I could not tell them anything and looked really like a stupid fool.

Parents who had not experienced any serious health problems with their children were also concerned about the lack of medical information, which they felt could prove vital in the detection and control of a disease before it develops to an incurable stage. A 1958 adoptive mother said:

> You don't know what could pop up and then you would like to know if the child's family had a history of any serious disease. It could be a

serious disease and may be caught in time if you know the child's genetic inheritance.

Update of Medical History

In the past, social agencies followed various practices for recording medical information and health history of the relinquishing birth mother. Variations occurred because genetic science didn't yet know about certain hereditary conditions. Certain life-threatening diseases that could be transmitted through generations were unknown by the available medical technology. Today, it has become standard practice with many agencies to obtain a detailed information concerning the health status of the child's birth relatives. Even so, records in many agencies are not updated. An information vacuum results from agencies' traditional policy of no contact with birth mothers once the adoption decree is entered. To be sure, the only source by which agencies could update information on health status and particularly on genetically transmitted diseases in the child's birth family is the birth mother, who may have information on the whereabouts or history of the birth father. We therefore asked the birth mothers about ways in which the department should contact them to update their medical histories. To obtain a range of ideas and suggestions we also posed a similar question to adoptive parents and adoptees. The resulting information is presented in table 5–7.

Table 5–7
Options to Update Medical Records on Birth Mothers
(*percentages*)

Department's Options	N =	Adoptive Parents (1958, 1968, 1978) (142)*	Birth Parents (1968, 1978) (77)*	Adoptees (51)*
1. Birth parent should be required to file periodically		3.6	6.5	21.6
2. Birth parent should be left alone to file periodically		8.7	23.4	27.5
3. Department should contact birth parent whenever needed		29.7	49.3	13.7
4. Department should not update		23.2	2.6	-
5. No suggestion or can't be done		34.8	18.2	37.3

*All those who agreed with release of medical history on birth parents in table 5–6

Suggestions by Birth Mothers

Significantly, almost one-half (49.3 percent) of the birth mothers agreed to periodic direct contact by the department for an update on medical history or for consent to contact their family physicians. However, they emphasized that the department should make sure that the medical information requested is vital for the child's health. Their eagerness to cooperate with the department was motivated by their central concern for the well-being of the relinquished child.

> The department should phone me and I would give my family doctor's name if it was going to help my child.

> I wouldn't want to see my child die; I'd rather see that the department get this information one way or the other.

> If there is something wrong with my little girl and the adoptive parents want to find out if there is anything in my family, the department should come to me.

> You'd have to get in touch with me if it concerns my child's health and if I cannot be found the department should contact the child's natural grandparents.

> If my child is in a car accident and she needs a transfusion the department should tell her my whereabouts so that my daughter can get my blood.

> If my daughter wants a kidney transplant or something that only her blood relatives can provide, the department should contact me.

Some birth mothers suggested that they be asked at the time of relinquishment for the names and addresses of their family doctors and their consent to release such information as needed. They said it would be relatively easier for the department to contact their family doctor, who would most probably know their whereabouts.

Less than one-quarter (23.4 percent) of the birth mothers would not allow contact by the department but were willing to file medical information as it became relevant.[1] Mandatory reporting was overwhelmingly rejected by all but five birth mothers (6.5 percent).

---

[1]In Minnesota, 85 percent of birth mothers who were located by an agency intermediary agreed to update medical and genetic information (Adoption Records Issue, 1986).

Close to one-fifth (18.2 percent) proffered no suggestions for updating medical histories or thought the task of locating and tracking down birth mothers was impractical. It is worthy of note that only two birth mothers (2.6 percent) did not want any part in updating their medical histories because, as they put it, "I don't want to do anything with the department."

Suggestions by Adoptive Parents and Adoptees

Despite their concern for updated and detailed medical histories, adoptive parents and adoptees were reticent in their support for periodic direct contact with birth mothers. Only a little over one-quarter (29.7 percent) of adoptive parents and one-tenth (13.7 percent) of adoptees endorsed this approach (see table 5–7). Their major consideration was the preservation of birth mothers' anonymity and freedom from intrusion in their lives. One 1958 adoptive mother said, "It would be too much poking and probing in the lives of birth parents." One male adoptee said, "Once she has given up the child, she is going to try to make her life. She would not like the social worker to knock at her door and ask her if anything new came up medical-wise."

Adoptees were almost equally divided between those who preferred voluntary reporting (27.5 percent) and those who favored mandatory reporting (21.6 percent) by birth parents. Adoptive parents, however, were far less inclined toward the mandatory option, with only 3.6 percent in favor. Adoptees in favor of compulsory reporting argued that the responsibility of birth parents toward the child's well-being did not end at relinquishment. They suggested that the birth mother be required to sign an agreement at the time of placement. To illustrate the point, this male adoptee used an analogy of a car manufacturer's obligation toward its product:

> I think it should be made known to birth parents that the child's health is their responsibility even after relinquishment, because they have created a biological body that might have a defect. It is the same as if Ford put out a car and its brakes failed two months later. It is still the responsibility of the motor company to let its owner know of the danger so that the person could take precautionary steps.

Another male adoptee made a similar point:

> Birth mothers should be required by law to fill out a questionnaire every so often, because they are playing with someone's life whether they chose to accept it or not. They are still responsible for the welfare of that child.

Adoptive parents countered that it would be unfair to force birth parents into doing something they might not want to do. They said, coercion might not guarantee cooperation and responsiveness; on the contrary, birth parents might resent the child and the department.

Almost one-quarter (23.2 percent) of adoptive parents disliked the idea of updating medical information because they were afraid that any contact with birth parents could lead to the possible revival of the child's past. They would rather feel content with the medical information they received at the time of adoption, however inadequate, than risk "opening a Pandora's box," as one 1978 adoptive mother put it. A 1968 adoptive mother was also averse to the idea of updating medical history because "it would mean the department has to keep in touch with the birth parents all the time."

A sizeable proportion of adoptive parents (34.8 percent) and adoptees (37.3 percent) recognized the enormous difficulties and expense involved in keeping track of birth parents years after they relinquished children. They feared these difficulties would render updating medical information almost impossible. Some parents and adoptees suggested that the department obtain detailed information from the birth parent(s) at the time of relinquishment and contact family doctors for a periodic update, but only with their prior consent.

Use Legal Means or Accept Birth Parent's Refusal?

Despite the department's or agency's pledge of noninterference, there are situations that could pose a serious threat to an adoptee's health and thus necessitate contact with his birth parents. In view of that, we asked our respondents if the department should use legal means in the event the birth parent refuses to cooperate. As shown in table 5–8, a huge proportion in each group (86 to 90 percent) favored legal action against an

Table 5–8
Use Legal Means or Accept Birth Parent's Refusal?
(*percentages*)

Department's Options	N =	Adoptive Parents (1958, 1968, 1978) (142)*	Birth Mothers (1968, 1978) (77)*	Adoptees (51)*
Use legal means		87.9	85.7	90.2
Accept refusal		8.5	14.3	9.8
Unable to answer		3.6	–	–

*All those who agreed with release of medical history on birth parents in table 5–6

uncooperative birth parent if the adoptee's health is at stake. These respondents felt strongly that the health of an adoptee should override all other considerations, including the birth parent's right of privacy. They contended that the department is justified to use any means, including legal, to force the compliance of a resistive birth parent having information deemed vital to save an ailing adoptee's life. This sentiment was echoed by a female adoptee:

> Tough luck! Use legal means especially when your life depends on her information. This person does not have any right to say, "I don't feel like doing it."

More interestingly, birth mothers gave their overwhelming approval, with 85.7 percent in favor of legal intervention if necessary. They thought it would be inhumane and callous for a birth parent to refuse to cooperate in a critical situation involving their child's health. Their disdain for refusal to provide medical information was voiced by a 1978 birth mother who viewed the uncooperative attitude as "almost like committing a murder." Another 1978 birth mother stressed her commitment to the well-being of the relinquished child in these words:

> I don't want any harm coming to my child. The department should get this information through whatever means is possible. It's a matter of life and death.

Those who disagreed with the legal option constituted less than one-tenth each of adoptees (9.8 percent) and adoptive parents (8.5 percent). They were realistic and understanding of the birth mother's reasons that make it difficult for her to cooperate at times. Adoptive parents thought legal action would be too costly and time consuming, and would not guarantee cooperation of recalcitrant birth parents. A 1958 adoptive mother asked, "Do you think by bringing them into court they're going to divulge the information?"

Female adoptees reflected a deep understanding of a birth mother's refusal, which they thought could be inspired by genuine difficulty and therefore should be respected. They regarded legal intervention as violation of birth parents' right to anonymity and privacy, equating it to the rights of certain segments of society to refuse treatment on religious grounds. This is what some of them said:

> Maybe there is something the birth mother does not want somebody to know about.

> As soon as you use legal means you have taken away her identity. If she refuses to give information, it is not a crime, it's a sin.

You have to respect a person's option and I don't think a court can change that.

A slender proportion (14.3 percent) of birth mothers who disapproved of legal recourse gave similar reasons: "The department cannot force the information out of the birth mother if she doesn't want to give it." "You have to respect them as human beings and respect their choice."

Nonidentifying Information to Adoptive Parents

Once the agency has approved the adoptive applicant and the placement of a child is mutually determined appropriate, the prospective parents are provided with information regarding the child's medical history and characteristics of the birth parents. Depending upon the agency's practice and the availability of such information, the nature and the extent of details vary. However, prospective parents may differ in their views of the significance of background characteristics depending upon their conviction in the role environment plays in the intellectual and social development of the child. Adoptive parents who think environment is important may react to the information with less anxiety because of their hope to be able to cast the child in "their own image" regardless of his genetic base.[2] Parents who consider heredity the determining component in shaping the child's behavior are likely to feel more discomfort about genetic influences and therefore regard such information highly significant. The reaction of prospective parents to the child's background information is also likely to be influenced by their recognition of the child's need for identity formation and their willingness to share such details with the child. On this reckoning, adoptive parents were asked if they were given social history on the child's bioparents (for example, physical description, marital status, age, race, religion, education, occupation, nationality, number of children) at placement and whether they found the information adequate. Table 5–9 shows that the percentage of parents who were given information on the child's background and health history progressively increased for each successive adoption period. This may be partly because of the department's gradual recognition of the importance of such information and its increased efforts to obtain a detailed history from the relinquishing birth parents. Two observations from the table deserve mention. First, the history in almost all cases pertained only to birth mothers; there was a

---

[2] In an English study of 160 adoptive families, Raynor (1980) noted that one of the factors associated with parental satisfaction with adoption was their ability to "mould the child to their ways" (p. 38).

Table 5–9

Nonidentifying Information on Child's Birth Parents Received
by Adoptive Parents

Type of Information Received	N=	Adoptive Parents by Year of Adoption			
		1958 (48)	*1968* (50)	*1978* (54)	*All Adoptive Parents* (152)
No information		31.2	18.0	3.7	
Social history (physical description, marital status, siblings, age, race, religion, education, occupation, nationality).		13.9	25.8	45.2	30.5
Personal and social characteristics		8.3	20.0	22.2	17.1
Health history		16.7	38.0	51.9	36.2
Psychiatric problems		12.5	12.0	35.2	20.4
Drug addiction or alcoholism		4.2	12.2	37.0	18.5

virtual absence of information on birth fathers. Second, the proportion of
parents who did not receive any information was the largest (31.2 percent) among the 1958 parents and the least (3.7 percent) among the 1978
parents. However, since the presentation by the adoption worker was
verbal, it is possible that some parents (especially in the 1958 year) could
not recall the details and so reported no information.

Nature and Adequacy of Background Information

Adoptive Parents' Views

Almost all adoptive parents in each group regarded medical history inadequate and had expected more detailed information on genetic diseases in
the child's birth family. In their view the medical history constituted the
highest priority in the background information. Their major concern was
the health of the child and they wanted to know if there was a history of
medical abnormalities that were likely to show in the child later in life.
They felt if they were made aware of genetically transmitted diseases they
could pass that information to the child's doctor, who would find it
helpful in monitoring the child's health and treating him, if necessary.
They were concerned especially for girls, who might have certain genetic
abnormalities that were contraindications for childbearing.

A lot of information might be important to the child. But I wouldn't care what religion her birth parents were or what education they had or anything like that as long as I had their health history, I mean if they had any medical or psychiatric problems. I'd like to tell my daughter before she got married and decided to have her own children if there was a history of blood or chromosome disorders in her biological family.

[1958 Adoptive mother]

The social worker asked me if we wanted to know the background of the child's biological parents and I said, no. The only thing I was interested in at that time was the health of the child and I wanted to know if his parents were healthy and that was all.

[1956 Adoptive mother]

Some parents wanted a detailed health history because their adoptive children had developed diseases of the blood and respiratory systems, which made them anxious. They (and sometimes their adult children) found it frustrating and embarrassing to admit their ignorance of the medical history because of the adoption status.

The health history might have been nice because Michell got a blood disorder indicating her blood is slow to clot. Every time I had to take her to see a doctor the first thing he would ask is if it's in the family and I said I got nothing on that. That's pretty embarrassing.

[1968 Adoptive mother]

I think the race and all that won't make a difference, but the department should have more information on health. When my daughter was small she did get rheumatic fever and we couldn't trace it back. After she got married and pregnant the doctor thought she was going to have twins and asked her if there is any twins in her family. She said that she was sorry she couldn't answer because she was adopted.

[1958 Adoptive mother]

I wouldn't want to know anything else other than the medical information. He wets the bed a lot and has a lot of problems with his stomach. One time I took him to a doctor and she said he could be diabetic. She didn't want to do any tests unless she knew more about my son's background.

[1978 Adoptive mother]

When asked if they would like to receive any information other than the medical history, the adoptive parents overwhelmingly (85 to 90 percent) in all subgroups showed a complete lack of interest. Their typical comments were: "I don't think I would have wanted to know Gary's background." "I wasn't interested in her birth parents." "I didn't want to know about his mother other than the medical history." Even when the background information was being presented by the adoption worker many of these parents found it unnecessary and turned a deaf ear, as this 1978 adoptive mother described:

> We always felt that any background information was unnecessary. In fact, I just sat there and listened when all this was going on and on. I didn't take a lot of it in except the medical history.

Another 1978 adoptive mother was also disinterested in their child's background:

> The social worker gave us some background information on Kevin's mother. But I didn't want to know who his mother was. Even if she is my next door neighbor I still don't want to know.

However, behind their apathy lay a marked discomfort from knowing about the child's past. They would like to pretend the child never had any other parents, but was 'as if' born to them naturally. The denial of the adoptive child's past represents these parents' attempts to resolve their anxiety stemming from the child's status. Kirk (1981) describes this phenomenon as 'rejection of difference,' which suggests that the adoptive parents by ignoring or suppressing the existence of the child's genealogical past could "wear the mantle of their longed-for status as parents pure and simple" (p. 72). This point was illustrated by the study parents' comments: "Now that I know very little about my son's background I never think of him as being anybody else's but my own." "I didn't want any information on Susan's parents because she was going to be my child." "I told the worker I was not interested in Lisa's biological parents because I want to raise her as my child and she was mine." They would like to believe that the most important component in the child's development is environment and upbringing, and they regarded the biological past as having little significance for the child.

> When I took him in my arms he was mine; I figured he would be me and my husband's and I would mould his life after me because it is said you grow like people you live with. I didn't tell him that he was adopted because we wanted him to be ours and Smiths'; that was it.
>
> [1958 Adoptive mother]

> I don't think the child's background is necessary because whatever the natural parents were it doesn't make any difference. It is the individual child and how he is raised that count.
>
> [1968 Adoptive mother]

These parents further dealt with their anxiety over adoptive status by repressing or forgetting whatever facts about the child's genealogy were given by the adoption worker.

> I forgot the next day what they told me; I was too excited to get out, to
> be left alone, and to get on with rearing the child.
>
> [1958 Adoptive mother]

> If there were things said about the birth mother I can't remember. All I
> could think about was the fun I was going to have with him.
>
> [1968 Adoptive mother]

Some parents were indifferent to background information. They said
they would feel jealous of the birth parents who might compare favorably
with them:

> I got the feeling the less I know about my son's parents, the better it is
> because I would be making comparison to them.
>
> [1978 Adoptive mother]

> I don't want to know anything about my child's birth parents. I figured
> if I knew they were smarter and had a university education or they had
> more money than we have, I'd feel bad.
>
> [1968 Adoptive mother]

Birth Mothers' and Adoptees' Views

Birth mothers and adoptees were unanimous that background information
should be provided to parents who adopt children. They regarded such
information as highly significant for the adoptive parents and adopted
children. They felt such information would help the parents understand
the child's personality traits, talents, and potentials, the knowledge essential in raising a child. The background information also would enable the
parents to answer the child's questions on genealogy once he or she is old
enough to understand adoption and begins to express identity concerns.
This female adoptee commented:

> If the adoptive parents knew this information they could make the child
> feel more like a whole person because they would be able to answer
> many questions and there wouldn't be that big dark hole of a question
> mark in the child's life.

However, they did not view all five items on nonidentifying information—
social history, personal and social characteristics, health history, psychiatric problems, and drug addiction or alcoholism—equally important for the
adoptive parents or for the child. That is to say, they were less favorable
toward releasing an overall social history of birth parents, such as physical
description, marital status, siblings, age, race, religion, education, occupation, compared to the information on health status and drug and alcohol
addiction. For instance, an overall two-thirds (64.5 percent) of adoptees
and three-fourths (74.8 percent) of birth mothers supported the release of

social history; however, a substantially higher percentage of them—90 percent (birth mothers) and 94 percent (adoptees)—favored sharing information that has bearing on health of the child. Birth mothers who disapproved of the release of their sociophysical profile felt such information was not important for adoptive parents or were afraid it could be used to locate and identify them. Adoptees who were opposed to the disclosure of such information regarded these details as unnecessary, irrelevant, and above all, too intrusive.

> I think everything that is determined to be useful in raising that child should be made available to the adoptive parents. But I don't want my adoptive parents to have an open book on my natural parents.
>
> [Male adoptee]

> I don't see what difference it makes to the adopting parents to know the physical description, marital status, age, occupation, religion, education of the birth parents. However, drug addiction, illness, and psychiatric problems, if serious, can do a number on the youngster later in life and these should be known to adoptive parents.
>
> [Female adoptee]

Some adoptees disagreed with disclosure of birth parents' social histories because adoptive parents who felt uncomfortable discussing the child's past might not feel ambivalent when queried by the child regarding his biological parents. Having no information on the sociophysical history of the birth parents would also spare adoptive parents from being curious every time they see lookalike faces. For all the disagreement on the scope of background information, adoptees were unanimous in declaring a few caveats: the department should share details on birth parents' background that, in its judgment, are relevant to the interest of the child and helpful to adoptive parents in their task as parents; it should use its discretion to filter out any items or details that are adverse to the child's well-being and are potentially embarrassing or incriminating. Illustrative of negative information are these excerpts:

> Some parents may not be able to handle information on the psychiatric history of the birth mother. Every time a child picked up a bread knife and wanted to cut off a slice, they'd say, 'He's just like her.'
>
> [Male adoptee]

> Some personal and social characteristics of the biological parents may indicate that the father was a drunkard and the mother was a lady of the night. To know something like this is not going to do any good.
>
> [Female adoptee]

Summary and Conclusion

Unlike identifying information, the disclosure of background information received overwhelming support from members of the triad. The strongest endorsement was expressed by birth mothers. Female adoptees were more supportive of such a policy than their male counterparts. The solid and unequivocal endorsement of this measure owes to the nature of the information, which does not disclose the identity of the adoption participants but satisfies the adoptee's curiosity, an unlikely prospect in developing a policy on identifying information.

All adoptive parents and half of adoptees felt that nonidentifying information should be provided to parents at the time of adoption. They argued that the adoptive parents can deliver the information to adoptees more appropriately than the department, while taking into account the time, situation, and relevance of the contents to the child's need and readiness. Adoptees and birth mothers suggested that the department screen the information for embarrassing items before it is made available to adoptive parents or an adoptee.

Unlike for identifying information, adulthood was not considered a necessary condition by the triad (especially by birth mothers and female adoptees) for the release of background information. Also, respondents were not in favor of requiring the birth parents' consent or adoptive parents' consent if the adoptee was an adult. Birth mothers held a more liberal view on the requirements of age and of adoptive parents' consent than did adoptive parents and male adoptees. However, they were opposed to surreptitious sharing of information with the adoptee and strongly felt that the adoptee should confide in his or her parents, to avoid any hurt feelings.

The support of the triad was even stronger and more unanimous for the release of medical information than it was for background information. They regarded medical information as far more important to adoptees than any other details. Respondents said this information should be given to adoptive parents at the time of adoption. Birth mothers expressed a heightened concern for the health of the relinquished children and agreed to periodic direct contact by the department for an update on their medical histories or for consent to contact their family physicians. They were also willing to file medical information on their own. Only two birth mothers said they would refuse to cooperate. All except eleven birth mothers favored legal intervention, if necessary, in case the birth parent refuses to provide medical information deemed vital to save the life of the adoptee. The level of support for such a move was almost the same among adoptive parents and slightly higher among male adoptees.

All three groups of adoptive parents received upon adoption background information on the birth parents of their children. However, the 1958 parents were presented fewer details than their 1968 and 1978 cohorts. Information on birth fathers was virtually nonexistent in all adoption periods. Almost all parents regarded the medical history and information as inadequate and considered this information the most important among items on background details. An overwhelming proportion of them in all groups were uncomfortable toward the birth parents' psychosocial profile. Their denial of the child's past represented their attempts to pretend that the child was born to them naturally, a phenomenon known as "rejection of difference." A large majority of these parents dealt with their anxiety over adoptive status by ignoring or forgetting whatever facts were presented to them at adoption about the child's genealogy.

Birth mothers and adoptees were unanimous that background information on birth parents should be provided to adoptive parents so they can better understand the child's potentials and answer his questions on genealogy. They regarded health and genetic information as highly significant. Adoptees strongly felt the department should share with the adoptive parents only the background details deemed relevant to the interest of the child and should filter out those items that are potentially embarrassing, incriminating, or that could cause discomfort to adoptive parents.

6
Release of Information about Adoptees to Birth Mothers

While it is increasingly recognized that the disclosure of information on the birth parent to an adoptee is vital to resolution of his identity concerns, the equivalent right of the birth parent to information regarding the adoptee is not accepted as legitimate and realistic. This is partly because of adoption agencies' claims that the birth parent waived all rights with the surrender of the child and partly because of the belief that the birth parent wanted to forget the child and be left alone. In this chapter we will discuss the birth mothers' attitudes toward release of information on the whereabouts and well-being of the relinquished child. The chapter also will address whether a birth mother should be given background information on the people who adopted her child.

Identifying Information to Birth Mothers

We asked respondents whether information concerning the adopted child's whereabouts should be made available to the birth mother. The resulting data, displayed in table 6–1, reveal varying degrees of support for such a policy. Strongest approval was given by birth mothers, who constituted almost 70 percent. Of significance, adoptees gave a marginal approval, with 56.6 percent. Not surprisingly, adoptive parents were overwhelmingly opposed, with almost three-fourths rejecting this measure. Contrast this with the level of support respondents showed for a policy permitting disclosure of the birth mother's identity to adoptees, which was much higher in all groups, ranging from 19.2 percentage points to 24.5 to 42.1 percentage points among birth mothers, adoptees, and adoptive parents in that order.

Table 6–1
Attitudes toward the Release of Adoptees' Identity to Birth Mothers
(*percentages*)

Degree of Agreement	N =	All Adoptive Parents (1958, 1968, 1978) (152)	All Birth Mothers (1968, 1978) (78)	All Adoptees (53)
Strongly agree to somewhat agree		27.6	69.3	56.6
Strongly disagree to somewhat disagree		72.4	30.7	43.4

Reasons for Disclosure of Adoptees' Whereabouts

Adoptees who supported this policy considered it natural for the birth mother to yearn for contact with her relinquished child, just as it is for them to desire reunion with her. They said they were the birth mother's flesh and blood, even though she did not raise them. The following statement by a female adoptee typifies this sentiment:

> Even though my birth mother has not been around for twenty-one years she did give birth to me and I'm still a part of her. I'm sure she would like to know about her child. You can't expect the adoptee to have curiosity to meet her mother and not the birth mother.

Some adoptees were motivated in their endorsement by an attitude of quid-pro-quo and fair play. They felt compelled by a sense of justice to extend birth mothers the same right to know as they want. "If an adoptee has the right to know about her birth mother, she has the right too." "It would be exactly the same as if it were the adopted child who was looking for her."

Some adoptees felt compassion toward the birth mother, since they felt her decision to surrender the child might have been motivated by compelling circumstances. These adoptees recognized the pain and guilt the birth mother might have suffered and regarded her desire to meet the relinquished offspring as genuine. They did not want to cause further distress to her by denying access. Their sympathetic attitude is reflected in this remark by a female adoptee:

> Maybe she made a mistake when she was young. Now she has probably gotten over it and feels guilty. She has more at stake than the adoptee.

Birth mothers favored disclosure of the adoptee's whereabouts because they yearned to see the birth child and wanted to be assured of its well-being. They accepted the fact that they had relinquished the right to the child. But they said they could not forget the child and often wondered what had become of it, and if it had been adopted and well cared for. Recognizing the adoptive parents' fear of losing the child's allegiance, many birth mothers gave assurance that they would not do anything to disrupt the child's identification with the adoptive family. They said they wanted to resume contact with the child, now adult, to explain the reasons for the adoption. They also would like to seek assurance of forgiveness from the child. A 1968 birth mother said:

> Just knowing what's happening to this child would give you some kind of feelings of comfort. Maybe things haven't turned out the way you were hoping, but even if the information you got was not good, you at least would know about him. I don't think any mother would try to get her child back.

Reasons against Release of Adoptee's Identity

The predominant reason given by members of the triangle who opposed such a policy was that the birth mother voluntarily surrendered the child, constituting abrogation of her right to resume contact. Adoptive parents who expressed strongest opposition to such a policy contended that with the adoption decree the parental rights and obligations were legally transferred to them. They said that in revealing the child's identity to the birth mother, the department would be giving legitimacy to her claim to the child. They believed such action would violate the department's pledge of noninterference. They maintained that any reunion should be initiated by the adoptee. The following excerpts reflect these parents' sentiments:

> It is none of her business. She carried the baby for nine months; she had many days after the baby was born to make up her mind. She shouldn't be entitled to meet him. If she made the decision, right or wrong, she should take it upon herself not to disturb this child's life.
> [1968 Adoptive mother]

> The birth mother gave the child up and I don't want anything to do with her. If my child wants to seek her, that's fine; but not her.
> [1968 Adoptive mother]

Adoptees were afraid that an expected appearance by the birth mother could be chaotic, especially to adoptees who were not aware of their adoptive status. They felt their interests would be better served if they were left unruffled. They contended there is no better demonstration of the birth mother's love and concern than to leave them alone.

Adoptees' opposition to disclosure of their whereabouts largely stemmed from feelings of resentment toward the birth mother's for abjuring her responsibility as parent. They did not feel convinced about the genuineness of her motive. In their view the birth mother has no justification whatsoever to a renewed relationship with a child who belongs to new parents. They abreacted their resentment in these statements:

> It's none of her business to look for me now, as she has got no right to me. I would ask why she gave me up in the first place. Now she wants to go back and see me. If she wanted me that strongly she should have kept me in the first place. She let me go and that was her decision. She has got a new family and now she wants me back. Forget it.
>
> [Male adoptee]

> When she gave me up she supposedly did not love me. But I didn't experience her love. The only time I experienced love in life was when it was given to me by someone else. I grew up with these people who gave me everything and made me what I am today. At the time my mother could have kept me if she were responsible enough. But she refused to do so and thus she lost her right to me.
>
> [Male adoptee]

Like adoptees, some adoptive parents did not find any bona fide reason for the birth mother's interest in her relinquished child. As far as they were concerned, the birth mother did not want the child in the first place and then never cared for several years. They regarded the birth mother's later interest in the child as disingenuous and irrational.

A considerable proportion of adoptive parents (44.5 percent) contended that resumption of contact with the child by his birth mother would not be in the child's best interests and were certain that the birth mother's appearance would likely to be upsetting. Another set of parents, they said, would undermine the concept of equivalence doctrine in the adoption, as this 1968 adoptive mother contended:

> When we adopted Lisa we understood that she had the same status as our two natural-born children. That's the way we feel and think about this child. So she is ours and the birth mother has no right to disturb our lives.

Some adoptive parents, however, would not oppose disclosure if the information is requested under special circumstances of the birth mother, such as serious illness. These parents said it is humane to allow a dying mother to meet her relinquished child should she request it. Interestingly, this exception was considered by only 1958 adoptive parents who, perhaps, because of their own age, could appreciate the need of a dying mother.

A small number of birth mothers (30.7 percent) who disapproved of disclosure of adoptees' whereabouts also feared excessive intrusion in adoptees' new home. They were afraid once they knew the whereabouts of the child they would be tempted to make repeated contacts because their desire, which they had learned to suppress, might become obsessive. One 1978 birth mother said: "The more you know, the more you're going to wonder and want to know about the child." Another 1968 birth mother echoed a similar concern: "If I knew where my boy was, I don't think I would let it rest at that. I'd want to find out everything about him." To obviate the risk of excessive involvement, these birth mothers would prefer that they not be permitted access to adoptees' records.

Grounds for Release of Adoptees' Identity

Respondents who supported a policy permitting disclosure of identity of adoptees and their adoptive parents stipulated that their support depended on age of the adoptee and consent of the adoptive parents and adoptee.

Age of Adoptee

As shown in table 6–2, there was a consensus that the adoptee should reach at least the minimum age of majority. However, the degree of support differed for legal age. Adoptees held the strongest support, with two-thirds (66.7 percent) endorsing this condition. Of these, more than one-third (37 percent) felt the adoptee should be at least twenty-one years of age. Over 60 percent of adoptive parents favored the age of majority. (Difference between adoptive parents and adoptees did not reach the level of significance.) Birth mothers expressed the weakest support for this idea, with less than half (48.1 percent).

Respondents who favored adulthood felt that at a younger age the adoptee was likely to be confused by the appearance of another mother. They said that as adults, adoptees can better appreciate the purpose of the birth mother's contact and make a rational decision about whether to

Table 6–2
Age of Adoptees for Release of Their Identity
(*percentages*)

Adoptee's Age	N =	Adoptive Parents (1958, 1968, 1978) (42)*	Birth Mothers (1968, 1978) (54)*	Adoptees (30)*
At any age		16.7	18.5	16.7
Only when mature		21.4	33.3	16.7
Only when adult		61.9	48.1	66.7

*All those who agreed with release of adoptees' identity in table 6–1

meet her, and are better equipped to handle the relationship and conflicts that might arise from the reunion.

Adoptive Parents' Consent

Approval in all three groups for disclosure of identifying information was contingent upon prior consent of the adoptive parents. However, respondents varied in the degree of support, depending upon the age of the adoptee, as shown in table 6–3. Adoptees and adoptive parents showed strongest support for requiring parental consent when the adoptee was a minor, with 70 percent and 64.3 percent respectively. Birth mothers endorsed this requirement but only with a lean majority—57.4 percent.

However, the percentage indicating approval of this condition dropped considerably among all groups when the adoptee reached adulthood. For example, a little over one-third (35.7 percent) of adoptive parents favored parental veto, followed by birth mothers and adoptees, who supported at almost one-quarter each. These respondents felt that an adoptee of legal age is considered mature enough to make rational decisions and accept consequences. They regarded it as an affront to the dignity of the adult adoptee to require consent from the parents to meet the birth mother. Interestingly, 60 percent of adoptees and about 40 percent of birth mothers felt adoptive parents should be notified as a matter of courtesy upon the release of the adoptee's whereabouts by the department. Adoptees expressed their views in these words: "I think the adoptive parents' feelings should be taken into consideration, but at age nineteen and over, the adoptee's decision is outside everybody's realm." "As an adult the adoptee can stand up for himself and decide whether information about him should be given to the birth mother or not. But he should tell the parents of his decision." Birth mothers echoed similar

Table 6–3
Prior Consent of Adoptive Parents
(*percentages*)

Degree of Agreement	N=	Adoptive Parents (1958, 1968, 1978) (42)*	Birth Mothers (1968, 1978) (54)*	Adoptees (30)*
Agree in case of adult adoptees		35.7	24.1	23.3
Agree in case of minor adoptees		64.3	57.4	70.0
Consent not required		-	18.5	6.7

*All those who agreed with release of adoptees' identity in table 6–1

sentiments: "Adoptive parents should be involved and given a careful consideration, but it should be the adoptee's decision when she is nineteen years old."

Adoptee's Consent

Respondents in all three groups overwhelmingly endorsed the adoptee's consent as requirement for the release of identifying information to the birth mother. As shown in table 6.4, the strongest endorsement came from adoptive parents, with 95.1 percent followed by adoptees and birth mothers in that order, with 80 percent and almost three-quarters (74.1 percent) respectively. However, all six adoptees and nine of the fourteen birth mothers who were opposed to mandatory consent indicated that the adoptee should be notified by the department if the birth mother is given identifying information. They felt that such notice would prepare the adoptee for the meeting, should it occur.

The triad supported the requirement of the adoptee's consent for various reasons. For birth mothers, prior consent of the adoptee indicates the child does not harbor any grudges or ill feelings and is receptive to a reunion. These statements are illustrative of birth mothers' desire for the adoptee's approval: "Not until I know my child's reaction; he might hate me or my unexpected call could confuse him." "You don't know what the child might be feeling, there could be a lot of bitterness." "Only if my son wants to see me." "If my child doesn't want to meet me, I won't face her."

Adoptive parents emphasized the right of the adopted person to make a decision on the desirability of reunion as the birth mother. These comments exemplify their feelings: "He has the right to say, just as the birth mother does, that he doesn't want his life invaded by someone he doesn't know." "Some adoptees may not have anything to do with the birth mother because she could upset them."

Table 6–4
Prior Consent of Adult Adoptees
(*percentages*)

Degree of Agreement	N =	Adoptive Parents (1958, 1968, 1978) (42)*	Birth Mothers (1968, 1978) (54)*	Adoptees (30)*
Strongly agree to somewhat agree		95.1	74.1	80.0
Strongly disagree to somewhat disagree		4.8	26.0	20.0

*All those who agreed with release of adoptees' identity in table 6–1

Adoptees supported their mandatory consent primarily because they wanted to be recognized as participants in their own right in the adoption process. They contended that they were not given a choice in being born and adopted, but would like an equal opportunity to decide whether they would like to regain contact with the birth mother. Another reason they gave was that they might not be in a position to establish any kind of relationship with the birth mother, at least for a certain time. It is possible, they said, that they might be going through a stressful period in life and a new relationship could exacerbate their situation. Their feelings were summed up by this female adoptee: "The birth mother made her decision over nineteen years ago. It's now the child's right to decide if his identifying information should be released."

Six adoptees and fourteen birth mothers (26 percent) who were against mandatory consent of the adoptee did so for different reasons. Adoptees believed curiosity about birth parents is almost universal and they thought it inconceivable that any adoptee would turn down a birth parent who wanted to meet for genuine reasons. This female adoptee wondered in almost disbelief: "I honestly can't imagine why an adopted child would not want to meet if his mother was interested." Birth mothers contended that the adoptee is their child and, like any mother, they should be entitled to unrestricted access to find out directly if the child was interested in resuming a relationship. The following statements illustrate their viewpoints: "I should be told anyway no matter if he is forty years old. If he refuses I still have the right to know who my child is." "It's your child; you gave birth to her, so you should know who she is and what she is." "If the birth mother wants to talk to her child, let her find out from the child how he feels."

Time Period for Seeking Adoptee's Consent. To underscore the importance of the prerequisite of the adoptee's consent, almost two-thirds each of adoptees and adoptive parents indicated the department should search indefinitely for the adoptee whose consent is required. Birth mothers showed weak support with a lean majority (52.3 percent) for the indefinite search, as shown in table 6–5. Another one-quarter to one-third of respondents in the three groups were also in favor of active search for the adoptee, but only for a limited time period not exceeding one year. It seems that a massive majority in each group, including adoptive parents, were opposed to restricting access to the information by searching birth mothers. Altogether, 88 to 100 percent favored an active search for the adoptee on behalf of the searching birth mother. Only one-tenth each of the adoptive parents and birth mothers would not like the department to act on the birth mother's request; none of the adoptees thought this way.

Table 6–5
Time Required for Seeking Adult Adoptees' Consent
(*percentages*)

Time Required to Locate	N =	Adoptive Parents (1958, 1968, 1978) (40)*	Birth Mothers (1968, 1978) (44)*	Adoptees (24)*
As long as it takes to locate		62.5	52.3	65.5
Locate up to a certain time period		25.0	36.4	34.5
Wait until adoptee contacts the department		12.5	11.4	–

*All those who agreed with release of adoptees' identity in table 6–4

Absence of Adoptee's Consent Because of Death. Respondents were asked what policy option the department should choose in the event the adoptee is dead or believed to be dead: Should it use its own judgment and release the identifying information to the birth mother, ask the court to appoint a guardian to represent the absent adoptee, or not release the information? Their responses, presented in table 6–6, show that a majority of respondents in each group approved of a policy allowing a waiver of the consent requirement if the adoptee was deceased. But they prefer to leave the final decision to the department. It is significant to note that adoptees endorsed this policy option more strongly, with 62.5 percent, than did adoptive parents (51.4 percent). Birth mothers, at 56.4 percent, did not differ significantly from adoptees. Adoptees felt that once they were dead it would not hurt them if the identifying information was revealed to birth mothers. Similarly, adoptees were less supportive of an unequivocal ban on the identifying information without their consent than were adoptive

Table 6–6
Options for Disclosure of Adoptees' Identity in Case of Their Death
(*percentages*)

Department's Policy Option	N =	Adoptive Parents (1958, 1968, 1978) (35)*	Birth Mothers (1968, 1978) (39)*	Adoptees (24)*
Act on its own judgment		51.4	56.4	62.5
Ask court to appoint guardian to represent adoptee's interest		28.6	41.0	25.0
Not release identifying information		20.0	2.6	12.5

*All those who agreed with search of adoptee in table 6–5

parents, who constituted one-fifth, compared with a little over one-tenth (12.5 percent) of the adoptees. Birth mothers were least in favor of such a move, with only less than 3 percent supporting an unqualified embargo on identifying information. This signifies birth mothers' abiding interest in learning about their relinquished children even though they are no longer alive.

Interestingly, while birth mothers were interested in the information they were least favorable toward its release without safeguards for the child's interest. As depicted in table 6–6, more than 40 percent favored a court-appointed guardian responsible for protecting the deceased adoptee's best interest and that of his surviving family members who might not welcome a visit by the birth mother. One-quarter each of adoptive parents and adoptees favored a court-appointed guardian.

Release of Information on Adoptees' Well-Being to Birth Mothers

Support increased dramatically among respondents in all three groups when the information requested by the birth mother pertains to her adopted child's health and development. As shown in table 6–7, members of the triad expressed an overwhelming approval, with 80 to 90 percent, for the release of such information to birth mothers. Birth mothers and adoptees expressed the strongest support, at almost 90 percent each, and adoptive parents were slightly less approving, with 81.5 percent. It is significant to note that one-fifth (20.4 percent) more birth mothers endorsed the release of such information than they did for the identifying information (see table 6–1). This reflects their belief that voluntary surrender of the child constituted waiver of their parental right to reconnect with the child.

Table 6–7
Attitudes toward Release of Adoptees' Well-Being to Birth Mothers
(*percentages*)

Degree of Agreement	N =	All Adoptive Parents (1958, 1968, 1978) (152)	All Birth Mothers (1968, 1978) (78)	All Adoptees (53)
Strongly agree to somewhat agree		81.5	89.7	88.7
Strongly disagree to somewhat disagree		18.5	10.3	11.3

Reasons for Release of Nonidentifying Information

The chief reason for the massive support of such a policy is the nature of the information, which is not likely to reveal the identity of the principals to each other, thus maintaining the existing adoption arrangement. Respondents also felt that such information does not violate any privacy interest. Respondents made these recurring comments: "This type of information is not going to harm the child and the adoptee is not going to know who this woman is and where she lives." "This information is not hurting anybody, but it would clear up a lot of things in her mind." "Since she is not going to get the names and addresses, it can't harm the child or the adoptive parents."

Birth mothers underscored their ongoing concern for the health and well-being of the relinquished child and contended that such information is vital to their peace of mind, while at the same time safeguarding the privacy of the adoptee and adoptive parents. Many birth mothers said: "What mother wouldn't want to know if her baby is dead or alive and well cared for?" The following statement by a 1968 birth mother typifies the birth mothers' concern for the child:

> Why shouldn't the birth mother be given this information? After all, you can't put that child out of your mind. It is always there, you always worry about it. I think if you knew it was doing fine, health-wise and school-wise, and it didn't have any problems, and it got better bringing up than you could have provided, you would feel better. You would be more happy with your decision.

Both adoptive parents and adoptees interpreted the birth mother's inquiry about the child's development as a positive indication of her caring attitude and genuine interest in the child. They found it reassuring that such a birth mother had not forgotten the child. They felt this information could provide the birth mother with mental peace. They regarded the birth mother's concern and desire to learn about the child's welfare as natural. The following excerpts are illustrative of the adoptive parents' and adoptees' sentiments:

> Probably it is gnawing at her all these years and she wonders if he is being well-treated or if he was abandoned again. I would have these haunting thoughts myself all through my life. I think that won't hurt to tell her that the child has done well, is very happy, and has been well taken care of. This information probably would be a source of comfort to the mother.
>
> [1958 Adoptive mother]

Because the birth mother has asked for the information about her child's well-being, she has obviously been troubled by this. By knowing this information she would be able to go on with her life. No matter what she is, she is this kid's mother and there will always be a maternal instinct for that child.

[Male adoptee]

A few adoptive parents, however, cautioned that nonidentifying information should be brief, infrequent, and screened for descriptions that are potentially identifying. Their typical comments were: "The department should give her a little bit of information just enough to let her know the child is alive, healthy, and happy." "If the department gives her information once or twice a year, I won't begrudge her." A similar caution was sounded by a few birth mothers against giving out facts about the child that are distressing. They said such information could traumatize them and make them obsessed with the thought of the child. Thus, they might frequently pester the department or the adoptive parents for more details.

Reasons against Release of Nonidentifying Information

Eight birth mothers (10.3 percent) who expressed opposition to the policy of releasing such information were just as curious to know the health and development of their adopted child as their counterparts who approved this policy measure. All of them indicated that they never forgot the child and would be eager to meet if their child someday searched for them after reaching adulthood. But they said they learned to repress their feelings and were afraid that the nonidentifying information would rekindle their desire to learn more about the child, driving them eventually to seek reunion. Since they wanted to avoid actual contact and still come to terms with their relentless desire, they rationalized that their birth child had been adopted into a good and loving home.

> Once the birth mother will ask a few questions, then she'll ask a few more. The information on her child probably would make her think about the child all the time. I'm sure he should be in a good home because the adoptive parents took the child they wanted.
>
> [1968 Birth mother]

> Of course, you don't forget about the child, but not knowing about him helps to forget it.
>
> [1978 Birth mother]

Five adoptees (9.5 percent) who did not support disclosure of nonidentifying information were skeptical about the genuineness of the birth mother's interest in the child. A male adoptee said: "I would ask why she wants to know now. If she had interest in me she could have kept me in the beginning." For these adoptees, such policy constitutes interference with their own and their adoptive parents' lives, because the department must obtain information by contacting them or their parents. Inquiries by the department can be traumatic, especially for adoptees who are not told of their status. A couple of them feared that a birth mother who has been given information once is likely to make repeated requests and thus place undue demands on the department and the adoptive family, as this female adoptee expressed: "You never know, you might have her down your neck again next month."

Twenty-eight (18.5 percent) adoptive parents did not support this policy step, chiefly because of the possibility that nonidentifying details could inadvertently leave clues leading to identification. While they acknowledged the birth mother's desire and emotional need to know the child's development, they had doubts that the social worker, however scrupulous and meticulous, would not be able to filter out identifying facts. A 1958 adoptive mother expressed her doubts this way:

> I know if I had given my child up, I would have these haunting thoughts all through my life and wonder if the child was treated well and if he was not abandoned again. Therefore, it's all very well for her to have the information. But I'm afraid she could find out by the answers she gets from the social worker where the child lives.

Some adoptive parents found the birth mother's anxiety needless. They felt she should trust the judgment of the department in handling the adoption placement and should not worry about the quality of the care the child received. A few older adoptive parents thought it imprudent for birth mothers to dwell upon the relinquished child. They felt that a few facts on the child would only ignite their desire, making them relentlessly compulsive for more information. They said it is best that the birth mother treat the event as if it never happened. A 1958 adoptive mother had this advice for birth mothers:

> As far as I'm concerned, the birth mother has put herself out of touch. If she got some information from the department, she is not going to stop thinking about the child. I think that would only torture her more.

Grounds for Release of Nonidentifying Information

As in the case of identifying information, respondents stipulated the requirements of age of the adoptee, his consent, and consent of adoptive parents for releasing information on the child's health and well-being.

However, given the nature of the information, these conditions were much less stringent than those specified for identifying information.

Age of Adoptee

Almost all respondents (90 to 95 percent) in each group placed no restrictions on the age of the adoptee. They said that since the information does not involve the adoptee or the adoptive parents, age of the adoptee should not be a significant determinant.

Adoptive Parents' Consent

Members of the triad overwhelmingly rejected the requirement of a parental veto, as depicted in table 6–8. Adoptive parents, birth mothers, and adoptees represented a little less than seven-tenths to three-fourths in their respective groups. The chief reason cited by respondents in all three groups was that such information doesn't threaten the privacy of the adoptee or the adoptive parents and therefore the department acts within the realm of its pledge when it releases nonidentifying information to birth mothers without parental consent. A few adoptive parents, especially older ones, took delight in the fact that the birth mother had continued interest in the well-being of her relinquished child. Some adoptees and birth mothers were afraid that certain adoptive parents might be insensate to the birth mother's emotional need for such information and thus use their veto to block its release. A female adoptee said: "Maybe the adoptive parents would get the wrong idea and feel threatened and refuse to cooperate with the department."

A few respondents who favored parental veto provided two major reasons. First, they felt it morally right that the adoptive parents should know and have their say in matters that involves sharing of information

Table 6–8
Prior Consent of Adoptive Parents to Release Adoptees' Well-Being
(*percentages*)

Degree of Agreement	N =	Adoptive Parents (1958, 1968, 1978) (124)*	Birth Mothers (1968, 1978) (70)*	Adoptees (47)*
Strongly agree to somewhat agree		32.2	22.9	23.4
Strongly disagree to somewhat disagree		67.8	77.1	76.6

*All those who agreed with release of adoptees' well-being in table 6–7

that pertains to them. They said adoptive parents are entitled to know why the birth mother is making an inquiry about the child's health and social development. Adoptive parents felt that as the adoptee's real parents they should decide whether it is in the best interest of the child to release this information to any person. Furthermore, any facts about the adoptee are not exclusionary and isolated, in that they are the part of the information shared with the birth mother. Their second reason involves obtaining updated information. Both adoptees and adoptive parents pointed out that the department must rely on the adoptive parents' cooperation to find out the child's progress and, therefore, their involvement in the decision is unavoidable. This female adoptee typified this concern: "I can't imagine that the department can obtain the information from anywhere unless it was made available by the adoptive parents or by me."

Adoptee's Consent

Respondents in each group disapproved of consent of an adult adoptee as a rationale for disclosing his health and developmental status to the birth mother. But unlike their disagreement on parental veto, the respondents differed widely in the magnitude of disapproval. As shown in table 6–9, adoptive parents rejected this requirement with a modest majority of about 55 percent, compared with a huge majority of 72.9 percent and 81 percent for birth mothers and adoptees, respectively.

The reasons advanced by these respondents for disapproving this condition were by and large the same as were advanced in rejecting adoptive parents' veto power. The most frequent was that the information does not violate the privacy right of the adoptee and therefore his interest is well-protected. Some birth mothers felt that although they transferred their parental rights to another parent, they continued to feel concerns for the health and well-being of a child who is their flesh and blood. They said

Table 6–9
Prior Consent of Adult Adoptees to Release Their Well-Being
(*percentages*)

Degree of Agreement	N =	Adoptive Parents (1958, 1968, 1978) (124)*	Birth Mothers (1968, 1978) (70)*	Adoptees (47)*
Strongly agree to somewhat agree		45.1	27.1	19.1
Strongly disagree to somewhat disagree		54.9	72.9	80.9

*All those who agreed with release of adoptees' well-being in table 6–7

that because of their irrevocable biological bond, they should not be denied this information regardless of the adoptee's feelings. A sizable number of adoptive parents were opposed to this requirement because they were afraid contact by the department might spark curiosity in the adopted child, a prospect threatening to the concept of equivalence. Their overriding message was to 'leave it alone' as was bluntly expressed by a 1958 adoptive mother:

> As far as I'm concerned the subject should never be brought up to our children. We don't want our children to even think of themselves as adopted. They are just not happy to think that they are adopted. This is a normal family like any family and that's the way we want it. I don't want our children to think that they are different. So the department should not come back to our house and ask for that information. I must say that Mrs. Birth Mother has to do without the information on my child. I wouldn't like my boys to know that you are from the Department of Social Services. If Brian came home I would introduce you as a friend of somebody else.

To safeguard against the possibility that the department might inadvertently contact an adopted person who has not been told or incite curiosity in an adoptee, some parents suggested that the department contact them for the information.

Nine adoptees favored their consent as a condition. They said that once they are adult they are more likely to manage their own life independent of their parents. That would mean the department must contact them if it wants to obtain more precise information on their health and development.

Birth mothers in favor of the requirement of the adult adoptee's consent thought it was only fair that the adoptee be made aware of such a disclosure. They also felt that an adoptee might not feel comfortable sharing certain facts about his life, either because he finds them embarrassing or he resents the birth mother, whom he might not want to become a part of his life. Adoptive parents agreed with the birth mothers that the information is part of the adopted person's life and he or she may not want to share with the birth mother.

Obtaining Information on Health and Development

In current adoption practice, the department maintains no contact with adoptive parents or adopted children following the adoption decree. Thus, the obvious source of information on the child's current health and developmental status is the adoptive parents. It stands to reason that the department can meet the birth mother's request only if the adoptive parents are willing to cooperate and provide information about their adopted child. It also means that some degree of intrusion in the adoptive homes is inevitable. We asked all respondents who agreed with release of information on adoptees' development to describe the manner in which the department can best obtain such information from the adoptive parents. The resulting data are presented in table 6–10.

It appears that a huge majority of adoptive parents (71.2 percent) were opposed to direct contact by the department to obtain such information. They viewed such follow-ups as an unwanted intrusion and discriminatory. They argued that they were led to believe that the adopted child was as if naturally born to them and their family was thus equivalent of the consanguineous kinship. An inquiry by the department concerning the adopted child is, therefore, discriminatory because natural children are not followed up for their social and physical progress. Besides, adoptive parents raise the child as if it is their own flesh and blood and a requirement or expectation that they should inform the department on the child's health and developmental status would be synonymous to their being foster parents. They said periodic contact by the department after the adoption decree would undermine their status as legal and psychological parents. It would also serve to remind them that their child is adopted, a reminder that would not be conducive to the adoptee's integration into

Table 6–10
Ways to Obtain Information on Adoptees' Development and Well-Being from Adoptive Parents
(*percentages*)

Manner of Obtaining Information	N =	Adoptive Parents (1958, 1968, 1978) (79)*	Birth Mothers (1968, 1978) (62)*	Adoptees (40)*
Encourage adoptive parents at adoption to voluntarily inform		71.2	42.1	22.5
Require adoptive parents to inform at various stages of development		3.8	8.2	7.5
Routinely contact adoptive parents at various stages of development		–	31.0	30.0
Contact adoptive parents only when information is needed		14.9	15.3	15.0
Unable to determine		10.1	3.4	25.0

*All those who agreed with update of records on adoptees' development

the new family. Their sentiment was cogently and candidly expressed by a 1978 adoptive mother:

> When you get the child you feel great and you are kind of relieved that you don't have anything more to do with social workers. Not that you don't like social workers, but that you are kind of relieved that there is no other appointment for the social worker to make sure that everything is all right. You start to live your own life and you're independent. The child is in your hands then.

This 1968 adoptive mother said:

> I wonder if that would not be considered an invasion of privacy in case the department tries to update records on children living in ordinary families. So why make an adoptive family feel different? Once they have adopted they are like any other family.

Only a small proportion (14.9 percent) were receptive to contact as needed. However, these parents preferred that the department use means that are less obtrusive, such as the child's school records, his family doctor, or the health department. Interestingly, parents who were amenable to follow-ups were mostly older parents, which suggested confidence and security in the adoptive relationship. The younger parents had not developed the degree of trust and bonding that usually occurs over time and therefore felt more protective of their child.

By contrast, close to one-half each of birth mothers (46.3 percent) and adoptees (45 percent) supported routine or periodic contact with the adoptive parents. However, like adoptive parents, they suggested that the department use less intrusive means to obtain the information, such as the health department and school records. They felt that adoptive parents usually would not welcome postadoption contact.

Birth mothers were more supportive of voluntary reporting than adoptees. Forty-two percent of birth mothers said adoptive parents should be requested at the time of adoption to inform the department on the child's development, compared with less than one-quarter (22.5 percent) of adoptees who felt this way.

Mandatory reporting by adoptive parents as a policy option was the least choice among all three principals—adoptees (7.5 percent), birth mothers (8.2 percent), and adoptive parents (3.8 percent). This female adoptee typified their objection to compulsory reporting:

> If the parents have to report to the department every now and then it almost seems like you're on probation and you are expected to check in for the rest of your life. That seems like the child is never yours.

Nonidentifying Information on Adoptive Parents to Birth Mothers

Some adoption experts contend that birth mothers often wonder about the people who adopted their children. They wonder what kind of homes their children have gone into, how they might be treated by the new parents, whether they have their own children, and if they would treat the adoptive children as their own. Others argue that birth mothers made a thoughtful decision to relinquish their children on their own volition and placed them in full trust of the adoption agency. They need not, therefore, feel wary of the decision the agency made in finding a suitable home for their children. Besides, they say, there is not much the birth mother can do to rectify the situation or reverse the agency's decision even if they disapprove of the adoptive home, because these children legally belong to other parents.

Respondents were asked if birth mothers routinely should be given background information on the parents who adopted their children and what kind of information should be provided. The resulting data, presented in table 6–11, shows that birth mothers and adoptees gave an overwhelming endorsement to such a policy measure, with 79 percent each. Adoptive parents supported the idea, but conservatively by comparison, representing six-tenths (61.8 percent) of all parents.

Table 6–11
Attitudes toward Release of Nonidentifying Information of Adoptive Parents to Birth Mothers
(*percentages*)

Agreement or Disagreement	N =	All Adoptive Parent (1958, 1968, 1978) (152)*	All Birth Mother (1968, 1978) (78)*	All Adoptee (53)*
Yes		61.8	79.5	79.2
No		38.2	20.5	20.8

Reasons for Release of Background Information

The triad did not differ on the kind of information and reasons justifying its release to birth mothers. They agreed that the relinquishing mother wonders about the child and is desirous to know of its well-being so that she may feel a sense of relief. They were also unanimous that the information should include statements on the stability of the adoptive home and the adoptive parents' ability to love and care.

Three observations are worth making. First, adoptive parents and adoptees emphasized that the information should be very limited and contain a general description of the adoptive home, the parents, and avoid any details that might border on specifics. Their repeated cautionary words were: "very minimum," "some and no details," "certain amount, but nothing nitty gritty." In their view, the limited information should refer to that which has bearing on the child's well-being. Such information should include adoptive parents' commitment to providing the child with loving care, their marital stability, financial security, mental and physical health, and any history of drug or alcohol abuse. Interestingly, birth mothers also were interested in general background information limited to relevant details bearing on the child's well-being. This 1978 birth mother sums up these mothers' concepts of background information on adoptive parents:

> I asked the social worker what kind of people they were and she told me that they had checked them out and gave me details on their income and several social qualities. All I wanted to know was what kind of home my son was going into—that is, if both parents work and if they drink or fight.

Second, birth mothers strongly emphasized they were chiefly interested in whether their child was well and if he was adopted. They said they were often concerned if their child was shunted between foster homes because the department could not find suitable adoptive parents. They said that although they assumed their child was placed in a loving, well-to-do home, they always had a lurking anxiety that their child might not have found a permanent home, but never had the courage to verify with the department. The following statement by a 1968 birth mother exemplifies this concern of the birth mothers:

> When I received your call regarding this study it gave me a big relief and I was sure that my child was all right. I got the feeling from the social worker that at the time of the adoption it would be impossible to find out anything about my child. I had always liked to know if she was adopted, was well, and if she was with a decent family. I made myself believe that she was with a decent family and was being looked after as well as I do my two girls.

Third, the birth mothers' need to know the background of the adoptive parents seems far more compelling than was perceived by the adoptees or the adoptive parents. They stressed that they feel a tremendous sense of anguish and guilt as a result of their decision to give up the child and contended that surrendering parental rights and responsibility did not automatically strip them off their right to know the child's welfare. They said that such information would ease their mind, relieve their guilt, and help them cope with their decision. This statement by a 1978 birth mother epitomizes the anguish and yearning of birth mothers to learn about their children:

> You gave your child up for adoption to have new parents but you really don't give your child away. She is still there with you and you have the right to know how your child is being taken care of and if her new parents are providing a good home. Such information would help you come to terms with what you have done and would be emotionally soothing to you.

Reasons against Release of Background Information

As indicated in table 6–11, almost four-tenths of adoptive parents and one-fifth each of birth mothers and adoptees were opposed to such a policy option. The main argument advanced by adoptive parents and adoptees was that once the birth mother decided to relinquish the child she signified her complete lack of interest and a desire to sever all connections with the child. They said the birth mother was fully aware that her consent to adoption meant permanent abrogation of her rights and her entitlement to any information on the child or the new parents. They pointed to the futility of such a policy measure since the adoptive arrangement is irrevocable and the adoptive parents' rights cannot be reversed even if the birth mother is not satisfied with the parents' background. Adoptive parents found such policy measures superfluous. One 1958 adoptive mother put it: "We are the child's parents and the birth mother can't change it even if she is not pleased."

Adoptive parents and adoptees were also of the opinion that the birth mother should have faith in the competence and professional judgment of the department and feel assured that her child was placed in a home judged most suitable to the child's needs. They said that before signing the adoption consent, the birth mother understood and accepted the process of selecting adoptive parents, who were subjected to rigorous criteria. They feel the birth mother has no apparent justification for getting background information on these parents.

Some adoptive parents and adoptees thought the information could not serve any useful purpose. They felt it might spawn fantasies about the adoptive home, thereby continually keeping her painful memories fresh. A couple of adoptive parents were afraid the birth mother might use nonidentifying information as a lead to trace their whereabouts. This 1968 adoptive mother said:

This city is such a small place, and I wouldn't want anyone phoning me, knocking at my door. I feel Michelle is ours and she's going to be ours.

Differences within Groups

This section will deal with salient differences between subgroups of adoptive parents and adoptees concerning their attitudes toward release of identifying information regarding adoptees to birth mothers. The two subgroups of birth mothers did not differ in any significant way on this issue. Furthermore, there was near unanimity among subgroups of the triad on disclosing nonidentifying information to birth mothers.

Adoptive Parents

Older adoptive parents (1958, 1968 adoption years) were more disapproving of a policy revealing their whereabouts (77 and 80 percent) than the younger parents (1978 adoption year), who represented six-tenths (see table 6–12). Their different levels of support may give the impression that the younger parents were less anxious about the intrusion by birth mothers than the older parents. However, when conditions for release were considered these figures belied this impression. The data show that the younger parents (1978 adoption year) favored making the disclosure more restrictive than the older parents. For example, while a little less than one-half each of the 1958 parents (45.5 percent) and the 1968 parents (47.6 percent) supported the release when the adoptee is a minor, only 10 percent of the 1978 parents thought this way. Similarly, a much higher percentage of the younger parents (81.1 percent) favored release contingent upon their consent, compared with about 60 percent of the older parents who supported this requirement. Also, a higher proportion of the

Table 6–12
Attitudes of Adoptive Parents toward Release of Adoptees' Identity to Birth Mothers
(*percentages*)

Degree of Agreement	N=	Adoptive Parents by Year of Adoption			All Adoptive Parents
		1958 (48)	1968 (50)	1978 (54)	(152)
Strongly agree to somewhat agree		23.0	20.0	38.9	27.6
Strongly disagree to somewhat disagree		77.0	80.0	61.1	72.4

younger parents (68.4 percent) insisted on the adoptee's consent, in contrast to 41.7 to 50 percent of the older parents.

Adoptees

More female than male adoptees approved of a policy permitting the release of their whereabouts to birth mothers. Three-fifths (60.5 percent) of female adoptees favored this policy, as contrasted with less than one-half (46.7 percent) of male adoptees. Not only were male adoptees less supportive of the disclosure, they also tended to impose more stringent conditions on its release. For example, they wanted the department to ascertain that the birth mother requesting this information was of stable mind, that the adoptee had been told of his adoption, and that he would be receptive to a meeting. A male adoptee said: "I think the biological parent should be screened because you don't want some fanatic going around saying, 'You're my kid.'"

Furthermore, slightly more male adoptees than females were in favor of the requirement of their consent, with 85.7 percent and 78.5 percent respectively. Females also differed significantly with their male counterparts on a policy permitting the release of background information on adoptive parents to birth mothers. More than eight out of ten females (84.2 percent) favored such a measure, compared with two-thirds males (66.7 percent), thus reflecting a greater sensitivity on the part of women toward the birth mother's continual feelings of pain and loss and her need to know the well-being of her child.

Summary and Conclusion

Support for release of adoptees' whereabouts to birth mothers was strongest among birth mothers, and only modest among adoptees. More female than male adoptees approved of this policy. Adoptive parents were overwhelmingly opposed to this policy measure. The older parents (1958 and 1968 adoption years) were, however, in favor of making the disclosure less restrictive than the younger parents (1978 adoption year). Adoptees were motivated in their endorsement by the equivalence of rights doctrine and recognized the pain and guilt birth mothers experience. However, their subdued support was largely caused by feelings of resentment toward the birth mother who surrendered them. Adoptive parents were opposed because they felt voluntary surrender of the child constituted abrogation of the birth mother's right to resume contact. Birth mothers favored the disclosure because they yearned to see the birth child and to get an opportunity to explain their reasons for adoption. However, support of adoptees and birth mothers was conditioned upon the adoptee's adult status and consent. A sizable proportion of adoptees favored the higher age for the adoptee. A strong majority of them also wanted the department to search for them indefinitely. Birth mothers consistently showed weak support for the adult age requirement and the indefinite search.

In contrast to their opposition or equivocal support for revealing identifying information, the triad overwhelmingly approved of a policy permitting release of information on adoptees' health and development to birth mothers, upon request. The strong support for such a policy was attributed to the nature of information, which was not likely to reveal the identity of the principals to each other, thus maintaining the status quo in the adoption arrangement. Since adoptive parents are the only avenue by which to obtain information on the health status and development of an adopted child, respondents were asked whether the department should contact them. A huge majority of adoptive parents were opposed to direct contact, viewing such follow-ups as unwanted intrusions. However, a sizable proportion (a little less than one-half) of birth mothers and adoptees favored routine or periodic contact with adoptive parents. But they insisted that the department use less obtrusive means, such as the child's school records, the family doctor, or the health department. Mandatory reporting by adoptive parents as a policy option was the least-favored choice among all three principals.

With regard to the policy permitting birth mothers to receive background information on adoptive parents, adoptees and birth mothers were overwhelmingly in favor of such measure, while adoptive parents supported the idea slightly conservatively in comparison. The support level was highest among female adoptees. The triad agreed the information should be limited, nonspecific, and should refer to only those items in the parents' profiles that have bearing on the child's well-being. Birth mothers stressed their need to know if their child was adopted and whether the new parents provided a loving and secure home. Birth mothers also contended that such information would give them great relief from pain and guilt over their decision.

The data in this chapter do not confirm the stereotypical view that birth mothers are selfish, uncaring, and insensitive or that given an opportunity they would not hesitate to intrude in the adoptive home. The accounts of the birth mothers demonstrated the contrary. It is clear that birth mothers never forget the child they relinquish and continue their quest to reconnect, but only if the child is expressly willing to meet. Like adoptees, they opposed mandatory parental consent for the revelation of the adult adoptee's identity. But they were sensitive to adoptive parents' feelings—one-half of them felt the adoptive parents should be notified as a courtesy should the department release the information to adoptees.

They were unsure of their right to regain contact with the child, but felt that they would be content to know the health and development status of the child. They made it clear they had no intention of claiming the child, but wanted to be assured of his or her well-being and affection. While, they were interested in information about their birth child, they were least favorable of the respondents toward its release without safeguards for the interest of a deceased child. Of the three groups, birth mothers represented the highest proportion in favor of a court-appointed guardian to safeguard the child's best interest after death.

A few birth mothers who were opposed to the release of adoptees' addresses and/or information on their development were equally interested in the child and were eager to meet someday "without reservation." Their ongoing emotional need to know was characterized by this 1968 birth mother: "There isn't any birth mother who has given up a child for adoption and doesn't wonder where and how it is." However, these birth mothers would like the contact initiative to come from the adopted child. They were afraid they might inadvertently disrupt the adoptive home or meet rejection. More often than not, they were caught in a dilemma between their loss of right to the child and their desire to learn about her or him.

> I know I gave up my rights when I signed the papers for his adoption and I'm not his mother anymore. But I really would like to know about him. Even if I looked down across the street and couldn't talk to him. I'll be satisfied with that. Because I have no right to go to him I want him to find me.
>
> [1968 Birth mother]

> I won't ever bother my child, but I would love to know where she is. I'll not intrude on her life and the life of her parents. I feel it's better for me to wait and hope that she'll come than barge ahead without knowing about her feelings and the feelings of her parents. I would meet her with an open arm if she contacted me.
>
> [1969 Birth mother]

> There are a lot of birth mothers who are willing and who want to see their children, but are reluctant because of their belief that they gave up the right to the people who got their children. They wonder about the child but may never go to the department voluntarily. But they want their child to come and look for them. I think it'll be a rare mother who'll say to the child, "I do not want to see you."
>
> [1978 Birth mother]

7
Release of Information about Adoptees to Birth Fathers and Siblings

Identifying Information to Birth Fathers

Although it took two to conceive the adopted child, the birth father is not accorded the same recognition in the literature as the birth mother, as well as among other players in the adoption drama. Usually, he is not involved in the decision regarding the disposition of the pregnancy and placement of the child, as he is often seen by the birth mother as irresponsible and exploitative, or he takes to his heels upon discovery of the pregnancy. Although a principal protagonist in the existence of the adopted child, the birth father is often viewed as a phantom figure, an illusory entity whose only justification for the linkage with the child is that hc helped this biological event happen. A 1958 adoptive mother characterized him thus: "Birth father is not a person in my estimation." Historically, social agencies have not attempted to seek his active involvement, sometimes out of convenience, in planning for the baby and in the greater concern about his responsibility afterward.

Given this backdrop it was not surprising that members of the triad were strongly opposed or ambivalent to disclosure of the adopted child's whereabouts to the birth father. This contrasts with their position on the birth mother, whose right to similar information was supported by adoptees and birth mothers (see chapter 6). Thc data in table 7–1 show that the strongest disapproval was voiced by adoptive parents, with every eight out of ten parents opposing such a policy. This proportion is higher than that opposed to giving such information to the birth mother (see table 6.1). Of significance, birth mothers were almost evenly divided, with 49 percent in favor of this policy measure and 51 percent rejecting it. Recall that almost seven out of ten (69.3 percent) birth mothers were in favor of gaining access to such information for themselves (see table 6.1). Birth mothers' desire for preferential right of access illuminates their resentment toward the birth father who, in their view, is not as entitled to information or contact with the child as they are.

Table 7–1
Attitudes toward Release of Adoptees' Identity to Birth Fathers
(*percentages*)

Degree of Agreement		All Adoptive Parents (1958, 1968, 1978)	All Birth Mothers (1968, 1978)	All Adoptees
	N =	(152)	(78)	(53)
Strongly agree to somewhat agree		16.4	48.7	52.8
		[27.0]	[69.3]	[56.6]
Strongly disagree to somewhat disagree		82.6	51.3	47.2
		[73.0]	[30.7]	[43.4]

Figures in brackets represent degree of support for release of identifying information to birth mothers.

One 1968 birth mother said:

> The girl is the one who got pregnant, carried it through nine months and took all the responsibility and the guy goes on about his business as usual. If he had stayed around there wouldn't have been adoption.

Like birth mothers, adoptees rejected the equivalence of rights of both biological parents. Unlike their clear support for birth mothers' right of access to their whereabouts, adoptees were equivocal on similar rights for birth fathers.

Reasons against Release of Identifying Information

Birth mothers (51.3 percent) who were opposed to making such information available to the birth father were resentful toward him because he deserted the young mother and child. They disagreed with the principle of coterminous of rights because they argued the birth father voluntarily abdicated responsibility for the care of the child and thus contemporaneously lost his right to learn the child's identity or to establish contact. Their outpouring indignation is epitomized in the following excerpt:

> It takes two to tangle. When he gave up his responsibility to marry me and care for the child he gave up all his rights as father. As far as I'm concerned there is no such thing as a birth father.
>
> [1968 Birth mother]

These birth mothers also wondered if the father would be really interested in the child since he never evinced any interest since the child was born. These 1978 birth mothers said:

If the birth father was not interested in the beginning, there is no sense in him coming around years later looking for information about the child. I'd just tell him to get lost.

The guy left me and he didn't care enough to stay around. So why should he care now?

A few birth mothers suspected that only a few fathers would ever return to the department. Their reasons were twofold. First, many fathers are not told by the mother that the child was put up for adoption. Second, those who are aware of the child might face the possibility of suspected paternity. That is to say, the department might find it difficult to determine if the applicant were truly the genetic father of the child. This point was exemplified in remarks by two 1968 birth mothers:

There are probably millions of fathers walking around who don't even know they have children adopted in the first place.

Most men don't even know if they have dozens of kids. They could have more kids than they realize. I'm sure these men don't want to go to the department and tell them they have a child; otherwise they might end up providing support for a lot of children.

Adoptive parents disapproved of sharing identifying information with the birth father for much the same reason as did birth mothers. They felt he did not show much concern for the predicament of the young mother and/or share responsibility for planning and care of the child. One 1968 adoptive mother said the birth father "washed his hands of" the whole affair and allowed the mother to put the child up for adoption. Some adoptive parents argued that the father was not a principal party to the adoption agreement consummated between the adoptive parents and the birth mother.

As noted earlier, adoptive parents expressed their strongest disapproval toward giving both birth parents access to the identity of the adopted child. They were somewhat more sympathetic toward the birth mother because as a young mother she was faced with agonizing choices without the benefit of a father's support. This explains why they showed different levels of support for the birth mother and the father, as is evident in table 7–1.

I agreed with the birth mother getting this information, because I feel she should have more right to it than the father because he didn't want to do anything with the child to begin with. If he had cared about the child he could have married this girl and been a father of this child. I don't think he is entitled to any information whatsoever.

[1968 Adoptive mother]

This 1958 adoptive mother who supported access right of the birth mother was quite indignant when she was asked if the father should be given such information.

> Give him hell. The girl got pregnant and the father did not want to make a home for the child or marry her. He left the poor girl in the lurch. He gave up all his obligations then; let him give up all his rights now.

In the minds of most adoptees, the birth father was a nonentity, a biological entity not to be reckoned with. He was referred to as "that person," "that man," "biological father." His genealogical past was generally symbolized by the birth mother and her family, as the following statements by male adoptees illustrate:

> I have never ever thought of a birth father. I know that sounds crazy. It is as though that person never existed. I know there must have been one. But I'm concerned only with my natural mother.

> God only knows about the birth father. The birth mother is the only real attachment I have. The circumstances could have been that Daddy came and Daddy went.

Essentially, underneath the adoptees' negation lay feelings of resentment, hostility, and strong negativism toward the birth father, feelings these adoptees tried to repress by denying his existence. They perceived him as an opportunist who exploited a young innocent girl. They blamed him for not assuming responsibility and thus forcing the mother to adopt out her child. They felt if he were genuine in his relationship and accepted his obligation, she could have married him; they could have had a home and the adoptees could be living with their biological parents.

> For me, if I had a biological father, I wouldn't be with Mom and Dad (adoptive mother and father) now. My mother wouldn't have given me up and they could be together and I would be with them.
>
> [Female adoptee]

> I'll just give an answer for the birth mother and leave the father out. [Why?] It could be anybody and she might not have had any feelings for the man at the time. It could have been her father who raped her. I've no feelings toward that person.
>
> [Male adoptee]

> As far as the birth father is concerned, he couldn't have been worthy if he walked off and left a sixteen-year-old child. She was probably better off without him anyway.
>
> [Female adoptee]

Reasons for Release of Identifying Information

Adoptees who supported the birth father's right to information were prompted by reasons of fairness, since they endorsed the right of the birth mother to such information. Their most recurring sentiment was voiced by this male adoptee working as a correctional officer: "Although I have no feeling toward that man I have to be fair to him. I think the same law should apply to him as it does to the natural mother." To our question, why the birth father should be given such information, these adoptees gave a laconic monotone responses: "Same as the birth mother, no distinction," or "Whatever applies to the birth mother, the same applies to the birth father."

Interestingly, adoptees were amnesic about the birth father and reacted with almost astonishment when he was mentioned. Their characteristic response was: "I never really thought of him. I don't know why." A female adoptee felt embarrassed when she admitted it: "I didn't ever think there was a father involved; it tells you something about my sex education." Similarly, a male adoptee revealed his negation of the birth father's existence: "I never thought I had a birth father. I know you have to have one in order to conceive."

Forty-nine percent of birth mothers who favored the release of the adoptee's identity to the father were motivated by contiguity of rights. They said he made a biological contribution, which provides the only justification for his entitlement, although he failed to meet his responsibility as parent and to share the trying task of decision-making.[1] They felt the child might want to meet both parents despite the father's lack of parental feelings. The typical reason: "He's, after all, the legal father."

> I feel I'm the mother, but probably he doesn't feel he is the father because he never went through the pain or signing any paper. But he is the legal father and should have just as much right to see the child or his information as I do.
>
> [1968 Birth mother]

> I know I had to make the decision and he did not care. He did not want to know about the child. But I don't see why it should be any different from the birth mother as far as the child is concerned. Besides, the child would like to know both the mother and the father.
>
> [1968 Birth mother]

---

[1]As the manuscript was being prepared, interestingly, the Divisional Court of Ontario ruled in a precedent-setting case that a male who gets a woman pregnant and then ignores his responsibility to the child does not qualify as a parent (The Globe and Mail, April 2, 1988). In the United States, the Indiana Supreme Court rejected the plea of an Indiana man who tried to stop his estranged wife from having an abortion, thus deemphasizing the father's rights (USA Today, November 15, 1988).

However, their support of the birth father's right was not meant to deflect their true feelings for him, which were different from those birth mothers who opposed such a policy. This group of mothers left no doubt that they felt they were victimized by the birth father and as such were resentful and disdainful toward him. Their contradictory feelings are typified by this 1968 birth mother:

> No matter what he's like; he could be a saint, but yet I would hate him. Nevertheless, he is the legal father and that should be enough as regards his right where this information is concerned.
>
> [1968 Birth mother]

Grounds for Release of Information

Age of Adoptee

Members of the triad were unanimous that the adoptee should be of legal age when his identity is released to the birth father, as is evident in table 7–2. However, adoptees and adoptive parents were more supportive of this requirement, with 60.7 percent and 64.0 percent respectively, compared with one-half (47.4 percent) of birth mothers who held this position. Furthermore, of the three principals, birth mothers were less rigid about the age requirement. An almost equal proportion of them (42.1 percent) rejected the legal age and felt that a mature adoptee can handle reunion with or knowledge of his father.

Adoptees' and Adoptive Parents' Consent

Respondents also imposed consent of the adoptee as a condition, while they rejected the requirement of parental consent for adoptees who had

Table 7–2
Age of Adoptees for Release of Identifying Information
(*percentages*)

Degree of Agreement	N =	Adoptive Parents (1958, 1968, 1978) (41)*	Birth Mothers (1968, 1978) (38)*	Adoptees (28)*
At any age		16.0	10.5	17.9
Only when mature		20.0	42.1	21.4
Only when adult		64.0	47.4	60.7

*All those who agreed with release of adoptees' identity in table 7–1.

reached adulthood. Interestingly, the proportion of respondents who supported these requirements was identical for birth fathers and birth mothers seeking whereabouts of the child (see tables 6–3, 6–4). Their characteristic answer was, "Same as for the birth mother."

Identifying Information to Siblings

Siblings do not share the "irresponsible," "wily" image of the birth father, nor do they represent the threat of a "disruptive" birth mother and rival parent. Still, they do not provide rationale for information that is as recognizable and justifiable as that of birth parents. One 1978 adoptive mother put it, "The sibling's request for information seems to go beyond emotional reasons." Besides, the birth sibling's status in the adoption configuration is not as discernible and compelling as those of both biological parents and the adopted child. In short, siblings are not recognized as one of the principals in the adoption triangle. Because of siblings' amorphous status, respondents gave a mixed reaction to the question of whether siblings should be provided with the identity of the adopted adult. Their responses are depicted in table 7–3.

The data show that birth mothers and adoptees expressed stronger support for this policy option than did adoptive parents. Adoptive parents favored the policy measure with a bare majority (52.7 percent), while birth mothers and adoptees represented 62 to 64 percent who were favorable. It is worthy of note that siblings received a much stronger support from members of the triad than did the birth father (see table 7–1). The favored support for siblings reflects the confidence of adoptive parents and adoptees, since siblings do not represent the same threat as do birth parents.

Table 7–3
Attitudes toward Release of Adoptees' Identity to Siblings
(*percentages*)

Degree of Agreement	N =	*All Adoptive Parents* *(1958, 1968, 1978)* *(152)*	*All Birth Mothers* *(1968, 1978)* *(78)*	*All Adoptees* *(53)*
Strongly agree to somewhat agree		52.7	64.1	62.3
Strongly disagree to somewhat disagree		48.3	35.9	37.7

Reasons for Release of Identifying Information

The primary reason cited by all three groups was that knowledge of the birth sibling would obviate the possibility for inadvertent romantic involvement between kin. This concern was exemplified by this 1958 adoptive mother: "A child could end up marrying his own sister and not knowing about it."

They all mentioned the exciting possibility of the adopted adult meeting a brother or sister. They thought a birth sibling would provide the adoptee with a sense of closeness to a blood relative, especially if he or she were the only child and the parents were deceased.

> In my case if I had a brother and sister I'd like to know. I think I'd be tickled to death if he or she came to see me.
>
> [Male adoptee]

> Everybody needs to know whether they have a brother or sister so that they are not alone in the world. If anything happened to the adoptive parents, the child, especially if he is the only child, would know that he had a brother or a sister to cling on to.
>
> [1958 Adoptive mother]

> Sometimes you could end up being closer to your brother and sister than your parents. It is a special relationship.
>
> [1978 Birth mother]

Reasons against Release of Identifying Information

Adoptive parents and adoptees were concerned that the involvement of siblings would only complicate interpersonal and familial relationships and exacerbate tension. They also feared that if disclosure is permitted beyond the birth mother it would open the possibility for involvement of other members of the birth family, creating a complex web of relationships. In other words, they were concerned about stretching the disclosure policy a bit too far. Their caution was sounded in these words: "You have to draw the line somewhere." "It's going to get really complex." "You'll be getting too many people involved." "Really and truly it could get out of hand." Some adoptive parents thought the adopted child would not have the same kind of emotional feelings for his siblings as he would for birth parents and therefore his interest in genealogical lineage should terminate with the parents. One 1958 adoptive mother commented:

> I think we should go as far as the mother and the father. When you bring brothers and sisters into it you'll get a whole pile of people looking for information and that would be an awful mess.

Birth mothers referred to two major problems that might ensue if the adoptee and his or her brother or sister knew of each others' existence. First, the adopted adult is likely to feel rejected again by the fact that the mother kept the sibling but not the adoptee. This could engender further embitterment toward the birth mother. Second, in sharing the information with the sibling the birth mother, in effect, will reveal a socially unacceptable and potentially embarrassing occurrence of many years past. Birth mothers were afraid they might be judged harshly by their children, who might not understand the circumstances surrounding the pregnancy.

Birth mothers also contended that search or contact between the sibling and the adoptee would inescapably resurrect painful memories of the past, which some mothers might have been trying to repress.

Grounds for Release of Identifying Information

Adoptee's Age

Adoptees and adoptive parents were much more in favor of releasing this information than were birth mothers only when the adoptee had reached adulthood. Almost seven out of ten adoptees and adoptive parents held this view, while only a slender majority of birth mothers (56 percent) thought this way. They maintained that the older the adoptee, the greater the chances that he or she will attain maturity necessary to make a responsible and well-considered decision on whether to meet the sibling. A sizable proportion of birth mothers (40 percent) thought a minor adoptee could be mature enough to handle new relationships with siblings. (See table 7-4.)

Table 7–4
Age of Adoptees for Release of Their Identity
(percentages)

Age	N =	Adoptive Parents (1958, 1968, 1978) (80)*	Birth Mothers (1968, 1978) (50)*	Adoptees (33)*
At any age		2.5	4.0	3.0
Only when mature		27.8	40.0	27.3
Only when adult		69.7	56.0	69.7

*All those who agreed with release of adoptees' identity in table 7–3

Adoptive Parents' Consent

Table 7–5 shows that respondents in all three groups overwhelmingly rejected the requirement of parental veto for disclosing whereabouts of

Table 7–5
Prior Consent of Adoptive Parents
(*percentages*)

Agree or Disagree	N =	Adoptive Parents (1958, 1968, 1978) (80)*	Birth Mothers (1968, 1978) (50)*	Adoptees (33)*
Agree in case of adult adoptees		18.2	11.6	10.7
Agree in case of minor adoptees		69.2	64.1	67.8
Consent not required		2.6	24.3	21.5

*All those who agreed with release of adoptees' identify in table 7–3

adoptees who have reached adulthood. The proportion of respondents in favor of this requirement represented only one-tenth in each group. However, respondents unanimously supported this condition if the adoptee was a minor at the time his identity was released. The proportion approving this prerequisite for a minor adoptee was 64 percent to 69 percent. It should be noted that fewer respondents in all groups required parental consent for disclosure of identity of the adult adoptee to siblings than those who supported this requirement when such information is released to birth mothers (see table 6–3). This reflects their more relaxed attitude toward siblings.

Adoptee's Consent

Respondents in all three groups overwhelmingly favored adoptees' consent as condition for release of his or her identity to siblings. Table 7–6 shows that adoptive parents expressed the strongest support, with 95 percent, followed by 84.8 percent for adoptees, and 82.0 percent for birth mothers. The chief reason for their support of mandatory consent was that adoptees, especially adults, should be entitled to make their own decision. Once contacted by the department, adoptees could assess their current circumstances and mentally prepare to meet the sibling.

A few adoptees and birth mothers who opposed mandatory consent of adoptees were, however, confident that adopted adults and their siblings could handle the encounter regardless of the circumstances. They were certain the sibling would use discretion and good judgment in contacting and arranging a meeting in a manner that would not prove disruptive to the adoptee. However, they suggested that the adoptee should be notified by the department in advance of contact by the sibling, so that he or she is mentally prepared for the meeting. This is how one male adoptee expressed his confidence:

Table 7–6
Prior Consent of Adoptees
(*percentages*)

Degree of Agreement	N =	Adoptive Parents (1958, 1968, 1978) (80)*	Birth Mothers (1968, 1978) (50)*	Adoptees (33)*
Strongly agree to somewhat agree		95.0	82.0	84.8
Strongly disagree to somewhat disagree		5.0	18.0	15.2

*All those who agreed with release of adoptees' identity in table 7–3

> I shouldn't feel threatened that somebody who is my brother or sister is looking for me. It might cause an emotional shock or dismay but there are a lot of other things in this world that are much worse and which I face unexpectedly.

Differences within Groups

There was no difference of any significance among subgroups of adoptive parents and birth mothers on the issue of releasing identity of adoptees to birth fathers and birth siblings. Male and female adoptees, however, differed in attitudes toward the birth father.

Male adoptees were more favorable toward the policy, with 60 percent permitting birth fathers right of access to their whereabouts, than were females, who represented one-half. Males also imposed less stringent criterion of age for birth fathers than they did for birth mothers. A little over one-half (55.6 percent) favored legal age of the adoptee as condition for the release of such information to birth fathers, compared with 71.4 percent who held this position for birth mothers. In contrast, female adoptees represented almost identical proportion, at 63.2 and 65.2 percent for birth fathers and mothers respectively. Note also that the reverse was true if the birth mother requested such information. Less than one-half (46.7 percent) of male adoptees were supportive of the birth mother's right of access, compared to 60.5 percent of females who would do likewise (see chapter 6). This pattern between male and female adoptees' views is consistently held throughout the study.

The different level of support appears to be caused by their different attitudes toward both parents. As noted earlier, female adoptees show a greater propensity to empathize and identify with the birth mother, while males tend to put greater onus on the mother for not providing a home, and therefore feel most resentful toward her. This female adoptee, a twenty-four-year-old correctional officer, epitomized this difference:

> I know female adoptees and everybody tend toward girls and tend on the side of their natural mothers more than they do toward the natural father.

Note also the contrast in their attitudes, reflected in the reasons cited by male and female adoptees for their respective positions on such a policy for both parents. This is how a male adoptee explains his rationale for supporting the right of access for birth fathers:

> The birth mother gave up the child and thus she gave up the right to know about him, too. The birth fathers perhaps did not know that the mother had the child and had given it up for adoption. They might have some interest in the child when they find out later on. I think they should be given this information so that they can meet their lost child.

This female adoptee had different views as to which parent should receive such information:

> I can understand the mother's position and have sympathy with her. But for the father I don't know what the situation was and I have no feelings toward him.

Another female adoptee:

> It is quite possible that the birth mother has suffered enough, as it is not a very easy thing to give up a child. She wonders all those years what happened to the child. I think she should be given the information. [What about the birth father?] Forget it—he doesn't deserve it. He never had the guts to stand up and take the responsibilities for it in the first place. Tell him to go to blazes.

Summary and Conclusion

Members of the adoption triad were either opposed or ambivalent to releasing identity of adoptees to birth fathers. Strongest opposition came from adoptive parents; birth mothers were evenly divided. Like birth mothers, adoptees were equivocal on access rights for birth fathers. Adoptees differed by gender. Male adoptees appeared more favorable toward extending those rights to birth fathers than were females. This was a reversal of their position on access rights for birth mothers.

The chief reason for the triad's opposition to this policy was the negative feelings they had toward the birth father. They were resentful that he deserted the birth mother and child, failing to provide a home for them. They argued that the birth father voluntarily abdicated responsibility for the care of the child and therefore lost his right to learn the child's identity or to establish contact. Birth mothers felt victimized because they got pregnant and had to make difficult decisions without benefit of a birth father's support. Adoptees were almost amnesic about the birth father and denied his existence in the adoption configuration.

Adoptees who supported the birth father's right of access to such information were motivated by fairness; they felt it was only right since they supported similar rights for the birth mother. Birth mother's support was due largely to their consideration of his biological participation. However, these respondents felt just as resentful toward him as did the respondents who opposed access rights of the birth father. Furthermore, their support was conditional upon the adoptee's attaining legal age and consenting to the release of his or her identity. Adoptive parents' consent as requirement was rejected in the case of an adoptee who has reached adulthood.

Birth siblings received much higher support than did birth fathers. In fact, adoptees and adoptive parents were more favorable toward the access rights for siblings than they were for birth mothers. Their favored support for siblings reflected their confidence that siblings do not represent the same threat birth parents do. However, they stipulated legal age of the adoptee and his prior consent as conditions for release of such information.

The primary reasons for their support were that the knowledge of the brother or sister would avoid the possibility of their inadvertent romantic involvement. Also, they said a blood relation would provide the adoptee with a sense of closeness with the past, especially after the adoptive parents are deceased.

Some concerns were voiced. Adoptive parents and adoptees were afraid involvement of siblings would complicate interpersonal and familial relationships, opening up possibility for involvement of other members of the birth family. Birth mothers worried that the adoptee might be more embittered because he or she was relinquished while the sibling remained with the birth mother.

8
Registry and Postadoption Service

Once a social agency has established a policy under which adoptees and birth parents can have access to identifying information about each other, it needs a mechanism known as registry to facilitate exchange of personal details and reunion between the interested parties. There are generally three registry systems: passive, active/passive, and fully active.

A *passive registry system* requires reciprocal consent between parties or matched inquiries before their identities are disclosed. The agency may or may not act as an intermediary to facilitate reunion. An *active/passive registry* gives primacy to adoptees' need to know and recognizes their right to search, provided the consent of the birth parent is obtained. The agency takes active but discreet initiatives on behalf of the adoptee only to locate the birth parent and seek her or his consent. Under a *fully active system* the rights and needs of both parties to search are regarded as coterminous and the agency undertakes search for either unregistered party.

As depicted in table 8–1, there was overwhelming support among all groups in favor of a mutual-consent provincial registry under which an adult adoptee and the birth parent voluntarily enter their personal data and state their willingness to meet. The support was strongest among adoptees and birth mothers, with identical proportions (92.4 percent), compared with adoptive parents, who accounted for less than three-quarters (73.7 percent).

Adoptive parents were not only less favorable, they were also equivocal and apprehensive. Their support was based on the assumption that searching adoptees are maladjusted in the adoptive family, emotionally disturbed, and driven by special circumstances, such as death of the adoptive parents. The following excerpts illustrate their perception of adoptees who are likely to benefit from the registry:

Table 8–1
Attitudes toward Registry System
(*percentages*)

Degree of Agreement	N =	All Adoptive Parents (1958, 1968, 1978) (152)	All Birth Mothers (1968, 1978) (78)	All Adoptees (53)
Strongly agree to somewhat agree		73.7	92.4	92.4
Strongly disagree to somewhat disagree		26.3	7.6	7.5

> The adoptee who wants to meet his natural parents because he is not getting along or because the adoptive parents are dead, would really need such registry.
>
> [1958 Adoptive mother]

> I feel if the children want to look for their parents they can't be very happy with the adoptive parents. If this is going to keep them, there should be registry.
>
> [1958 Adoptive mother]

Adoptive parents' support for registry is hedged with ambivalence and apprehension, as typified by the following excerpts:

> It is a good idea but there would have to be a lot of thought put into this before any decisions are made by the child. On the one hand there is somebody he thinks is his mother all his life and on the other hand there is somebody he had never met and he wants to meet. That could make the adoptive mother feel all kinds of things.
>
> [1968 Adoptive mother]

> I don't see anything wrong with it, but I hope this information is not easily available to them. I also hope that Evelyn will never want to know her real parents and she looks upon me and Bob as her real parents.
>
> [1978 Adoptive mother]

Reasons Supporting Registry

The most frequent reason cited by respondents referred to the lessening of red tape that the registry is supposed to achieve. They hoped this system would dispense with agonizing bureaucratic delays in facilitating sharing of information between parties. The birth mothers' recurring comments were, "It would save a lot of trouble and fuss." "At least you know where to go directly to look for information instead of being pushed through a number of people." Adoptive parents felt that the system, in the words of one adoptive mother, "would cut out a lot of racing around for adoptees who have set their minds on searching." Adoptees and birth mothers felt the existence of the registry signified the government's formal commitment to permitting them access to background information and thereby minimizing the risks of facing disappointment should they decide to seek reunion. Their sense of relief and optimism is exemplified by these remarks: "It's still up to yourself, but at least it's something to look forward to, the day you'll see your child." "We know there's a choice now if registry is set up."

For birth mothers, registry is an uncumbered device by which an adopted child can signal to them. They said the initiative by the adoptee would encourage them to reciprocate without running the risk of being rejected or inadvertently interfering in the adoptee's life. As this 1978 birth mother put it: "This way I could meet my daughter if I knew she wanted to meet me." Adoptive parents also thought that since this system implies mutual consent it would protect an adoptee from directly confronting his birth mother, who might be unwilling to meet.

Some adoptive parents thought the registry would prevent the possibility of an unwanted and embarrassing appearance by a birth mother at the adoptive parents' home. As one 1978 adoptive mother put it, "Better this way, than all of a sudden having someone on your doorstep."

The older adoptive parents from the 1958 year particularly felt they did not have many years to live and their adopted children, especially only children, would be left alone in the world. They found the registry useful for their children, who could resume contact with members of their birth family.

Reasons Opposing Registry

As noted in table 8–1, adoptive parents represented the largest proportion (26.3 percent) among the three groups who were opposed to registry. Only six birth mothers (7.6 percent) and four adoptees (7.5 percent) disapproved of the system. The reason for the adoptive parents' opposition was that they did not want the resurgence of their adopted child's past. They viewed the registry as a potential threat to their efforts toward preserving the doctrine of equivalence—that is, they wanted to believe that the child was born to them naturally, and as a 1958 adoptive mother stressed, "Nobody from his birth family should even be involved."

Some adoptive parents had foreboding anxiety that the knowledge of the registry might spark desire to search in their adopted children. They maintained that their children were fully assimilated into the adoptive home and that family harmony could be disturbed by the registry. They were afraid the existence of the registry might stir up their child's interest in birth parents and make him or her feel dissatisfied with the adoptive home. In their judgment, the registry was fraught with many problems and was limited in serving any real need of adopted children. One 1958 adoptive mother summed up the 'let sleeping dogs lie' attitude of these parents by referring to the distressing experience of an adoptee in Ontario:

> I hope you'll never open the registry in this city and do a damage to our children. I've heard several horrifying cases in Ontario where they have a registry. One girl was so depressed after finding out about her parents that she took an overdose. This is what worries me.

Six birth mothers who were opposed to registry were concerned that reunion could prove disruptive in the lives of all participants in adoption. In fact, four preferred that adoption information remain sealed permanently. They contended that the mere possibility of access to the information could tempt even the most unconcerned adoptee or birth mother to feel curious about each other. Their typical comments were, "It could cause a lot of problems for a lot of people—their own family, adoptive parents, and friends," or "If your child came into your mind, it would be a hard decision not to call in the registry."

More significantly, four of these birth mothers told us that they had thought of the child very frequently or occasionally since relinquishment, but were afraid to regain contact because it might resurrect the painful feelings of loss they experienced at relinquishment, which they had been trying to repress. Two mothers said they would not meet because they were apprehensive of negative reactions by their husbands and children, should they happen to learn of their past pregnancy. Four adoptees (7.5 percent) who were against the registry expressed concern about their adoptive parents, who would feel hurt if the child desired reunion with birth parents.

Active vs. Passive Registry

Respondents who supported the concept of registry were asked if they preferred fully passive, active/passive, or fully active registry. The reader is reminded that this question was asked in relation to sharing of information and/or actual meeting between an adult adoptee and his birth mother, although registry can be used for contact between adopted adults and their other members of the birth family. As stated in chapter 1, the literature and the records of social agencies indicate that in most cases adoptees undertake search for birth mothers before they meet other birth relatives. However, the views expressed by the respondents with respect to birth mothers should not be applied to other members, since the data show they have different feelings toward birth fathers and siblings (see chapter 7).

As is evident in table 8–2, respondents in all three groups overwhelmingly favored an active registry on behalf of adoptees. Interestingly, birth mothers expressed the strongest support, with almost nine out of ten approving of an active search for the unregistered birth mother at the request of the adoptee. More significantly, despite equivocal support among adoptive parents for registry, a large proportion of them (79.5 percent) endorsed an active search on behalf of adoptees. Adoptees represented the third largest group, with 71.4 percent, to hold this position.

However, support for the quid pro quo when a birth mother requests the search on her behalf dropped considerably among all but one group—birth mothers. Only 57 percent and 58 percent of adoptees and adoptive parents, respectively, approved of this policy measure. Birth mothers supported this policy with an overwhelming majority—three-fourths, but did not consider they had the reciprocal right of access to identifying informa-

Table 8–2
Options for an Active-Passive Registry
(*percentages*)

Policy Options	N =	Adoptive Parents (1958, 1968, 1978) (112)*	Birth Mothers (1968, 1978) (72)*	Adoptees (49)*
1. If adoptee has registered department should notify birth mother		79.5	88.9	71.4
2. If birth mother has registered department should notify adoptee		58.0	75.0	57.1
3. If birth mother cannot be located department should release identity of birth mother to adoptee		47.2	65.6	42.9
4. If adoptee cannot be located department should release identity of adoptee to birth mother		29.2	51.9	35.7
5. Wait until birth mother contacts department		20.5	11.1	28.6
6. Wait until adoptee contacts department		42.0	25.0	43.0

*All those who agreed with registry system in table 8–1

tion or contact. As noted earlier, a significantly higher proportion of birth mothers—almost 90 percent—favored an active search on behalf of adoptees.

The primacy of adoptees' right to identifying information was also evident when respondents were asked if the department should release the information to parties in situations where, after a search has been conducted for a reasonable length of time, the person whose consent is required cannot be located. Less than one-half each of adoptive parents (47.2 percent) and adoptees (42.9 percent) supported release of information to an adoptee when the birth mother is not traceable. The comparable proportion favoring this measure for birth mothers was less than one-third (29.2 percent) and a little over one-third (35.7 percent), respectively. Birth mothers, too, gave preferential support to adoptees' right to information. Two-thirds of birth mothers tipped on the side of adoptees' right, versus one-half for their own right.

The data in table 8–2 also show that respondents in all groups rejected a passive registry under which the department does not conduct searches for the unregistered party. However, their level of disapproval for a passive registry varies depending upon whether the unregistered party is an adoptee or a birth mother. For example, if an adoptee seeks information or contact, only a small percentage in each group—about one-tenth to one-quarter—were opposed to the search for the unregistered birth mother. But if the reverse is true, a much higher percentage (25 to 43 percent) thought it would be intrusive for the department to search out the adoptee. In short, members of the triad were strongly in favor of a fully active registry, but they regarded adoptees' right to identifying information or contact as supreme. However, birth mothers were far less inclined to favor the hierarchy of rights between themselves and adoptees than were the other two principals.

Reasons for Adoptees' Primacy Right to Information

Adoptees and adoptive parents believed that birth mothers know their origins and also know who their children are, whereas adoptees do not know the identity of the women who bore them and who symbolize their past. Therefore, they argued, adoptees' need to know should supersede birth mothers' right of privacy. They found it ironic that a birth mother should be uneasy in revealing her identity to the child she gave birth to and should feel threatened by her own flesh and blood. Their frustration at the secrecy of birth mothers' identities is reflected in the following statement by a male adoptee:

You may explain all you want, but you can't justify that I can't get the name of the woman who bore me. I keep running it in my head as to why there is such great sin to know this woman and why she wants to keep her identity a mystery from the son she gave birth to. I'm not a threat to her.

Adoptees and adoptive parents also maintained that it was the birth mother's voluntary decision to relinquish the child, which also meant a contemporaneous loss of her right to that child. An adoptee, they said, may not have any interest in the birth parent because he or she is happily adjusted into the new home and contact by the department on behalf of the birth mother could be too intrusive and disruptive. Adoptive parents were concerned that contact by the department might stimulate desire in the child, who may have learned to repress it. It is also possible that the adoptee has not been told of his adoption and such contact could be disastrous for the child. These risks, they contended, do not attend on the birth mother when she is contacted. Besides, the birth mother is a lot older and more mature than the adoptee and, therefore, should be able to handle intrusion better than the adoptee. They also wondered why a birth mother would like to seek out her child whom she relinquished. But as far as their own reasons for wanting to see the birth mother, these are clearly justifiable:

I can understand the reason of the adoptee for his wanting to see his birth mother. But she does not have any reason to seek the child now. I mean she gave it up for some reasons and that should be it. I think it should be the child who should seek the mother and not the other way around.

[Female adoptee]

I'm totally on the side of the child. If he decided that he wants to meet his real mother he should be given identifying information. The birth mother made her decision when she signed the papers, but the child was not involved in the decision.

[1968 Adoptive mother]

Birth mothers agreed with adoptees and adoptive parents that they renounced their right to the child, but they said they did not rid themselves of feelings of loss and anguish and their wish to know. They said they wished to resume contact with the birth child, now adult, but would not initiate search either because they believed they waived their right or they feared that they might disrupt the child's life. Also, they were afraid the adoptee might not be receptive. Some birth mothers were apprehensive that the child might not be aware of the adoptive status or they might hear bad news about him or her. However, these birth mothers were willing to meet if contacted by their birth child, as is demonstrated by our data. The following remarks illustrate why birth mothers would prefer to be contacted:

> A lot of times I've been at the welfare office and I often thought of going upstairs (adoption department) to ask about my child. But I'd draw back because in my heart I knew I wouldn't get anywhere and it would hurt me more. So the only thing I could do is think about him and hope and pray that one day he will come and look for me.
>
> [1968 Birth mother]

> The way the laws are, the adoption information is confidential and you are not supposed to find your child. So although most birth mothers would be willing to meet with their child, they won't think about it enough to put their names in the register until someone phones them and says, "Your child from thirty years ago would like to meet you."
>
> [1968 Birth mother]

Some birth mothers said that if they were asked at the time of placement for their consent so that their adopted child could gain access to their identifying information or make contact with them, it was highly unlikely that they would have agreed. They said it was only after the experience with the pregnancy and adoption had been resolved that they were able to make a rational decision, as this 1968 birth mother explained:

> When you give up the child and the social worker asks you if you would like to meet the child, chances are that a lot of birth mothers don't want to ever see her again. It is only after some time has passed and they have given some consideration that they will agree. But they are not going to think about it unless someone has approached them.

Suggestions for Making the Registry Effective

Members of the triangle advanced certain suggestions for making the registry effective and successful in sharing information and assisting in reunions.

1. The registry should be widely publicized so that its policy provisions and service programs can be fully understood by potential searchers. They said knowledge of the registry will represent formal commitment of the provincial government to a new policy permitting disclosure of information and facilitating reunions between consenting parties to adoption. They said lack of awareness might

cause some adoptees and birth mothers to miss the opportunity to register, which could be interpreted by the other party as being uninterested, possibly reinforcing a sense of rejection.

2. The department should conduct a search and make initial contact in a manner that is discreet and subtle, so that the action does not jeopordize the sought party's anonymity. Extreme caution is needed in contacting adoptees, to allow for the possibility that some may not know they are adopted.

3. The approach to the party whose consent is being sought should not imply any pressure or obligation to agree to disclosure or a meeting. Furthermore, the person contacted should be permitted sufficient time to reflect and give a rational and well-considered decision. Some birth mothers maintained that they had an ongoing parental concern for the relinquished child but did not remain preoccupied with these thoughts for fear of evoking painful memories. Besides, since they did not see any hope of reuniting they found it senseless to dwell on the matter. Therefore, their initial reaction to approach might be indifferent and apathetic, perhaps negative. They warned, however, that the initial response can be misleading, as it may not represent their true desire to meet, which usually surfaces after reflection and careful consideration.

> Normally, birth mothers do not dwell on the child enough to motivate them to register because they have been told for years that they lost their right, or in most cases it is a painful experience they try to put to the back of their mind. Most do not think of the possibility of ever meeting their child again. So, when the department calls, the mother may not be thinking and therefore may not sound enthusiastic.
>
> [1968 Birth mother]

> There are a lot of birth mothers whose first reaction can be one of shock and they may show a 'go away, leave me alone; I've my own life' attitude on the initial contact, because they have not been thinking about the reunion. But when they have a chance to think about it they may change their minds. So I don't think the matter should be dropped at that.
>
> [1978 Birth mother]

4. The search for the nonregistered party should be thorough and exhaustive and should allow a reasonable time before disclosing the identity of that party. They thought a reasonable length of time for search should not exceed one year.

Intermediary

Once matching registration has taken place and an adopted adult and his birth mother have consented to meet, the parties may approach on their own or involve the department to act as an intermediary to arrange and facilitate the first meeting. Members of the triad were overwhelmingly in favor of an intermediary for their initial encounter, as is evident in table 8–3. The strongest support was expressed by adoptees, with almost three-fourths (73.5 percent) favoring involvement of the department as an intermediary. Birth mothers and adoptive parents accounted for almost equal proportions, at two-thirds each.

The chief reason for their support of an intermediary was that the adoptee and the birth mother are complete strangers and are likely to be overwhelmed with anxiety and nervousness. The intermediary can be of great help in breaking the ice and putting them at ease. Birth mothers and adoptees were concerned that they would experience mixed emotional feelings and felt the intermediary should provide them with brief background information on each other before the meeting. They also would like the department to provide them with helpful suggestions for keeping their composure. However, they were unanimous that department involvement should not extend beyond the first meeting and the parties should be left on their own to arrange any subsequent meetings. Typical of this viewpoint was expressed by two 1968 birth mothers:

> It would be better if you had a third person to set up the meeting because I wouldn't know how to approach him on it and probably he wouldn't either.

> I think an intermediary is a good idea for the first meeting. The person would know what my reaction is going to be or what I feel. I

Table 8–3
Attitudes toward Department as Intermediary
(*percentages*)

Degree of Agreement N =	Adoptive Parents (1958, 1968, 1978) (112)*	Birth Mothers (1968, 1978) (72)*	Adoptees (49)*
Department should be involved	62.5	66.7	73.5
Contact should be left to searching parties	35.7	33.3	26.5
Uncertain	1.8	–	–

*All those who agreed with registry system in table 8–1

probably would get so excited I might just flake right out. This person could help me to handle myself.

A little over one-third each of adoptive parents and birth mothers and about one-quarter (26.5 percent) of adoptees were opposed to mandatory involvement of the department as an intermediary. They considered the meeting between an adoptee and his birth mother a private matter that should be pursued by two adults in privacy, and felt the involvement of an intermediary would be too intrusive. Birth mothers and adoptees said a reunion with the child is a once-in-a-lifetime occurrence and to experience this event fully both parties should be freely expressive in their emotions, which is not possible in the presence of an intermediary, a stranger. They felt the third party might not have the sensitivity and concern appropriate for such occasions.

> Meeting with your mother or father could be a highly emotional experience for either or both. I would like to keep it personal and I don't need to have somebody who means nothing to either of us and could get in the way of saying hello.
>
> [Female adoptee]

> It should be up to the individual where and how they would like to meet. It's something you would like to experience between each other rather than have someone else there sitting between you and seeing how you feel.
>
> [1978 Birth mother]

A few adoptees regarded the requirement of an intermediary as offensive and an expression of a lack of confidence in them as adults. To them it would undermine their ability to handle a meeting with their parents. Their indignation is evident in this typical statement: "I would rather have the government stay out of it and I don't need an escort or the department's advice."

Prereunion Counseling

Mandatory counseling for adoptees and birth mothers who wish to meet was highly favored by adoptive parents and birth mothers, and was marginally approved by adoptees, as shown in table 8–4. A little over 60 percent in each of adoptive parents (60.8 percent) and birth mothers (62.5 percent) said the release of identifying information should be accompanied by mandatory counseling, compared with only one-half (51 percent) of adoptees who held this view. However, a large proportion of adoptees (42.9 percent) favored making counseling service available for searching

Table 8–4
Desirability of Counseling as Required, Optional, or Unnecessary
(*percentages*)

Desirability of Counseling	N =	Adoptive Parents (1958, 1968, 1978) (112)*	Birth Mothers (1968, 1978) (72)*	Adoptees (49)*
Should be required		60.8	62.5	51.0
Should be optional		13.4	18.1	42.9
Not necessary		25.9	19.4	6.1

*All those who agreed with registry system in table 8–1

adoptees and birth mothers, but only on a voluntary basis. Among those who rejected counseling altogether, adoptees accounted for the least proportion—6.1 percent.

Those who favored compulsory prereunion counseling saw its value in helping the searching parties to dispassionately examine their motives and their expectations for the new relationship. They expected the counselor would assess whether the parties were aware of the potential frustrations and implications of the reunion. The counselor could prepare them on how to handle an outcome that might be unsavory.

Since most birth mothers assumed that the initiative to contact would most likely come from the adoptee, they discussed the value of counseling from the point of view of searching adoptees. They expected the counselor to ensure that the adoptee did not have negative feelings toward the birth mother and that the search was not motivated by vengeance or resentment. As a 1978 birth mother put it: "A counselor can tell if the child is simply on an ego trip or he sincerely wants to find his parents." Interestingly, adoptees, too, felt a counselor could discern injurious motives of a searching adoptee. This female adoptee expressed her conviction in the value of prereunion counseling in these words:

> A counselor can screen motives of adopted children and filter out their bitterness. There might be some crazy fools who want to go and shoot their parents. That's a little too risky, I'm sure a lot of work is involved for the department, but it's really worth it.

Respondents in all three groups who thought counseling service should be available but not imposed upon the searching individuals gave identical reasons for their positions. They argued that some individuals are capable of making decisions after a thoughtful appraisal of their circumstances and motives, and have a strong conviction in the desirability of their action. They doubted that counseling could change the minds of individuals who are determined to pursue the search. They, however, stressed that the counseling component should be an integral part of the registry and that searching parties should be informed of this service. As one 1968 adoptive mother said, "These are intelligent and mature people who know what exactly they want and why they want and they are ready to accept calmly whatever the consequences."

Significantly, respondents who opposed counseling gave essentially the same reasons as those who thought it should not be required. These respondents were confident in the ability of the individuals who have made up their minds. Their rationale was reflected in this remark by one 1978 adoptive mother; "If the people involved feel strongly enough about meeting each other, they will work out their problems themselves."

Who Should Provide Counseling?

Adoptive parents had more confidence in the quality of service of the department than did birth mothers or adoptees, as shown in table 8–5. For example, while almost two-thirds (64.2 percent) of all adoptive parents expressed their confidence in the department, 58.6 percent of birth mothers and less than one-half of (47.6 percent) adoptees agreed with this view. Adoptive parents also differed with birth mothers and adoptees on the choice of a qualified counselor outside the department. While adoptive parents stressed the academic qualifications and training of a counselor, birth mothers and adoptees thought sensitivity and experience in searching and reunion were more important. For instance, about one-third (30.9 percent) of adoptive parents considered a psychologist or a doctor competent for this job, but birth mothers (32.8 percent) and adoptees (42.9 percent) thought an adoptee or a birth mother who has had experience in searching and reunion could provide a competent counseling service. Their rationale was that these nonprofessionals can better appreciate the feelings and are more sensitive to the needs and difficulties of the searching indi-

Table 8–5
Choice of Counselor
(percentages)

Choice of Counselor	N =	Adoptive Parents (1958, 1968, 1978) (81)*	Birth Mothers (1968, 1978) (58)*	Adoptees (46)*
Department of Social Services		64.2	58.6	47.6
Any qualified counselor searching person wishes to choose		30.9	32.8	42.9
Any other person		4.9	8.6	9.5

*All those who agreed with counseling service in table 8–4

viduals. Three birth mothers and two female adoptees said they would feel comfortable with a priest, who could approach the issue from a religious perspective, with compassion and sympathy. They thought social workers were too swamped with heavy caseloads to devote time required to provide efficient counseling.

Differences within Groups

Adoptive Parents

The younger parents (1978 and 1968 years) were more favorable to the registry than their older cohorts (1958 adoption year). Their respective proportions were 81.5 percent (1978 parents), 76.0 percent (1968 parents), and 62.5 percent (1958 parents). The difference between the 1968 parents and the other two groups approached, but did not achieve, statistical significance. Interestingly, their level of support was consistent with the position they took on the release of identifying information to adoptees (see table 4–8). Recall that the younger parents' support was more apparent than real and reflected their underlying anxiety. Similarly, their strong endorsement for registry was attenuated by anxiety and uncertainty, as is illustrated in these statements: "I hope Michelle will never want to know her real parents." "If it's going to affect them psychologically, it's just as well to find out their birth mothers and get it over with." A 1978 adoptive mother would avoid any discussion with her adopted daughter: "I'm not sure yet whether or not I should tell my daughter that she is adopted."

In contrast, older parents were confident about the adopted children's bond with the new family, as this 1958 adoptive mother exemplified: "I don't see anything wrong with it. I think if the child is adopted for twenty years, there shouldn't be any reason why parents should feel threatened if their children found the long-lost other parents." These parents were also more liberal than their younger cohorts toward releasing identifying information to the adult adoptee or the birth mother when consent of the other party was not available. For example, almost 40 percent of 1958 parents said information should be given to the birth mother when the adoptee's consent is not available, compared with only one-quarter each of the 1968 and 1978 parents who favored this measure.

Older adoptive parents also differed with their younger cohorts on the question of whether adult adoptees need the assistance of the department in arranging their first meeting with the birth mother. A higher proportion of older parents (46.7 percent) felt confident in the ability of adoptees to handle the first encounter on their own than did the younger parents, who accounted for nearly one-third each (31.6 percent).

There was unanimity among the three groups of adoptive parents with almost identical proportion—about 70 percent—who favored providing counseling to adoptees and birth mothers seeking reunion. But they differed on whether counseling should be mandatory. More younger parents, 62 to 64 percent, thought counseling should be required than did older parents, 53.3 percent.

On the question of who should provide counseling, older parents had the highest degree of confidence in a department social worker, while more younger parents (1978 year) expressed the least confidence. More than eight out of ten (80.9 percent) of the 1958 parents said department social workers are competent to provide this service, compared with one-half of the 1978 parents who held this view. The 1968 parents took the middle position, with 69.2 percent. Viewed another way, older parents were less likely to prefer a counselor outside the department than were either the 1968 or 1978 parents. About 31 and 42 percent, respectively, of the 1968 and 1978 parents thought searching parties should seek counseling from a qualified worker outside the department, while only 14.3 percent of the 1958 parents felt this way. The following remarks illustrate their perceptions of a competent counselor:

> I think the department does have counselors who are trained for that sort of thing and they understand both sides of the issue.
>
> [1958 Adoptive mother]

> It should be a psychologist because this professional knows most about the emotional needs of people. Psychologists have done a lot of courses in human behavior and they know the anxiety and frustration levels of a person.
>
> [1968 Adoptive mother]

> I think they should speak to whomever they feel more comfortable with. They could get the same kind of counseling from the clergy or adoptive parents. It depends on the relationship.
>
> [1978 Adoptive mother]

It is conceivable that the low preference among the younger parents for a department social worker may not be related to the qualifications and competence of the worker, which has progressively improved since the 1950s, but may reflect resentment toward the department. As the availability of healthy white infants became more scarce in the late 1960s and 1970s, the department progressively tightened its criteria for the selection of adoptive parents. As a consequence, the 1978 parents were subjected to a more rigorous scrutiny of their eligibility than were the older parents in the 1950s. A number of prospective parents found the new assessment procedures too intrusive. It could partly explain why these parents do not want to deal with the department.

Birth Mothers

There was no difference between the 1978 and 1968 birth mothers in their level of support for the registry. However, the two groups differed on whether the release of identifying information should be subject to compulsory prereunion counseling. The older birth mothers (1968 year) were less inclined to support this option than the younger mothers (1978 year). Less than 60 percent (57.1 percent) of the 1968 birth mothers favored mandatory counseling, compared with close to 70 percent (67.6 percent) of the 1978 birth mothers who felt this way. Weaker support for mandatory counseling among the 1968 birth mothers could be attributed to the fact that a large majority of these mothers were married and living with their husbands, with whom they could discuss their feelings. Thus, they did not see the need for formal counseling, as did their younger cohorts. It is also possible that the younger birth mothers were more oriented to professional counseling than they were to an informal support system of family and friends.

Not only did the younger birth mothers favor compulsory counseling but they also preferred that this service be provided by a department social worker. A much higher proportion of the 1978 birth mothers (71 percent) expressed their choice in favor of the department, compared to less than one-half (44.4 percent) of the 1968 birth mothers. Similarly, while younger birth mothers thought department social workers are well-qualified and professionally trained in the area of reunion counseling, older birth mothers had more confidence in an adoptee or a birth mother as a counselor. More than 40 percent (40.7 percent) of the 1968 birth mothers expressed a preference for a nonprofessional person, an adoptee or a birth mother, compared with only one-quarter (25.8 percent) of 1978 birth mothers who held this view. A higher level of support for this position among the 1968 birth mothers could be because six of these mothers have had contact with Parent Finders in Toronto and were quite impressed by their quality of service, while none in the 1978 group had any exposure to such support-search group.

Adoptees

Support for the registry was stronger among female adoptees, with almost all of them (97.4 percent) in favor of it, compared with male adoptees, who accounted for 80 percent. This difference is consistent with their respective positions on the disclosure of identifying information. However, more males (83.3 percent) than female adoptees (70.3 percent) would definitely prefer the involvement of the department as an intermediary to arrange the first meeting between them and the birth mothers. This may reflect the characteristic uneasiness of males in being able to express themselves. Females generally are less inhibited in verbalizing their emotions and therefore have less need to rely on a third party for breaking the ice. This female adoptee illustrates her ease in reaching out to her birth mother: "Although you don't know each other, you do have a common bond. Give me her phone number and I would do my own arrangement."

Female adoptees were consistently less inclined than males to favor compulsory involvement of a third party as counselor. While three-fourths of the males were in favor of mandatory counseling service for searching parties, only a little over 40 percent (43.2 percent) of females held this view. They also differed as to who was competent to provide prereunion counseling. While males expressed supreme confidence in the competence of a department social worker, female adoptees and birth mothers thought an adoptee or a birth mother who has gone through the searching and reunion experience would be more qualified for counseling. For example, seven out of ten males gave their vote of confidence to the department social worker, compared to only four out of ten of the females. Twice as many female adoptees (60.0 percent) preferred an experienced adoptee or birth mother than did male adoptees (30 percent). Four female adoptees were receiving counseling from Parent Finders in Toronto at the time of follow-up, which could explain a high preference among females for such service.

Summary and Conclusion

There was overwhelming support among all groups in favor of a mutual-consent provincial registry under which adult adoptees and birth parents voluntarily enter their personal data and state their willingness to meet. Support was strongest among adoptees and birth mothers, compared to adoptive parents. Although younger adoptive parents (1968 and 1978 year) were more favorable to the registry than their older cohorts (1978 year), they were nevertheless equivocal and apprehensive in their support. In contrast, older parents appeared to be confident about the adopted child's bond with the new family. They were more liberal than their younger cohorts toward the policy of revealing information without the consent of either party. Adoptees also differed by gender in their support for the registry. Female adoptees gave a stronger endorsement than did their male counterparts. There was no difference of any significance among the two groups of birth mothers. The most frequent reason given by respondents for supporting a mutual-consent registry referred to the frustrating bureaucratic red tape that currently exists. They felt it would facilitate sharing of information and would minimize risk for adoptees and birth mothers of facing a direct confrontation or rejection by the other party.

All three parties in the triangle showed a strong preference for a fully active registry on behalf of adoptees. Adoptive parents and adoptees, however, tended to be more favorable toward the right of the adoptee to search than they were toward the right of the birth mother to search. Birth mothers did not advocate their rights to be equivalent to those of the adoptee. Members of the triangle suggested that for the registry to be effective it should be widely publicized and searches should be thorough, exhaustive, and conducted in a discreet and subtle manner, but should not exceed a maximum period of one year.

All three groups were overwhelmingly in favor of the department to arrange the first meeting and to act as intermediary to facilitate the initial encounter. The strongest support was expressed by adoptees.

Members of the triad agreed that the release of identifying information should be accompanied by prereunion counseling by the department. This requirement was highly favored by adoptive parents and birth mothers but only marginally by adoptees, who supported voluntary counseling. Among adoptive parents and birth mothers, the younger cohorts were more supportive of mandatory counseling than were their older counterparts. More female adoptees than males were opposed to compulsory counseling. On the question of who should provide counseling, adoptive parents expressed the strongest preference for a department social worker, followed by birth mothers. Adoptees were almost divided between their preference for the department social worker or a nonprofessional but experienced person, such as an adoptee or a birth mother.

The data highlight two important observations. First, we find further evidence shattering the prevailing myth that birth mothers are unconcerned about the child they relinquished. Among members of the triad, birth mothers were most supportive of a fully active registry signifying their willingness to be found and met. Only one-tenth (11.1 percent) would not favor a contact, and this represented the lowest proportion among the three groups. It also means that by and large birth mothers feel a continuing sense of loss and would like to reunite with their child, but are reluctant to take the first step for fear they might be rejected or inadvertently cause disruption in the child's life. They enthusiastically favored registry because it permits them to learn if their child has expressed a willingness to meet. Their sentiment was expressed by a 1968 birth mother: "Most birth mothers would be willing to meet their child but wouldn't even start to think until a contact has been made."

Birth mothers did not claim equal rights with those of adoptees, as is often believed. They agreed with the supremacy of adoptees' needs and their right to realize a sense of identity. Thus, birth mothers were less concerned about their identity being disclosed if they could not be located for consent, than they were for the disclosure of adoptees' identity in a similar situation.

9
Attitudes of Social Work Personnel

A government can enact a policy, but how equitably it is applied to the constituencies it intends to serve, and how actively it is implemented, depends upon the attitudes of the frontline workers and the support of the managerial staff, collectively called the organizational environment. Even a well-intentioned policy can flounder in an unresponsive and hostile environment. We wanted to gain an understanding of the sensitivity of the Department of Social Services to the need for reorienting its traditional policy of sealed adoption records. Thus, we sought the views of social work personnel responsible for adoption services on a policy permitting more openness in adoption and their understanding of its implications in terms of new services and resources. It also seemed desirable to find out if the personnel responsible for services perceived any difficulties and recognized responsibilities and challenges associated with a more relaxed policy on adoption disclosure. The social work personnel, numbering seventeen, included a broad section of officials responsible for policy formulations and decision making (minister, deputy minister, assistant deputy minister), policy interpretation (regional and district manager) and for policy implementation (adoption workers). The questions used to elicit their responses were open-ended to permit a full expression of views.

Adoptees' Right to Know

All respondents recognized that the need to know genealogy is omnipresent among adoptees and it is their basic right to gain access to the biological heritage. Some felt that denying such information to adoptees is discriminatory and unfair since nonadopted people know their genetic past. A few of them felt highly distressed about the practice of sealing the adoption records. This official at a ministerial rank was indignant when he said:

> When I see this research completed it'll lift from me a burden that has been longstanding. I have sat and pondered many times how awful it

must be for people who don't clearly know who they are and who cannot go to their roots, whatever that uncovers.

Another official holding a ministerial rank stressed the rights of adoptees to know:

> There are not many things in life that are as basic as where you came from and who your parents were. To have a general public policy that prohibits an individual from that to me is not very acceptable.

This ministerial officer emphasized the rights of adoptees by identifying with them and by tuning into their feelings:

> When I go back to the place where I was born and grew up it gives me some thrill. I'd feel up in the air if I did not know where I was born. I think it's one of those basic human needs.

Another official with a ministerial position endorsed the rights of adoptees to know as being a fundamental human need:

> I've always felt that it's the birth right and the basic need of every person to know where they came from. I don't think it's necessary that when you're adopted you should be completely cut off from where you came from.

A senior social worker supported the rights of adoptees to genealogical information as being a natural and basic desire among all human beings:

> The reality is that somebody else gave birth to you and you would like to know something about that person. I don't believe in the adoptive parents' reasoning, 'Let's pretend that you didn't exist before you come to us.

Release of Nonidentifying Information to Adoptees

All respondents seemed unanimous in supporting the release of nonidentifying information on birth parents to adoptees. However, their endorsement was hedged with conditions. They wanted disclosure to be contingent upon these criteria:

1. Adoptees' desire for information is genuine and compelling rather than a plain curiosity.

2. Adoptees' motives are positive, and are assessed as being legitimate to satisfy their identity concerns.
3. Adoptees' possess an emotional strength to be able to cope with the information, especially if it's negative and potentially distressing.

Respondents felt the information should be screened for content that might prove embarrassing or incriminating, such as incest, psychiatric problems, or bad character of the birth parents. One senior worker, however, was in favor of sharing "all sorts of information" with adoptees because, as she put it, "reality is reality." Although a vast majority (thirteen) would consider a minor adoptee who is mature and is supported by the adoptive parents as eligible for gaining this information, respondents tended to favor the age of majority as the requirement. They felt that the older the adoptee, the more emotionally stable. A little less than majority (seven) felt that adoptive parents should be involved in the decision and adopted adults should be encouraged to discuss their desire with adoptive parents, thus avoiding any impression of the parents' being ignored or slighted by the department. One senior manager said the involvement of adoptive parents would be a clear measure of the department's commitment to the pledge of confidentiality made at adoption placement.

Release of Medical Information to Adoptees

Respondents were unequivocal in their endorsement of a policy permitting release of information concerning medical and hereditary diseases. As a matter of fact, the department has been following this policy since 1940. This was based on the department's commitment to the overall well-being of the adopted child, who may need medical information for treatment, diagnosis of degenerative diseases, or to save his or her life. The department provides, on request from adoptees' physicians, information on the health status of their birth parents. However, these officials pointed out that the department does not have a great deal of medical history to share because the information contained in the files is extremely limited. Sometimes the department receives requests from female adoptees who are planning to get married or to have children to find out if there is anything in their heredity that could prove fatal to their offspring. The department has no mechanism in place to ensure that the information obtained from birth parents at relinquishment is updated periodically. On occasion, under medical emergencies, the department has contacted birth mothers.

Release of Identifying Information

Respondents were more guarded and equivocal in their approval of sharing identifying information with adoptees than they were in releasing nonidentifying information. While a majority (eleven) favored such a policy, they stressed several conditions to accompany release of this information:

1. Adoptee has attained the age of majority.
2. Adoptee is emotionally mature and stable enough to handle the information and/or the reunion experience.
3. Adoptee's desire is so persistent that the denial of the information is likely to result in serious emotional problems.
4. Adoptee's motives are positive and are not intended to seek vengeance or harm the birth parent.
5. Birth parent must provide consent to release her or his identity.

Involvement of the Department in Search for Birth Parents

All but one respondent favored active department involvement in locating and identifying the birth parent. They felt that without the department's initiative birth parents may not register their consent on their own for the following reasons: Birth parents may not be aware of their adopted child's desire to establish contact with them; they may not know the registry exists and that they are invited to participate in sharing information with adoptees; or they might have repressed the memories of the relinquished child, believing they would never reunite. Respondents, however, were divided almost equally between those who supported an indefinite search for the birth parent and those who thought the search should be limited to one year, and if the birth parent cannot be located, the department should release the identifying information to the adoptee. Significantly, both groups of respondents were confident that given the province population, it would be likely that the party would be found if the search is thorough and exhaustive, or, in the words of one senior administrator, "if we have combed the Earth."

One respondent, a senior manager, was opposed to the department's initiative because he felt most birth mothers would like to forget the child after relinquishment and would not like their past to be dredged up. In his personal experience he learned that most birth mothers were eager to sign the consent to adoption and have it "done and over with."

I think birth mothers wonder about what's happened to their children but gradually these feelings wear off with years . . . A lot of girls do not want to use the waiting period of seven days before they give their consent. They would ask, "Why can't we sign the consent now and have it over with?"

Involvement of Adoptive Parents

Only three respondents (one middle manager and two social workers) favored adoptive parents' consent as requirement for release of identifying information to adoptees. They feared a surreptitious search by adoptees could jeopardize the adoptive relationship. All others contended that such a requirement would be offensive to the dignity of the adoptee, who is now an adult. However, they were in favor of adoptive parents' involvement in the decision as a courtesy, since they are the child's legal parents. Recognizing that the department cannot make participation mandatory in the decision of adult adoptees, they tried to encourage open and honest communication between adoptees and their parents. These respondents felt morally obligated toward adoptive parents and felt ill at ease with a policy that would permit the release of adoption information in a surreptitious manner. This senior administrator summed up the department's attitude:

> We have been advising adoptive parents that through adoption the child becomes legally theirs and any link with the birth parent has disappeared. But adoption disclosure runs counter to that promise. To me there is something wrong. I believe that if they are aware of what is taking place they tend to accept and support what we are doing.

Four resondents (one middle manager and three senior social workers) were opposed to disclosure of birth parents' identity except under conditions of dire emergency, such as terminal illness or inheritance. They were largely concerned that the impact of the disclosure might destabilize the adoptive home life and distress adoptive parents. One senior manager described the reaction of an adoptive parent to this study:

> A friend of mine who had adopted a child five years ago and was contacted for this research study told me that up until that point she had not even thought that disclosure as an issue would ever be considered. Ever since that time she has had a knot right in the pit of her stomach. And she's a professional person and her sister happens to be a social worker.

Release of Information to Birth Mothers about Adoptees

While respondents were highly sensitive to the right and need of the adoptee to know, they did not consider the birth mother's rights equal to those of the adoptee. They contended that the birth mother made a conscious decision to relinquish the child and so forfeited her rights to learn about or have access to that child. Their attitude was that the adoptee did not ask to be born and adopted. Thus, he or she is a passive recipient of the birth mother's decision. They felt that once the adoptee is a person he or she has an absolute and inalienable right to total information about the genetic past. A ministerial officer ranked in order the hierarchy of rights among the adoption triad, giving highest priority to the child and then the adoptive parents. The birth mother was given lowest priority. The following statement by an administrator with a ministerial rank typified these respondents' feelings on the rights of adoptees and birth mothers:

> Birth mothers do not have the same claim and the demand with the strength that the child would. She knows who she is but this child doesn't know his identity.

Respondents viewed birth mothers' motives with suspicion and were concerned that they could disrupt the adoptive homes and try to reclaim the adopted child. The following statements by a middle manager and a social worker illustrate their deep suspicion of birth mothers' intent:

> You wouldn't give a burglar the combination of your safe because you know he'd break in. To be sure that that wasn't going to happen I would have to be sure of her motives.

> If you really get a persistent natural birth mother whose motive is to track down the child using this bit here and there, then I think we have to be careful of them and alert the adoptive parents that the natural mother can make contact with their child and warn them to be prepared.

Against this backdrop it is understandable that the respondents found it acceptable to provide birth mothers with nonidentifying information but were reticent about divulging the whereabouts of the child. Only five respondents expressed their categorical agreement for the release of identifying information to birth mothers. The rest were either uncertain or opposed to such a policy. Furthermore, those approving of this policy made disclosure of identifying information conditional that (1) the adoptee has attained legal age; (2) the adoptive parents have given their approval;

(3) the consent of the adoptee has been obtained; (4) the birth mother's motives are thoroughly assessed for possible negative purposes.

Service Implications

All respondents recognized that relaxation of the existing policy on sharing adoption information is inexorably associated with significant staffing and service implications for the department. It would mean an increased caseload for already overworked social workers, if additional staff were not hired. They felt the need for a strong commitment to provide adoption workers with specialized knowledge and skills to deal with inquiries from adoptees and birth parents. Some officials anticipated a dramatic rise in the number of inquiries as members of the adoption triad become aware of the new policy. They all recognized that this is a highly complex and sensitive area involving conflicting rights and needs of the parties to the adoption. Thus they stressed that the approach should be extremely cautious, discreet, and circumspect.

Summary

There was a great deal of sensitivity among the sample personnel of the Department of Social Services toward adoptees' need to know their genealogical past. Officials were increasingly cognizant of the urgency to revise the existing adoption policy in terms of greater openness. They deemed it essential that a well-defined, uniform policy be developed to serve as guidelines in handling requests from adoptees and birth parents. The urgency for bringing about a relaxed policy was stressed by this administrator holding a ministerial rank:

> A person's identity is essential for peace within mind and soul. If it can make this person happier then surely we must not pinch pennies in bringing it about.

Another administrator in a ministerial position emphasized "the right of the individual to know" and declared his commitment to "personally favor moving toward an opening of this process." However, all respondents stressed caution, discretion, and a limited reform. They were by and large highly supportive of making nonidentifying and medical information on birth parents available to adoptees who are minors, but mature and supported by the adoptive parents. But they were reticent in divulging the birth parents' identity, which they felt should be subject to stringent criteria. They were far more conservative in their support for releasing the identity and whereabouts of adoptees to birth mothers, whose need and claim to information they regarded as secondary. They argued that birth mothers lost their rights to know and/or contact once they relinquished the child. In effect, they considered the right of the adoptive parents to be involved in the decision more important than the birth mother's need to know. They contended that the child legally belongs to the adoptive parents, who are likely to feel undermined if the department takes a surreptitious route in disclosing the information. Their reluctance to permit birth mothers access to identifying information also stems from their view of birth mothers' motives, which they regarded as highly suspect.

All respondents recognized the implications of a revised adoption policy in terms of increased staffing, need for training, and specialized knowledge. This, they thought, was imperative to provide effective service to adoptive parents, returning adoptees, and birth parents.

10
What Does This All Add Up To?

This research was undertaken to generate recommendations that could serve as a positive instrument for rational policy and procedures for dealing with requests for adoption information. By now it should be evident that the issue of opening sealed records is highly complex, involving conflicting rights and needs. It brings into focus a serious task of formulating a policy protecting the rights, needs, and guarantees of each party to the adoption. It should be emphasized that the policy recommendations offered in this chapter are based on research finding and do not reflect the investigator's personal views. A few prefatory comments, however, would provide the rationale for such policy options.

First, because of the in-depth, personal interviews that permitted us to go beyond simple yes-or-no, agree-or-disagree answers from our randomly selected respondents, the information obtained represents nuances of views and concerns on the issue of adoption disclosure. Thus, it is hoped that these recommendations offer an effective framework for designing a policy to deal with various situations. Second, as noted from the data, certain concerns and reservations of the triad are attributable to fictional beliefs and unsubstantiated fears about the other party's motives. It is anticipated that with growing empirically based information and increased experience, the triad will find fewer compelling reasons for maintaining secrecy and privacy rights. This probably will pave the way for greater acceptance of openness in adoption. Consequently, these recommendations are futuristic in that they anticipate the gradual lessening of resistance of the triad toward changes in traditional adoption practices.

Third, there was no consensus among members of the triangle on any aspect of the issue, nor was it expected. They held widely divergent views on some issues; on others they did not differ much. Given the diversity of views, it is difficult to find a perfect middle ground upon which all polarized conflicts are resolved. Thus, in bringing forth the recommendations, the guiding principle was that these should serve the interest and needs of the greater good. However, care is taken that members of the triad who do not benefit from this policy are protected by certain safeguards, such as the establishment of an appeal process designed to arbitrate their interests and rights, and the consideration of exceptional circumstances.

To recapitulate the study findings, a few highlights are presented, followed by recommendations.

Highlights of the Study Findings

Release of Identifying Information to Adoptees

1. Birth mothers and adoptees showed a strong support for release of identifying information to adult adoptees with 88.5 percent and 81.1 percent, respectively, endorsing such measure. Female adoptees and the younger birth mothers (1978 adoption year) expressed stronger approval than did male adoptees and the 1968 birth mothers.

   Adoptive parents also endorsed this policy measure with a strong majority (69.7 percent), but their support was more apparent than real; it was hedged with reservations, anxiety, and conditions. This was more true for the younger parents (1968 and 1978 adoption year). To deal with their anxiety, some adoptive parents denied their children's interest in genealogy and avoided the issue.

   The older adoptive parents (1958 adoption year), however, were less apprehensive and their support was less equivocal, since they felt more secure in their relationship.

2. Adoptive parents and the adoptees preferred the adoptee to be in his twenties to be eligible for identifying information. Birth mothers represented a lean majority (58 percent) who favored this condition. In addition, consent of the birth mother as requirement was approved by an overwhelming majority of the triad. The support of this requirement was strongest among adoptive parents, with 84 percent, followed by birth mothers (75 percent) and adoptees (69.8 percent).

3. All respondents overwhelmingly supported an active search for the unregistered birth mother on behalf of the searching adoptee. Only a lean majority in each group favored an indefinite search. Far more female adoptees than males were in favor of an indefinite search.

4. A large majority in all groups—two-thirds to seven-tenths—favored the release of the birth mother's identity without her consent if she is deceased.

5. Adoptive parents' consent as condition for release of identifying information to adopted adults was supported by more than one-third (36.8 percent) of adoptive parents. Another one-quarter (23.6 percent) would like to be consulted on a voluntary basis. The strongest opposition to this requirement was voiced by adoptees, with 90.7 percent disagreeing with it.

6. In addition to the requirements of age and consent of the birth mother, almost all respondents stressed an assessment of the adoptee's motives, emotional maturity, and psychological readiness for such information.

Release of Nonidentifying Information to Adoptees

7. Support for disclosure of background information on birth parents not only was consistently high among members of the triad but also was less prescriptive. A massive majority in all groups (83 to 94 percent) approved the release of nonidentifying information to adoptees at any age.

8. All adoptive parents and one-half of adoptees felt nonidentifying details should be provided to parents at the time of adopting the child. Birth mothers also endorsed this policy option with a strong 80 percent. Both adoptees and birth mothers, however, suggested that the department should screen the information in terms of its embarrassing items before it is made available to either the adoptive parents or the adoptee.

Release of Medical and Background Information on
Birth Parents

9. The respondents were almost unanimous, with 94 to 99 percent, in their support for the release of information on medical history of birth parents, preferably to adoptive parents at adoption. Almost one-half (49.3 percent) of birth mothers were agreeable to periodic direct contact by the department for an update on their medical histories or for consent to contact their family physicians. The rest were willing to file medical information on their own.

10. All but eleven birth mothers favored legal intervention, if necessary, in case the birth parent refuses to provide medical information deemed vital to the health of the adoptee.

11. All adoptive parents received at the time of adoption background information on the birth parents of their children, but they regarded medical history the most important among items on background details. An overwhelming proportion in all three subgroups (85 to 90 percent) were indifferent toward the birth parents' psychosocial profile because of their marked discomfort with the child's past, which this information represents.

Release of Adoptees' Identity and Whereabouts to Birth Parents and Siblings

12. Support for a policy permitting the disclosure of adoptees' whereabouts to birth mothers was strongest at 69.3 percent among birth mothers and only modest among adoptees at 56.6 percent. More female (60.5 percent) than male adoptees (46.7 percent) favored this policy option. Adoptive parents were overwhelmingly opposed, with almost three-quarters rejecting this measure. Approval of adoptees and birth mothers was, however, contingent upon the consent of an adoptee who has reached at least adulthood.

13. Members of the adoption triad were either opposed or ambivalent to releasing identity of the adoptee to birth fathers. Strongest disapproval was voiced by adoptive parents, with every eight out of ten parents opposing such policy. Birth mothers were almost evenly divided on this policy. Adoptees, too, were equivocal, with a bare majority (52.8 percent) approving the right of access for birth fathers. More male than female adoptees were favorable. Adoptees, however, required that this information be released only when they have reached at least the legal age, and with their consent.

14. Birth siblings received much higher support from the members of the triad than did birth fathers. Birth mothers and adoptees were more favorable, with an almost identical two-thirds each agreeing with the release of adoptees' identity to birth siblings, compared with adoptive parents, who represented a bare majority (52.7 percent). Like birth fathers, the disclosure of such information to siblings was subject to legal age of the adoptee and his or her prior consent.

Release of Background Information on Adoptees and Adopted Parents to Birth Parents

15. In contrast to their opposition or equivocal support for identifying information, the triad expressed an overwhelming approval, 80 to 90 percent, for a policy permitting release of information on adoptees' health and well-being to birth mothers, upon request. The use of less obtrusive means, such as the child's school records, family doctor, or the health department, were preferred avenues for updating background information on adoptees.

16. Adoptees and birth mothers overwhelmingly endorsed (79 percent each) a policy measure permitting birth mothers access to background information on adoptive parents. Adoptive parents supported the idea but conservatively, representing six-tenths (61.8 percent) of all parents. The triad, however, felt unanimously that the scope of the information should be limited, nonspecific, and should refer only to those items that bear on the child's well-being.

Registry and Postadoption Service

17. Registry as a means of sharing personal details and establishing contact between interested parties was overwhelmingly favored by respondents in all three groups. The support was strongest among adoptees and birth mothers, with identical proportions (92.4 percent), compared with adoptive parents, who accounted for three-fourths (73.7 percent). Adoptive parents were not only less favorable, they were also equivocal and apprehensive. Female adoptees gave a stronger endorsement than did their male counterparts.

18. All three parties in the triangle showed a strong preference for a fully active registry on behalf of adoptees. Adoptive parents and adoptees, however, tended to be more favorable toward the right of the adoptee to search than they were toward the right of the birth mother to search. Birth mothers did not advocate their rights to be equivalent to those of the adoptee.

19. Members of the triad suggested that the registry should be widely publicized, and felt searches should be thorough, exhaustive, and conducted in a discreet and subtle manner, but should not exceed a maximum period of one year.

20. All three groups overwhelmingly favored the department is ar-

ranging a first meeting between adoptees and their birth relatives and acting as intermediary to facilitate the initial encounter. The strongest support was expressed by adoptees, with almost three-fourths (73.5 percent) favoring department involvement.

21. Members of the triad agreed that the release of identifying information should be accompanied by prereunion counseling by the department. This requirement was highly favored by birth mothers (62.5 percent) and adoptive parents (60.8 percent), but only marginally by adoptees (51 percent), who supported voluntary counseling. More female adoptees were opposed to compulsory counseling than were males.

22. On the issue of who should provide counseling, adoptive parents expressed the strongest preference for a social worker of the department. Birth mothers followed. Adoptees were almost divided in their preference for a department social worker or a nonprofessional but experienced person, such as an adoptee or a birth mother.

Attitudes of Social Work Personnel

23. There was a great deal of sensitivity among social work personnel toward adoptees' need to know their genealogical past. Officials were increasingly cognizant of the urgency to revise existing adoption policy in terms of greater openness. However, all respondents stressed caution, discretion, and limited reform. For example, they were highly supportive of making nonidentifying and medical information on birth parents available to adoptees who are minors but mature and supported by the adoptive parents. But they were reticent and equivocal in divulging birth parents' identity, which they felt should be subject to stringent criteria.

24. They were far more conservative in their support for releasing the identity and whereabouts of adoptees to birth mothers, whose need and claim to information they regarded as secondary. They considered the right of adoptive parents to be involved in the decision more important than the birth mothers' need to know.

25. All social work personnel interviewed for this study recognized the implications of a revised adoption policy in terms of increased staffing, need for training, and specialized knowledge. This, they thought, was imperative to provide effective service to adoptive parents, returning adoptees, and birth parents.

Recommendations

Identifying Information about Birth Parents or Birth Relatives (Siblings, Grandparents) to Adoptees

Definition. Identifying information is any information that would lead or likely lead to the identity of a particular person. Name, address, place of birth, place of residence, date of birth, and job title are examples of such information.

It is recommended that identifying information be released through the Adoption Disclosure Registry to adoptees provided that:

A. *The adoptee is twenty-one years old or older.*

B. *The consent of the birth parent/birth relative whose identity is sought is obtained before such release.*

C. *The consent of the adoptive parents/guardians is obtained, in case the birth sibling whose identity is being sought is a minor and is living with his or her adoptive parents or guardian.*

D. *The consent of the birth parent is obtained if the sibling lived with the parent until the age of eighteen.*

Procedures for Obtaining Consent. 1. In the event the birth parent/birth relative has not registered a desire to meet, the department would undertake an active but discreet search of the unregistered party, so as not to jeopardize her or his anonymity. The search would be conducted for a period not exceeding one year, and at the end of this period the available identifying information be released to the adoptee without the other party's consent, if she or he could not be located.

[It should be noted that a consistent majority among respondents in all three groups (54 to 59 percent) supported an indefinite search for the unregistered birth parent (see table 4–5). But the arguments advanced by those favoring a time-limited search seem more compelling than those in support of the interminable search option. We accept the argument that protracted search would be costly and arduous as well as potentially injurious to adoptees' right to know, especially to those adoptees who need this information to relieve their sustained emotional distress.]

2. The department would make sure the search was thorough and exhaustive and was not limited to any geographical area before disclosing the information.

3. At least two contacts should be made, fifteen days apart, with any birth parent/birth relative who refused permission. This recommendation is made in view of the revelation by the sample birth mothers that their initial negative response could be precipitous and therefore should not be treated as final. Furthermore, they said they would need time to reflect on the request, assess their circumstances, and prepare themselves for a possible contact by the adoptee.

4. The final refusal of the birth parent/birth relative should be accepted and communicated to the adoptee with the reasons provided.

5. In case the birth parent/birth relative is dead or believed to be dead, the identifying information should be released to the adoptee, provided the department decides the adoptee is not likely to abuse the information.

E. *Disclosure of the information should be accompanied by counseling by a qualified social worker.*

Purpose of Counseling. A counselor would assist searching adoptees to examine their motives, their expectations from the reunion and the new relationship, and its impact. The counselor would assess their emotional ability to cope with a revelation that might prove unsavory. She or he would make adoptees aware of and prepare them for potential frustration and implications for existing relationships. Adoptees would be assisted in the conduct of approaching and meeting the birth parent/birth relative with sensitivity and discretion; they would be encouraged to use the department as an intermediary, if reunion is intended. The counselor would encourage adoptees, where appropriate, to discuss their desire with the adoptive parents.

Explanations. These recommendations permit adult adoptees access to identifying information, while safeguarding the privacy rights of the birth parent. The adoptee at twenty-one years of age is more likely to have attained maturity and independence—emotional and financial—from the adoptive parents, thus making it easier to pursue search without interference or possible guilt. Adoptive parents would feel reassured that the child would grow under their care and integrate with the new family without being confused by a second set of parents. The recommendations also would open the possibility of the adoptive parents' involvement and support in the adoptee's decision to search. The recommendations offer birth parents protection from disclosure of identity to a minor child and from fear of disruption in their lives by an irresponsible, immature youngster.

Counseling would help safeguard birth parents from an intrusion by an unscrupulous adopted adult having negative motives.

Nonidentifying Information about Birth Parents/Birth Relatives to Adoptees and Adoptive Parents

Definition. Nonidentifying information is background description that would not lead or likely lead to identification of the birth parent/birth relatives. Examples of such information include personal history (such as physical description, education, marital status, number of siblings, etc.) and social history (such as occupation, hobbies, interests, talents, etc.).

It is recommended that as full non-identifying as possible information be provided to adoptees on request. Such information could be made available *at any age* of the adoptee, subject to determination by the department that:

a. Consent of the adoptive parents/guardian is obtained, in case the adoptee is a minor.
b. The information is not potentially identifying.
c. The adoptee has the emotional ability to handle information, particularly if it is embarrassing, damaging, or sensitive.

It is recommended that adoptive parents be given, at the time of adoption, personal and social background on the child's birth family. The department would use its discretion in screening the items for information that might be potentially embarrassing.

Explanation. These recommendations provide adoptees open access to background information through adoptive parents during their growing-up period and directly from the department when they are adults. While they ensure an optimum availability of background information, they protect the anonymity of birth parents and other birth relatives by screening items that could ascertain the identity of an individual. This easily could be a potential problem, particularly in small communities. This means the department would use discretion in defining nonidentifying information in relation to the size of a given community. Recognizing that some adoptees would like to know everything in their birth parents' background, while others might find certain pieces distressing, the provision of discretionary authority vested with the department would protect those adoptees unable to cope with stigmatizing disclosure such as rape, incest, sexual abuse, criminal offense, or disreputable occupations. The requirement of adoptive parents'/guardians' consent for minor adoptees reflects the agreement of all three parties, especially the adoptees in the study, and ensures that the adoptee will not be adversely affected by the revelation.

Medical Information to Adoptees and Adoptive Parents

It is recommended that as detailed a medical history as possible on birth parents and other birth relatives be made available upon request to the adoptee, and to spouse and offspring if the adoptee has died.

It is recommended that as detailed a medical history as possible be provided to adoptive parents at the time of adoption placement.

It is recommended that the department encourage birth parents at the time of placement to file names and addresses of their family doctors, along with consent for the physician to release medical information, if required, and to periodically update their addresses and any new medical conditions that may affect the health of the child.

It is recommended that the birth parent be contacted by the department as needed. However, it should make certain that the information required is critical for the health of the adoptee and that contact is unavoidable. In the event the birth parent refuses to provide medical information vital to the health of the child, the department should use legal means, if necessary, to obtain such information. The department should make every effort to ensure that its approach is nonintrusive and discreet, so as not to jeopardize the anonymity of the birth parent.

Identifying Information about Adoptees to Birth Parents and Birth Siblings

It is recommended that identifying information about the adoptee be released to the birth parent/birth sibling through the Adoption Disclosure Registry, provided that:

A. The birth sibling has reached a minimum age of twenty-one.
B. The adoptee has reached twenty-one years of age,
C. Consent of the adoptee is obtained before disclosure of his or her identity.

> **Procedures for Obtaining Consent.** The department would conduct an active but discreet search of the adoptee, if unregistered, to locate and seek consent. It is assumed that the department might contact adoptive parents of the adoptee as one of the avenues. The information would not be released unless consent of the adoptee has been obtained.
>
> At least two contacts with an adoptee who refuses permission should be made. The initial contact would allow the adoptee to

reflect on the request, as well as on current circumstances, and to make a thoughtful, dispassionate decision.

The adoptee's refusal to disclose should be accepted and conveyed to the birth parent along with the reasons.

The consent requirement be waived in the event the adoptee is deceased or believed to be deceased.

D. The disclosure of information should be accompanied by counseling.

The counselor would assist the birth parent/birth sibling to examine his or her reasons, expectations of the reunion, if it is sought, and its potential implications.

Where the consent of the adoptee has been obtained the department would encourage the adoptee, where appropriate, to discuss with the adoptive parents the desire to meet the birth parents.

[It is recognized that respondents in all three groups in the study did not uphold the access right of birth fathers or they were equivocal in their support. Even those who marginally approved (such as adoptees) did so for no other convincing reasons other than "to strike a balance with the access rights of the birth mother." Besides, they were highly antagonistic toward him because they felt he failed to assume responsibility toward the child and the mother.

The birth father's status as a parent was also recently challenged in the Divisional Court of Ontario, which ruled on April 1, 1988 that a man who gets a woman pregnant and then ignores his responsibility to the child does not qualify as a parent. However, the arguments by one-half of the adoptees and birth mothers in the study favoring coterminous of rights between both biological parents deserve consideration. Yet, as maintained by study birth mothers, it is expected that the number of inquiries from birth fathers will be extremely minimal.]

Explanation. These recommendations recognize the equivalence of rights of birth parents to identifying information about adopted adults, while at the same time safeguard the privacy rights of adoptees through the requirement of their absolute prior consent. They stipulate an active involvement of the department through search and counseling, which would provide adoptees with protection from an unwarranted intrusion in their lives. Active search of the adoptee would considerably increase the probability that the birth parent will succeed in the search. The recommendations also minimize the possibility of traumatizing an adoptee who might not have been told of his or her adoptive status. The adoptee is urged to confide in the adoptive parents. By raising the minimum age of the adoptee as requirement, the recommendation allows the adoptee to gain greater maturity and independence from the adoptive parents, thus improving the ability of the adoptee to cope with the new relationship and dispelling the adoptive parents' anxiety over the possibility that their child might get hurt.

Nonidentifying information about Adoptees and Adoptive Parents to Birth Parents

Definition. Nonidentifying information here means any information pertaining to the health and development of the adopted child; it also means financial and educational status, personality characteristics (such as their ability to give love and affection) and marital relations of adoptive parents, and overall quality of the adoptive home.

It is recommended that the birth parent be provided with information regarding the adoptee's health and development upon request.

It is recommended that the birth parent be given background information, as defined, concerning adoptive parents at the time of placement. In case an adoptive home has not been selected at relinquishment such information should be provided to the birth parent(s) soon after the adoption is finalized. Such information be made available to the birth parent(s) provided that:

A. The information about the child does not contain items that could prove distressing;

B. The information about adoptive parents does not lead to or is not likely to lead to identification of the adoptive parents.

It is recommended that adoptive parents and adult adoptees be encouraged to periodically update nonidentifying information, as defined. In exceptional circumstances, such as interminable illness of the birth parent, the department may contact adoptive parents and/or adult adoptee for an update. However, the adoptive parents or the adoptee may refuse to reveal or share the information. But the department would do its best to urge and persuade them to provide the information requested.

[It may be noted that the sample birth mothers and adoptees showed a stronger support for routine contact with adoptive parents for an update than they did for contact on a need basis (see table 6–10). The recommendation is being made in favor of contact only when needed for a trial period on the assumption that adoptive parents and adoptees would generally respond to the voluntary measures.]

Explanation. These recommendations recognize that the information on the relinquished child's health and well-being is vital to the peace of mind of the birth parent, and she or he should have unrestricted access to it. Disclosure of such information does not violate privacy of the adoptee or the adoptive parents, as it does not reveal the identity of the principals. Privacy of the adoptee and adoptive parents is further protected through the provision of voluntary updating of their files, barring exceptional circumstances. Through screening of contents, the recommendations obviate the possibility of psychological injury to the birth parent.

Waiver. Notwithstanding the above recommendations, the director of child welfare should be given discretionary authority to waive the requirement of age and consent, if in his or her judgment the circumstances of the individual are compelling enough to warrant the release of the information requested.

The negative decision of the director or department should be appealable, first to an impartial body appointed by the minister of Social Services, and then to the courts.

Postadoption Services

It is recommended that the department establish a fully active Adoption Registry, signifying the department's commitment to changes in the adoption disclosure status, with the appointment of a coordinator. The registry should be widely publicized in and outside the province.

It is recommended that the department act as an intermediary between parties wishing to meet the first time. In facilitating the meeting, the department should provide the parties with brief background information (via pictures, photographs, and verbal descriptions) of each other, arrange the initial meeting, and assist in handling the meeting with sensitivity.

It is recommended that the department provide postreunion service on a voluntary basis to those parties who have had reunion and experienced psychological and/or relational concerns, thus having an adverse effect upon them.

It is recommended that the department hire additional adoption workers so that the delay in processing of applications is minimal and the search for unregistered parties is not protracted beyond the reasonable time period.

It is recommended that the department provide an intensive training program for workers involved in handling requests for disclosure of information, searching, and in providing intermediary and counseling services. Efforts should be made to involve representatives of adoptive parents, birth mothers, and adoptees in training programs and in the implementation of the revised disclosure policy.

It is recommended that the department launch an educational campaign in the province through seminars, workshops, and meetings with constituencies likely to be affected by the policy changes. These forums should be held in advance of the enactment of the new policy and would be used to interpret and explain alterations in the adoption disclosure policy and to address concerns of the members of the adoption triad.

Application of the Policy

The provisions of this policy should be applied retroactively, whereby all adoptions consummated before and after the enactment of this policy are covered.

It is recommended that the department henceforth discuss with the relinquishing birth parents that the law provides for the release of identifying information with consent and determine if they would file a waiver of confidentiality. The birth parents may revoke this decision anytime by filing a new affidavit. The department should also inform prospective adoptive parents of the reality that the department would not provide them with an ironclad guarantee of anonymity. The change is needed in view of the fact that adopted children have two sets of parents and might one day seek information on their birth parents and/or contact them.

NATIONAL REGISTRY

It is recommended that a national mutual consent voluntary registry be established and operated by the Adoption Desk in Canada or a similar national body. The registry may be available to adoptees, birth parents, birth relatives, and adoptive parents. The registry will facilitate matching and involve placing agencies in the contact-consent process.

Legislative Update on Access to Adoption Records in the United States: An Overview*

STATE	PROVISIONS FOR DISCLOSURE OF INFORMATION	REQUIREMENTS AND PROCEDURES
Alabama	Original birth certificate is available for inspection by an adoptee and adoptive parents, upon demand.	Adoptee must reach the age of majority.
Alaska	1. Allows adoptees access, upon demand, to a copy	1. Adoptee must be eighteen or older.

STATE	PROVISIONS FOR DISCLOSURE OF INFORMATION	REQUIREMENTS AND PROCEDURES
	of original birth certificate and attached information about any changes in birth parents' name and address.	
	2. Grants adoptees access to nonidentifying information (physical characteristics, education, and social history) and medical history of biological parents and relatives.	2. Same as 1.
	3. Birth parents permitted access to names and identities of adoptive parents or adoptee.	3.(a) Prior consent of adoptee is required. (b) Consent of adoptive parents is required if adoptee is under fourteen.
	4. Allows release of medical history on birth parents to adoptees.	4. Adoptee is eighteen or older.
Arizona	1. Adoption records are sealed. Access to identifying information may be granted to adoptees only by court order.	1. Adoptee is at least eighteen.
	2. Agency may provide medical and background information on birth parents to prospective adoptive parents and adoptees.	2. Adoptee is at least eighteen.
	3. Health history and background information on birth parents may be	3. Adoptee is deceased.

*I gratefully acknowledge the assistance of Mr. William Pierce, President, National Committee for Adoption, Washington, D.C., who generously provided the most updated information and their publication, *NCFA Summary of States' Laws*. I am also appreciative of him for making available the article "1988 Survey of State Laws on Access to Adoption Records," by Jeffery Rosenburg in *The Family Law Reporter*, 14(40), 1988, which I found extremely helpful. This discussion is also based on summary legislative update assembled by the National Adoption Information Clearing House, Washington, D.C., and their assistance is also gratefully acknowledged.

STATE	PROVISIONS FOR DISCLOSURE OF INFORMATION	REQUIREMENTS AND PROCEDURES
	available to adoptee's spouse and/or offspring.	
Arkansas	1. Provides for establishment of a mutual consent voluntary registry by the Department of Human Services and by any voluntary adoption agency.	1.(a) Adoptee is at least twenty-one. (b) Individuals who enter in the registry must accept at least one hour of counseling by a professional social worker.
	2. Contacts are arranged between adoptees, birth parents, and second-degree genetically related individuals (defined as birth siblings, aunts, uncles, cousins, and grandparents of adoptee).	
	3. Placing agency is required, upon request, to provide written health, genetic, and social history to adoptive parents and adoptee.	3. Adoptee should be at least eighteen.
	4. Agency may provide information as described in 3 to adopted person's spouse or children.	4.(a) Adoptee's child is at least twenty-one years old. (b) Adoptee is deceased.
California	1. Permits adoptees access to identifying information about biological parents, including most current address.	1.(a) Adoptee is at least age twenty-one. (b) Agency must receive prior written consent from birth parent in the form of an affidavit.
	2. Adoptive parents may receive identifying information about biological parents.	2.(a) Adoptee must be younger than twenty-one. (b) Agency must determine that disclosure of such information is war-

STATE	PROVISIONS FOR DISCLOSURE OF INFORMATION	REQUIREMENTS AND PROCEDURES
		ranted by medical necessity or other extraordinary circumstances.
	3. Contact between an adoptee, biological, and adoptive parents may be arranged upon request.	3. Parties must file an affidavit waiving parents' right to confidentiality before any contact occurs.
	4. Allows sharing of identifying information between adoptees and birth siblings.	4.(a) Adoptee is twenty-one or older. (b) Waiver of confidentiality is required. (c) Reciprocal consent and matched inquiries are required.
	5. Requires agencies to provide adoptive parents and adoptees' with written reports on health and medical information about the child.	5.(a) Adoptee is married or is at least eighteen. (b) Such information may be released to adoptees under eighteen if the court determines medical necessity.
	6. Permits agencies to share letters, photographs, or other items of personal property in their custody with birth parents and adoptees.	6.(a) Adoptee is eighteen or older. (b) If adoptee is younger than eighteen, materials are shared with adoptive parents. (c) Written consent of parties who deposited such material is required.
	7. A biological parent is permitted access to identifying information about adoptee.	7.(a) Adoptee is at least twenty-one. (b) Agency must obtain prior consent of adoptee.
	8. A biological parent may request, at any time after adoption, information regarding well-being of the relinquished child.	8. Information is screened for identifying information about adoptive family.

STATE	PROVISIONS FOR DISCLOSURE OF INFORMATION	REQUIREMENTS AND PROCEDURES
	9. Requires agencies to inform relinquishing biological parents that the law provides for release of identifying information with consent and to find out if they would agree to such disclosure. Also, agencies must encourage birth parents to periodically update their addresses and any new medical condition that may have bearing on the child's health.	9. Applies to adoptions completed on or before January 1, 1984.
Colorado	1. Provides for a mutual consent voluntary registry allowing sharing of identifying information between birth parents and adoptees.	1.(a) Adoptee is at least twenty-one. (b) Registration of both biological parents is required, unless the birth certificate lists only one biological parent or biological parent is deceased or consent of at least one biological parent cannot be obtained because he or she could not be located despite a thorough search.
	2. Relatives of deceased biological parents and relatives of deceased adoptees may also register.	
Connecticut	1. An adoptee or an adoptable person (that is, not adopted but for whom parental rights were terminated) can be	1.(a) Adoptee and adoptable person are at least eighteen. (b) Adoption agency or the Department of Children

STATE	PROVISIONS FOR DISCLOSURE OF INFORMATION	REQUIREMENTS AND PROCEDURES
	granted access to identifying information.	and Youth Services is required to search for biological parents to seek consent. (c) Each biological parent who was party to the adoption must consent.
	2. Adoptee or adoptable person may petition the court for release of identifying information in the event biological parent being sought could not be located.	
	3. Permits the Department of Health Services to release a copy of original birth certificate to adoptable person.	3. Adoptable person is eighteen or older.
	4. Makes available genetic, social, and health history of biological parents to adoptees, adopted persons, and adoptive parents.	4. Adoptee and adoptable persons are at least eighteen.
	5. Genetic, social, and health history of birth parents may be released to minor adoptees for medical necessity.	5. A court order is required.
Delaware	1. Adoption records are sealed and may be made available only by court order.	
	2. Genetic and health history may be released to an adoptee or to an authorized person on his or her behalf, if minor, for medical necessity only.	
	3. Permits release of non-	

STATE	PROVISIONS FOR DISCLOSURE OF INFORMATION	REQUIREMENTS AND PROCEDURES
	identifying information to any party to the adoption.	
District of Columbia	1. Adoption records are sealed and may be made available only by court order.	
Florida	1. Provides for establishment of a mutual consent voluntary adoption registry for adoptees and birth parents. It is also available to adoptive parents and biological grandparents.	1.(a) Adoptee is at least eighteen. (b) For adoptees under eighteen, consent of parents is required. (c) Voluntary counseling on a fee-for-service basis is available.
	2. Identifying information may be disclosed for "good cause" to any party to the adoption upon court order, in the absence of consent to disclosure.	
	3. Requires agencies to make available nonidentifying medical and social history concerning birth parents to adoptive parents before adoption is finalized.	
	4. The information as described in 3 may be released to adoptees.	4. Adoptee is at least the age of majority.
Georgia	Adoption records are sealed and may be opened only by court order.	
Hawaii	1. Adoption records are sealed.	
	2. Access to identifying information is available to adoptees.	2.(a) Adoptee is eighteen or older. (b) Birth parent(s) has filed consent to disclosure.

STATE	PROVISIONS FOR DISCLOSURE OF INFORMATION	REQUIREMENTS AND PROCEDURES
		(c) Court order is required where consent is not available.
	3. Permits an adoptee access to nonidentifying information concerning birth parents.	3. Adoptee is at least eighteen.
Idaho	1. Provides for a mutual consent voluntary adoption registry under auspices of the State Registrar of Vital Statistics. Registrants may include adoptees, birth parents, and birth siblings.	1. Adoptee is eighteen or older.
	2. Biological relatives of adoptees may also register with the state registry.	2.(a) Consent of both birth parents is required for release of identifying information unless other parent is not listed on the original birth certificate or is deceased or cannot be located.
		(b) Both adoptee and birth parents are deceased.
		(c) Government employees are prohibited from soliciting consent or registration from any of the parties.
Illinois	1. Authorizes the Department of Health to establish a mutual consent voluntary adoption registry available to adoptees and birth parents.	1.(a) Adoptee is at least twenty-one.
		(b) Written consent of adoptive parents is required if the adoptee is under twenty-one but older than eighteen.
		(c) Reciprocal consent must be on registry file.

STATE	PROVISIONS FOR DISCLOSURE OF INFORMATION	REQUIREMENTS AND PROCEDURES
		(d) Adoptive parents may request nonconsent on behalf of an adoptee under twenty-one.
	2. Adoptees or birth parents may obtain identifying information without consent of the other party.	2. Court order is required.
	3. Adoptees under twenty-one may receive identifying information.	3. Written permission of adoptive parents is required.
	4. Agencies are required to obtain a statement from relinquishing birth parents whether they wish to consent, not consent, or are uncertain as to disclosure of their identifying information to adopted child upon reaching twenty-one. Birth parents can change this decision any time in the future.	
	5. Permits adoptees access to nonidentifying information, upon request.	5. Adoptee is at least eighteen.
Indiana	1. Provides for a mutual consent voluntary adoption registry and is accessible to adoptees, birth parents, and adoptive parents.	1.(a) Applies to adoptions that occurred before July 1, 1988. (b) Adoptee is twenty-one or older. (c) Registrants must specify whether they are consenting to the release of identifying or nonidentifying information or both and the person who should receive such information.

STATE	PROVISIONS FOR DISCLOSURE OF INFORMATION	REQUIREMENTS AND PROCEDURES
	2. Relatives of adoptees and birth parents may also register with the registry.	2. Adoptee and birth parents must have died.
	3. Allows release of non-identifying information to adoptees, upon request.	3. Applies to adoptions that occurred after July 1, 1988.
	4.(a) Requires birth parents to file with the adoption petition information regarding the health status and medical histories of child and their own.	
	(b) Agencies are required to supply a copy of the report containing information stated in 4(a) to adoptive parents at time of adoption.	
Iowa	1. Adoption records are sealed and access may be granted only by a court order.	
	2. Genetic and medical history may be released in case of medical necessity; that is, to save the life of adoptees or to prevent offspring from fatal disease.	
Kansas	1. Permits the release of original birth certificate on demand of an adoptee.	1. Adoptee is eighteen or older.
Kentucky	1. Grants adoptees access to identifying information	1.(a) Adoptee is twenty-one or older.
		(b) Prior consent of birth parents is required.
		(c) Cabinet for Human Resources is required to obtain a statement

STATE	PROVISIONS FOR DISCLOSURE OF INFORMATION	REQUIREMENTS AND PROCEDURES
		from relinquishing birth parents on whether they consent to the inspection of adoption records, or to both when he or she becomes an adult.
		(d) Birth parents can file consent or revoke it any time.
		(e) If prior consent is not on file, the court shall require the agency to search for each birth parent identified on adoptee's original birth certificate, notify them, and seek their consent.
	2. Adoptees may be permitted access to adoption records without consent of birth parents.	2.(a) Adoptee is twenty-one or older.
		(b) A court order is required.
	3. Permits adoptees to register with the Cabinet for Human Resources their names, addresses, and willingness to personal contact by preadoptive siblings.	3.(a) Adoptee is eighteen or older.
		(b) Siblings is eighteen or older.
		(c) Siblings must also voluntarily register their desire to meet.
	4. Requires agencies to provide medical information about birth parents to adoptive parents before adoption becomes final.	
	5. Adoptees may request medical history concerning birth parents.	5. Adoptee is twenty-one or older.
Louisiana	1. Provides for establishment of a mutual consent voluntary adoption registry under the auspices	

STATE	PROVISIONS FOR DISCLOSURE OF INFORMATION	REQUIREMENTS AND PROCEDURES
	of the Department of Health and Human Resources. 2. Contacts may be arranged between adoptees, birth mothers, and birth fathers. 3. Requires relinquishing parents to provide in writing their medical history. 4. Requires agencies to provide adoptive parents with medical information about child's birth parents at time of adoption. 5. Adoptees may request medical history concerning their birth parents.	2.(a) Parties wishing contact must register with department registry. (b) Adoptee is twenty-five or older. (c) Birth father must have formally acknowledged paternity and signed his consent to adoption. 5. Adoptee is eighteen or older.
Maine	1. Provides for a mutual consent voluntary adoption registry operated by the State Registrar of Vital Statistics. 2. Contacts may be arranged between adoptees, birth parents, and adoptive parents.	2.(a) Parties wishing contact must register with the Registrar. (b) Adoptees is eighteen or older. (c) Adoptive parents wishing to sign with the registry have children younger than eighteen.
Maryland	1. Provides for a mutual consent voluntary adoption registry.	

STATE	PROVISIONS FOR DISCLOSURE OF INFORMATION	REQUIREMENTS AND PROCEDURES
	2. Contacts may be arranged between adoptees, birth mothers, birth fathers, and birth siblings.	2.(a) Parents wishing to meet must register. (b) Adoptees is at least twenty-one.
	3. Agencies are required to obtain medical history from relinquishing parents.	
	4. Permits release of medical history for reasons of medical necessity to adoptees or their off-spring.	
Massachusetts	1. Allows Department of Social Services or private agencies to share identifying information between adoptees, birth parents, and adoptive parents.	1.(a) Adoptee is twenty-one or older. (b) A written mutual consent of the parties is required. (c) Consent of the birth parent must be on file at least thirty days prior to release of information and the birth parent must be surviving. (d) Written consent of adoptive parents is required if adoptee is younger than twenty-one.
	2. Allows adoptees and birth parents access to non-identifying information concerning medical, ethnic, socioeconomic, and educational status.	2. Adoptee is eighteen or older.
	(a) Adoptive parents can obtain such nonidentify-ing information about birth parents.	(a) Adoptee must be younger than eighteen.
	(b) Agency may at its discretion release noni-	

STATE	PROVISIONS FOR DISCLOSURE OF INFORMATION	REQUIREMENTS AND PROCEDURES
	dentifying information regarding circumstances surrounding the adoptee's relinquishment for adoption.	
Michigan	1. Permits a placing agency, court, or the Department of Social Services to release identifying information to adoptees.	1.(a) Adoption occurred prior to September 12, 1980. (b) Adoptee is eighteen or older. (c) Both birth parents have filed consent to disclosure; or One birth parent has filed consent and other parent has filed denial of consent to release or has failed to file denial of consent; or A birth sibling of adoptee has filed statement of consent, in the event one birth parent is deceased and other birth parent has filed denial of consent; or Both birth parents are deceased and child was placed for adoption because of their death.
	2. Agencies may release identifying information to adoptees without consent of birth parents.	2.(a) Adoption occurred on or after September 12, 1980. (b) Adoptees must be at least eighteen. (c) Neither birth parent has filed an objection to the release of such information.

STATE	PROVISIONS FOR DISCLOSURE OF INFORMATION	REQUIREMENTS AND PROCEDURES
	3. Requires agencies to provide nonidentifying information to adoptive parents at time of adoption. Nonidentifying information shall include name of hospital where adoptee was born and time of birth.	
	4. Allows adoptees to obtain nonidentifying information.	4. Adoptee is eighteen or older.
Minnesota	1. Requires a placing agency to provide available identifying information to adoptees, birth parents, and adoptive parents, and/or facilitate meeting between requesting parties.	1.(a) Adoption occurred after August 1, 1977 and before August 1, 1982. (b) Adoptee is at least nineteen. (c) Agency shall conduct a confidential search to establish contact with the other party and obtain consent. (d) Agency must contact adoptive parents if adoptee is a minor.
	2. Exchange of information or contact may be arranged between adoptees and birth siblings.	2.(a) Sibling is at least nineteen. (b) Confidentiality of birth parent must be protected, or birth parent must file written consent to such information or contact.
	3. Agency may release birth parents' names, last known addresses, birth places and birth dates to adoptees.	3.(a) Adoption occurred on or after August 1, 1982. (b) Adopted person is at least twenty-one. (c) Birth parent has not signed an affidavit

STATE	PROVISIONS FOR DISCLOSURE OF INFORMATION	REQUIREMENTS AND PROCEDURES

denying such disclosure.

(d) Agency must complete search for birth parent within six months of request to determine consent or objection information to such disclosure.

(e) Upon death of birth parents and verified by agency. This condition applies to situation where agency has on file from birth parent an affidavit of nondisclosure.

(i) Adoptees may petition the court for access to such information if birth parent has filed a nonconsent to release.

Birth parent is required to demonstrate to the court that nondisclosure of such information is more beneficial to the parent than disclosure to the adoptee.

4. Agencies may release a copy of the original birth certificate *with a court order.* Applies to adoptions that occurred before August 1, 1977.

5. Agencies may release a copy of the original birth certificate to adoptees *without a court order.* Applies to adoptions that occurred on or after August 1, 1977.

4&5.(a) Neither birth parent has filed denial of consent.

(b) Agency must attempt to contact each biological parent listed on the certificate and get consent or denial of consent.

(c) Consent of both birth parents is required if both are located and contacted.

STATE	PROVISIONS FOR DISCLOSURE OF INFORMATION	REQUIREMENTS AND PROCEDURES
	6. Permits release of nonidentifying information to adoptees.	6.(a) Adoptee is at least nineteen. (b) Adoptee younger than nineteen requires consent of adoptive parents.
	7. Provides, upon request, significant medical history (physical or mental) of genetic relatives to adoptees and adoptive parents. An adoptee or biological parent will be informed if either one dies or has terminal illness.	7. Age requirement of adoptee is the same as in 6.(a) & (b).
Mississippi	1. Adoption records are sealed and may be opened to inspection only by court order. 2. Adoption petition must accompany a physician's certificate describing physical and mental condition of child.	
Missouri	1. Adoptees may seek access to identifying information about birth parents by petitioning court. (i) Agencies or court personnel are required to contact adoptee's adoptive parents, if living and not incapacitated, and seek their written permission.	1.(a) Adoptions occurred after August 13, 1986. (b) Adoptee is twenty-one or older. (i) Adoption decreed before August 13, 1986. (ii) Consent of birth parents is required. Agency or court personnel must search for birth parents within three months of request and notify them. (iii) If birth parent cannot be located, release of

STATE	PROVISIONS FOR DISCLOSURE OF INFORMATION	REQUIREMENTS AND PROCEDURES
		information may be forbidden. Either birth parent may refuse to file consent. In that case information may not be released.
	2. Adoptees may petition court for release of identifying information about birth siblings.	2.(a) Adoptee is eighteen or older. (b) Birth sibling is eighteen or older. (c) Consent of birth sibling is required. (d) Court must determine that such information is necessary for "urgent health-related purposes."
	3. Adoptive parents or legal guardians may obtain nonidentifying information regarding the child's birth parents.	
	4. Adoptees may request release of nonidentifying information about birth parents.	4. Adoptee is eighteen or older.
Montana	1. Adoption records are sealed. Identifying information may be available only by court order.	
	2. Agencies may provide medical and social history of birth parents to adoptive parents.	
Nebraska	1. Allows adoptees access to identifying information.	1.(a) Adoption occurred before September 1, 1988 (b) Adoptee is twenty-five or older.

STATE	PROVISIONS FOR DISCLOSURE OF INFORMATION	REQUIREMENTS AND PROCEDURES
		(c) Written permission of adoptive parents is required if adoptee is younger than twenty-five, but older than eighteen.
		(d) Consent of birth parents is required.
		(e) Department of Social Services must search for birth parents and seek their consent.
	2. Adoptees may request the Bureau of Vital Statistics for release of original birth certificate and the names of birth relatives.	2.(a) Adoption occurred on or after September 1, 1988.
		(b) Adoptee is twenty-one or older.
		(c) Birth parent has not filed with the Bureau denial of consent to release.
	3. Adoptees may be permitted access to identifying information regarding birth relatives.	3. Birth relative must agree to release to such information and/or contact by adoptee.
	4. Contact between an adoptee and birth relatives may be arranged by the Department of Social Services.	4.(a) Birth relatives have not filed objection to such contact.
		(b) Department may assist adoptee in locating a birth relative and finding out relative's willingness to meet.
Nevada	1. Provides for a mutual consent voluntary registry and is operated by the state welfare division of the Department of Human Services. It is available to adoptees and birth parents.	1. Adoptee is eighteen or older.

STATE	PROVISIONS FOR DISCLOSURE OF INFORMATION	REQUIREMENTS AND PROCEDURES
New Hampshire	1. Permits adoptees access to identifying information.	1.(a) Adoptee is at least twenty-one. (b) Birth parent has filed consent to disclosure. (c) In case no nonconsent has been filed, the agency shall try to locate and contact the birth parent and determine his or her desire to be contacted.
	2. Allows adoptees to obtain nonidentifying information. 3. Allows adoptive parents to obtain nonidentifying information.	
New Jersey	1. Adoption records are sealed. Access is permitted only by court order. 2. Agencies are required to provide prospective adoptive parents with all available information relevant to child's development, personality, temperament, and medical history of birth parents.	
New Mexico	1. Permits sharing of identifying information between adoptees and birth parents. 2. Adoptees may request the release of nonidentifying information.	1.(a) Adoptee has reached the age of majority. (b) Consent of the other party is required. 2. Adoptee is an adult.
New York	1. Operates a mutual consent voluntary adoption registry available to adoptees, birth parents, and adoptive parents.	1.(a) Adoption occurred before January 1, 1984. (b) Adoptee is twenty-one or older. (c) Requires registration

STATE	PROVISIONS FOR DISCLOSURE OF INFORMATION	REQUIREMENTS AND PROCEDURES
		and consent of adoptee, adoptive parents, and each birth parent who signed a consent to the adoption.
		(d) Registration and consent of adoptive parents is waived if they are deceased.
	2. Registry is available to adoptees and birth parents for sharing of identifying information.	2.(a) Adoption occurred on or after January 1, 1984.
		(b) Age requirement of adoptee is the same as in 1(b).
		(c) Adoptee and each birth parent who entered the adoption decree must register and consent.
	3.(a) Requires birth parents to include child's medical history in petition for adoption.	
	(b) Requires agencies to make available to adoptive parents child's medical history at time of adoption.	
	4. Prohibits agencies from referring to the child having been born out of wedlock.	
North Carolina	1. Adoption records are sealed. Access is allowed only by court order.	
	2. Adoptees may obtain nonidentifying information about birth family.	2. Adoptee is twenty-one or older.
	3. Adoptive parents may obtain health history of the child's birth family.	

STATE	PROVISIONS FOR DISCLOSURE OF INFORMATION	REQUIREMENTS AND PROCEDURES
	4. Agencies must notify adoptive parents when both birth parents have been adjudged insane or incompetent.	
North Dakota	1. Permits adoptees access to identifying information concerning birth parents.	1.(a) Adoptee is twenty-one or older. (b) Consent of both birth parents is required. (c) Either birth parent has not filed denial of consent to the release. (d) Agency must search and make reasonable efforts to locate birth parents and seek their consent. If birth parents cannot be located agency will not release information.
	2. Adoptees may request identifying information regarding a birth sibling.	2.(a) Adoptee is twenty-one or older. (b) Sibling is twenty-one or older. (c) Written consent of sibling is required. (d) Written consent of sibling's birth parents is required, if he or she knows their identity.
	3. Permits release of non-identifying information concerning child's birth parents to adoptive parents.	
	4. Allows adoptees access to nonidentifying information about birth parents.	4. Adoptee is twenty-one or older.
Ohio	1. Adoptees may petition probate court for release of identifying information	1.(a) Adoption occurred before January 1, 1964. (b) Adoptee has reached

STATE	PROVISIONS FOR DISCLOSURE OF INFORMATION	REQUIREMENTS AND PROCEDURES
	about birth parents.	twenty-one or older. (c) The birth parents must have filed with the Department of Health a consent to disclosure of such information.
	2. Adoptees may be permitted access to identifying information about birth siblings.	2.(a) Adoptee is twenty-one or older. (b) Consent of birth sibling is required.
	3. Nonidentifying information regarding child's birth family may be available for inspection by adoptees and adoptive parents upon court order.	
	4. Permits release of medical and social history of birth family to adoptees and adoptive parents. (a) Medical records may be available upon court order for inspection by adoptive parents and adoptees where birth parents are required to undergo physical examination.	
	5. Adoption records are sealed for adoptions completed on or after January 1, 1964. Access is available only by court order.	
Oklahoma	1. Adoption records are sealed. Access is only by court order.	
	2. Provides for mutual consent voluntary adoption registry and is available only to persons	

STATE	PROVISIONS FOR DISCLOSURE OF INFORMATION	REQUIREMENTS AND PROCEDURES
	adopted through the public agency. 3. Requires relinquishing birth parents to file with the adoption petition medical history of their own, the child, and the child's grandparents.	
Oregon	1.(a) Mutual consent voluntary registry is available to adoptees and birth parents. (b) Registry is also available to adoptive parents, birth siblings, and adoptee's grand-parents. 2. Makes available nonidentifying information to adoptees, birth parents, and adoptive parents. 3. Provides nonidentifying information to adoptee's spouse and offspring. 4. Requires relinquishing birth parents to file their medical history and that of the child. (a) Agencies may provide medical history to adoptive parents at time of adoption. (b) Agencies may make available medical history to adoptees.	1.(a) Adoptee is twenty-one or older. (b) Adoptee and birth parents are deceased. 2. Adoptee is eighteen or older. 3.(a) Adoptee is deceased. (b) Adoptee's children are eighteen or older. 4.(b) Adoptee is eighteen or older.
Pennsylvania	1. Identifying information about birth parents may be available to adoptees through petition to the court or directly from the placing agency.	1. Adoptee is eighteen or older.

STATE	PROVISIONS FOR DISCLOSURE OF INFORMATION	REQUIREMENTS AND PROCEDURES
	2. Adoptive parents or legal guardians may petition court or agency for release of information as described in 1.	2.(a) Adoptee is younger than eighteen. (b) Consent of both birth parents is required. (c) The placing agency or a county agency appointed by the court shall search for birth parents and contact them for consent. (d) If only one birth parent consents to disclosure, only information pertaining to that parent may be released. (e) Agency or court may deny request to search if it deems search and contact would disclose to persons other than birth parents the existence of adoptee and his or her relationship to the birth parents.
	3. Permits adoptees access to information contained in original birth certificate.	3.(a) Adoptee is eighteen or older. (b) Birth parent must file with court or Department of Health consent to release such information.
	4. Adoptive parents or legal guardians may have access to information contained in adoptee's original birth certificate.	4. Adoptee is younger than eighteen.
	5. Requires agencies to make available to adoptive parents upon request nonidentifying information	

STATE	PROVISIONS FOR DISCLOSURE OF INFORMATION	REQUIREMENTS AND PROCEDURES
	about child's birth parents.	
	6. Permits adoptees access to nonidentifying information.	6. Adoptee is eighteen or older.
	7. Requires agencies to obtain medical history with adoption petition from relinquishing birth parents.	
Rhode Island	1. Adoption records are sealed. Access is granted only by court order.	
	2. Nonidentifying information may be released at the discretion of the chief officer of an adoption agency.	
South Carolina	1. Makes available a mutual consent voluntary adoption registry to adoptees, birth parents, and birth siblings.	1.(a) Adoptee is twenty-one or older. (b) Mandatory counseling accompanies release of identifying information. (c) Requires agencies to notify adoptive parents of adoptee's registration. (d) Adoptive parents have not filed objection to release within thirty days of notification.
	2. Nonidentifying information may be shared at the discretion of chief executive officer of the agency between adoptive parents, birth parents, and adoptees.	
South Dakota	1. Provides for a mutal consent voluntary adop-	1. Adoptee is eighteen or older.

STATE	PROVISIONS FOR DISCLOSURE OF INFORMATION	REQUIREMENTS AND PROCEDURES
	tion registry operated by the Department of Social Services and available to adoptees and birth parents.	
	2. Makes available nonidentifying information to adoptive parents and adoptees.	2. Adoptee is eighteen or older.
Tennessee	1. Permits adoptees access to identifying information.	1.(a) Adoptee is at least twenty-five. (b) Department of Human Services will search to locate birth parents and seek consent. (c) Either birth parent must consent. (d) Consent is waived if birth parents cannot be found.
	2. Contact is arranged between adoptees and their birth siblings.	2. Adoptee and siblings are eighteen or older.
	3. Adoptees may request nonidentifying information about birth families.	3. Age requirement is the same as in 2.
Texas	1. A mutual consent voluntary adoption registry is operated by the Department of Human Resources and licensed agencies. It is available to adoptees, birth parents, and birth siblings.	1. Adoptees must be twenty-one or older.
Utah	1. Establishes a mutual consent voluntary adoption registry available to adoptees and birth parents.	1.(a) Adoptee is twenty-one or older. (b) Adoptee and birth parents must register with a court or an adoption agency.

STATE	PROVISIONS FOR DISCLOSURE OF INFORMATION	REQUIREMENTS AND PROCEDURES
		(c) Birth sibling raised in the same family must also be twenty-one or older.
	2. Matching registry is also available to siblings. 3. Permits release of health, genetic, and social history of adoptee to adoptive parents, legal guardian, and adoptee's spouse, children, and birth siblings.	2. Sibling is twenty-one or older.
Vermont	1. Provides for a mutual consent voluntary adoption registry permitting release of identifying information to adoptees and birth parents. 2. Nonidentifying information is made available to adoptees and adoptive parents upon written request.	1.(a) Adoptee is at least twenty-one. (b) Reciprocal consent by adoptee and birth parent must be filed with the court.
Virginia	1. Adoption records are sealed. Identifying information may be available to adoptees only upon court order.	1.(a) Court will authorize a private agency to search for birth parent named on adoption petition, locate and seek the parent's consent. (b) Court will determine if information requested does not adversely affect adoptee.
Washington	1. Adoption records are sealed and identifying information may be available only by court order.	

STATE	PROVISIONS FOR DISCLOSURE OF INFORMATION	REQUIREMENTS AND PROCEDURES
	2. Allows adoptee to obtain nonidentifying information.	2. Adoptee must prove medical necessity.
	3. Requires agencies to release medical history containing any information on birth parents' mental, physical, or sensory handicaps, if any, to prospective adoptive parents before placement of the child.	
West Virginia	1. Adoption records are sealed. Access to identifying information may be available by court order.	
Wisconsin	1. Grants adoptees access to identifying information about birth parents.	1.(a) Adoptee is twenty-one or older. (b) Consent of both birth parents is required unless one of the biological parents was unknown at time of adoption. (c) If consent of birth parent(s) is not on file at Department of Health and Social Services or placing agency, department will, upon request, search for biological parent(s) and seek consent. (d) Department must locate and obtain consent from at least one of the known biological parents.
	2. Makes nonidentifying information and health history of adoptee	

STATE	PROVISIONS FOR DISCLOSURE OF INFORMATION	REQUIREMENTS AND PROCEDURES
	available at time of adoption.	
	3. Access to nonidentifying information and health history is available to adoptees.	3. Adoptee is eighteen or older.
Wyoming	1. Adoption records are sealed. Access to identifying information is granted only by court order.	
	2. Requires agencies to provide medical history of child and birth parents to adoptive parents once adoption decree is entered.	

Adoption Records Status at a Glance

Sealed Records: Identifying Information is Accessible by Court Order

Seventeen states

Arizona; Delaware; District of Columbia; Georgia; Hawaii; Iowa; Mississippi: Montana; New Jersey; New Mexico; North Carolina; Oklahoma; Rhode Island; Virginia; Washington; West Virginia; Wyoming

Mutual Consent Passive Adoption Registry*

Twenty-two states

Arkansas; California[1]; Colorado; Florida; Idaho; Illinois; Indiana; Louisiana; Maine; Maryland; Massachusetts[1]; Michigan; Nevada; New Hampshire[1]; New Mexico[1]; New York; Oregon; South Carolina; South Dakota; Texas; Utah; Vermont.[2]

---

[1]Release of identifying information to adoptees and birth parents with prior mutual consent.

[2]Identifying information is shared with mutual consent; search is not conducted for either party.

*Parties voluntarily register their consent; search is not conducted for either party.

Active/Passive Search and Consent Procedure*

Ten states   Connecticut; Kentucky; Missouri; Nebraska; New Hampshire; North Dakota; Pennsylvania; Tennessee; Virginia; Wisconsin)

*Search conducted by a representative of the state or an adoption agency on behalf of adoptees only.

Active Search and Consent Procedure*

One state   Minnesota

*Search conducted at request of either party.

Identifying Information Available to Adoptees on Demand

Three states   Alabama; Alaska; Kansas

Agencies or Departments Acting as Intermediary between Adoptees and Birth Parents

Eight states   Arkansas; California; Louisiana; Maine; Maryland; Minnesota; Nebraska; Tennessee

Identifying Information or Personal Contact Between Adoptees and Birth Siblings

Fifteen states   Arkansas; California; Colorado; Idaho; Indiana; Kentucky; Maryland; Minnesota; Missouri; Nebraska; Oregon; South Carolina; Tennessee; Texas; Utah

Registries Available to Adoptive Parents

Five states   California; Indiana; Maine; Minnesota; New York

Registries Available to Birth Relatives

Six states	Arkansas; Colorado; Florida; Idaho; Indiana; Oregon

*Adoptive Parents' Right to Veto When Adoptee is
Under Twenty-one*

Five states	Illinois; Massachusetts; Nebraska [older than eighteen and less than twenty-five]; New York; South Carolina [compulsory notification to adoptive parents of adoptee's registration])

*Adoptive Parents' Right to Veto When Adoptee is
Twenty-one Years Old or Older*

One state	Missouri—applies to adoptions decreed before August 13, 1986.

Requirement That Adoptee is at Least Twenty-one

Twenty-three states	Arkansas; California; Colorado; Illinois; Indiana; Kentucky; Louisiana [twenty-five years old]; Maryland; Massachusetts; Missouri; Nebraska [twenty-five years old]; New Hampshire; New York; North Carolina; North Dakota; Ohio; Oregon; South Carolina; Tennessee [twenty-five years old]; Texas; Utah; Vermont; Wisconsin

References

Adoption Records Issue: A Position Paper. 1986. Committee Regulations for the Placement of Children in Family Homes. District of Columbia, Department of Human Services.

American Academy of Pediatrics. 1971. Committee on Adoption, Identity, and Development in Adopted Children. Evanston, Ill.: Dependent Care 47:948–49.

Anderson, C.W. 1977. "The Sealed Record in Adoption Controversy." *Social Service Review* 51:141–154.

Anglim, E. 1965. "The Adopted Child's Heritage—Two Natural Parents." *Child Welfare* 44:339–343.

Askin, J. 1982. *Search: A Handbook for Adoptees and Birthparents*. New York: Harper and Row.

Aumond, S.A., and M.C. Barrett. 1984. "Self-Concepts and Attitudes Toward Adoption: A Comparison of Searching and Nonsearching Adult Adoptees." *Child Welfare* LXIII [3]: 251–259.

Babbie, E. 1986. *The Practice of Social Research*. 4th ed. Belmont, Calif.: Wadsworth.

Bailey, K.D. 1987. *Methods of Social Research*. 3rd ed. New York: The Free Press.

Barinbaum, L. 1974. "Identity Crisis in Adolescence—The Problem of an Adopted Girl." *Adolescence* 9:547–554.

Barth, R.P., et al. 1988. "Predicting Adoption Disruption." *Social Work* May–June: 227–233.

Bedger, J.E. 1980. *Teenage Pregnancy: Research Related to Clients and Services*. Springfield, Ill: Charles C. Thomas.

Bernard, V. 1953. "Application of Psychoanalytic Concepts to Adoption Agency Practice." In A. Smith (ed.) *Readings in Adoption*. New York: Philosophical Library.

Blalock, H.M. 1960. *Social Statistics*. New York: McGraw-Hill.

Blum, L.H. 1976. "When Adoptive Families Ask for Help." *Primary Care* 3(2): 214–249.

Borgman, R. 1982. "The Consequeneces of Open and Closed Adoption for Older Children." *Child Welfare* LXI [4]: 217–226.

Boult, B.E. 1987. *Adoption: Salient Experiences of a Sample of Adult Adoptees.* Unpublished master's theses. University of Cape Town, South Africa.

Bradley, T. 1966. *An Exploration of Case Workers' Perception of Adoptive Applicants.* New York: Child Welfare League of America.

Brieland, D. 1984. "Selection of Adoptive Parents." In Paul Sachdev (ed.) *Adoption: Current Issues and Trends.* Toronto: Butterworths.

———. 1959. *An Experimental Study of the Selection of Adoptive Parents at Intake.* New York: Child Welfare League of America.

Brown, E.G. 1980. *Selection of Adoptive Parents—a Videotape Study.* Unpublished Ph.D. thesis. School of Social Science Administration, University of Chicago, August.

Burke, C. 1975. "The Adult Adoptee's Constitutional Right to Know His Origins." *Southern California Law Review* 48 [5]: 1196–1220.

Carter, J.R. 1978. "Confidentiality of Adoption Records: An Examination." *Tulane Law Review* 52: 817–855.

Champion, D. 1970. Basic Statistics for Social Research, Scranton, Pa.: Chandler.

Child Welfare League of America. 1976. *Standards for Adoption Service.* [Revision adopted on December 1.] New York: Child Welfare League of America.

Children's Home Society of California. 1977. "Report of a Research Project." *The Changing Face of Adoption.* (mimeograph). Los Angeles.

Clothier, F. 1943. "The Psychology of the Adopted Child." *Mental Hygiene* 27: 222–230.

Collins, T., B.E. Endo, P. Kaska, F. Kurrle, and M.J. Rillera. 1981. *Organization Statistical Study, 1980–81.* Calif.: Triadoption Publications.

Colon, F. 1973. "In Search of One's Past: An Identity Trip." *Family Process* 52: 429–438.

Costin, L. 1963. "The History Giving Interview in Adoption Procedures." In A. Smith (ed.). *Readings in Adoption.* New York: Philosophophical Library.

Dawe, M. 1984. *Adoption Disclosure: A Policy Submission.* Report prepared for the Department of Social Services, Newfoundland and Labrador, November 9, 1984.

Day, C. 1979. "Access to Birth Records: General Registrar Office Study." *Adoption and Fostering* 98(9): 17–28.

Day, C., and A. Leeding. 1980. "Access to Birth Records." *Adoption and Fostering,* London. Association of British Adoption and Fostering Agencies.

Department of Health. 1983. *Report on Births, Marriages, and Deaths in the Province of Newfoundland for the year 1982.* Table 1, p. 8.

Depp, C.H. 1982. "After Reunion: Perceptions of Adult Adoptees, Adoptive Parents, and Birth Parents." *Child Welfare* LXI [2]: 115–119.

Deykin, E.Y., L. Campbell, and P. Patti. 1984. "The Post-Adoption Experience of Surrendering Parents." *American Journal of Orthopsychiatry* 54(2): 271–280.

Douvan, E., and J. Adelson. 1966. *The Adolescent Experience.* New York: Wiley.

Dusky, L. 1979. *Birthmark.* New York: M. Evans.

Erikson, E.H. 1968. *Identity: Youth and Crisis.* New York: W.W. Norton.

Farber, S. 1977. "Sex Differences in the Expression of Adoption Ideas: Observations of Adoptees from Birth Through Latency." *American Journal of Orthopsychiatry* 47(4): 639–650.

Fiegelman, W., and A.R. Silverman. 1983. *Chosen Children: New Patterns of Adoptive Relationships*. New York: Praegar.
———. 1986. "Adoptive Parents, Adoptees, and the Sealed Record Controversy." *Social Case Work* 67 (April): 216–226.

Fisher, F. 1972. "The Adoption Triangle—Why Polarization? Why Not an Adoption Trinity?" Paper presented at North American Conference on Adopted Children, St. Louis, Mo.

Fisher, F. 1973. *The Search for Anna Fisher*. Greenwich, Conn.: Fawcett Crest.

Freud, A. 1958. "Adolescence." *Psychoanalytic Studies Childhood* 13.

Frisk, M. 1964. "Identity Problems and Confused Conceptions of the Genetic Ego in Adopted Children During Adolescence." *Acta Paedo Psychiatrica* 31: 6–12.

Gawronski, A., L. Landgreen, and C. Schneider. 1974. "Adoptees' Curiosity about Origins—A Search for Identity." Unpublished master's thesis. University of Southern California, School of Social Work.

Geissinger, S. 1984. "Adoptive Parents' Attitudes toward Open Birth Records." *Family Relations* 33(u), 579–585.

Gonyo, B. 1984. "Genetic Sexual Attraction." Paper presented at American Adoption Congress, Seattle, Washington, May 31–June 3.

Gonyo, B., and K.W. Watson. 1988. "Searching in Adoption." *Public Welfare* Winter: 15–22.

Gorman, S.A. 1975. "Recognizing the Needs of Adopted Persons: A Proposal to Amend the Illinois Adoption Act." *Loyala University (Chicago) Law Journal* 6 (1), Winter.

Groth, M., D. Bonnardel, D.A. Devis, J. Martin, and H.E. Vousden. 1987. "An Agency Moves toward Open Adoption of Infants." *Child Welfare* LXVI [3]: 247–257.

Grow, L.J., and D. Shapiro. 1974. *Black Children—White Families: A Study of Transracial Adoption*. New York: Child Welfare League of America.

Haimes, E. and N. Timms. 1985. *Adoption, Identity, and Social Policy: The Search for Distant Relatives*. London: Bower.

Haley, A. 1976. *Roots*. New York: Doubleday.

Harrington, J.D. 1986. "Adoption and the State Legislatures 1984–1985." *Public Welfare* 44 (Spring): 18–25.

Hoopes, J., E. Sherman, E. Lawder, R. Andrews, and K. Lower. 1970. A Follow-up Study of Adoptions Post-Placement Functioning of Adoptive Children. Vol. II. New York: Child Welfare League of America, Inc.

Horrocks, J.E., and S.A. Weinberg. 1970. "Psychological Needs and Their Development During Adolescence." *Journal of Psychology* 74:51–69.

Hubbard, G.L. 1977. "Who Am I?" *The Child* 11:130–133.
———. 1947. "Who Am I?" In A. Smith (ed.) *Readings in Adoption*. New York: Philosophical Library.

Jaffee, B. 1974. "Adoption Outcome: A Two-Generation View." *Child Welfare* 53:211–224.

Jaffee, B., and D. Fanshel. 1970. *How They Fared in Adoption: A Follow-Up Study*. New York: Columbia University Press.

Joanes, E.F., et al. 1986. *Teenage Pregnancy in Industrialized Countries*. New Haven: Yale University Press.

Jones, M.A. 1976. *The Sealed Adoption Record Controversy: Report of a Survey of Agency Policy, Practice, and Opinion*. New York: Columbia University Press.

Kadushin, A., and J.A. Martin. 1988. *Child Welfare Services*. 4th ed. New York: Macmillan.

Kadushin, A. 1978. "Children in Adoption Homes." in Henry S. Maas (ed.). *Social Service Research*. Washington, D.C.: NASW, 39–89.

Kinsey, A.C., W.B. Pomeroy, C.E. Martin, and P.H. Gebhard. 1953. Sexual Behavior in the Human Female. Philadelphia: Saunders.

Kirk, D.H. 1964. *Shared Fate: A Theory of Adoption and Mental Health*. New York: The Free Press.

———. 1981. *Adoptive Kinship: A Modern Institution in Need of Reform*. Toronto: Butterworths.

Kornitzer, M. 1971. "The Adopted Adolescent and the Sense of Identity." *Child Adoption* 66:43–48.

———. 1976. *Adoption*. London: Pulnam.

Kowal, K.A., and K.M. Schilling. 1985. "Adoption through the Eyes of Adult Adoptees." *American Journal of Orthopsychiatry* 55(3): 354–362.

Krugman, D. 1964. "Reality in Adoptions." *Child Welfare* 43:349–358.

Lamski, D. 1980. *The Search for Identity: A Problem of the Adopted Child*. Ph.D. thesis. California School of Professional Psychology. University of Southern California, Berkley, Los Angles, 4–5A.

Lawrence, M.M. 1976. "Inside, Looking Out of Adoption." Paper presented at annual meeting of American Psychiatric Association, Washington, D.C.

Leeding, A. 1980. "The Local Authority Experience." *Fostering Agencies Research Series* 1, Association of British Adoption and Fostering Agencies: 9–20.

Lemon, E.M. 1959. "Review Mirror—An Experience with Completed Adoptions." *Social Worker* 27, No. 3:41–51.

Lifton, B.J. 1979. *Lost and Found: The Adoption Experience*. New York: Dial Press.

Lion, A., and S. Gillon. 1976. "A Survey of Fifty Adult Adoptees Who Used the Rights of the Israel 'Open File' Adoption Law." Paper presented at annual meeting of International Forum on Adolescence, Jerusalem, Israel.

Lithgow, P.A. 1980. "The Adoption Disclosure Registry: The First Year." *Journal: Ontario Association of Children's Aid Society* 23 (September): 1–3.

Livermore, J. 1961. "Some Identification Problems in Adopted Children." Paper presented at annual meeting of American Orthopsychiatic Association, New York.

MacDonnell, S. 1981. *Vulnerable Mothers, Vulnerable Children*. Halifax, N.S.: Nova Scotia Department of Social Services.

Mann, P. 1976. "The Adopted Child Establishes His Identity." *Journal of the Institute of Health Education* 15 (2).

Marcus, C. 1979. *Adopted? A Canadian Guide for Adopted Adults in Search of Their Origins*. Vancouver: International Self Counsel Press Ltd.

———. 1981. *Who Is My Mother?* Toronto: Macmillan of Canada.

McWhinnie, A.M. 1967. *Adopted Children—How They Grow Up*. London: Routledge and Kegan Paul.

————. 1969. "The Adopted Child in Adolescense." In G. Caplan and S. Lebovici (eds.) *Adolescence—Psychosocial Perspectives.* New York: Basic Books, 133–142.

Mech, E.V. 1973. "Adoption: A Policy Perspective," in B.M. Caldwell and H.N. Ricciuti (eds.) *Review of Child Development Research.* Vol. 3. Chicago: University of Chicago Press, 467–507.

Ministry of Social Services and Housing. 1984. Background paper on the establishment of an adult adoption disclosure registry in British Columbia. September 1984.

Musser, S.K. 1979. *I Would Have Searched Forever.* Bala Cynwyd: Jan Enterprise.

Norvell, M., and R.F. Guy. 1977. "A Comparison of Self Concept in Adopted and Non-Adopted Adolescents." *Adolescence* 12 (47): 443–448.

Offord, D.R., et al. 1969. "Presenting Symptomatology of Adopted Children." *Archives of General Psychiatry* 20:110–116.

Pannor, R., and E.A. Nerlove. 1977. "Fostering Understanding Between Adolescents and Adoptive Parents through Group Experiences." *Child Welfare* LVI, (8):537–554.

Pannor, R., and A. Baran. 1984. "Open Adoption as Standard Practice." *Child Welfare* LXII [3]: 245–250.

Paton, J. 1954. *The Adopted Break Silence.* Acton, Calif.: Life History Study Center.

Payne, J. 1977. "Adoptees: Have We Forgotten That They Are Humans Also?" *Southern University Law Review* 4(1) 104–113.

Potts, M., P. Diggory, and J. Peel. 1977. Abortion. Cambridge, England: Cambridge University Press.

Prager, B., and A.S. Rothstein. 1973. "The Adoptee's Right to Know His Natural Heritage." *New York Law Forum* 19:137–156.

Rautman, A.L. 1959. "Adoptive Parents Need Help Too." *Mental Hygiene* 33:424–431.

Raynor, L. 1980. *The Adopted Child Comes of Age.* London: George Allen and Union.

Reynolds, W.F., and D. Chiappise. 1975. "The Search by Adopted Persons for Their Natural Parents: A Research Project Comparing Those Who Search and Those Who Do Not." Paper presented at the meeting of the Psychology-Law Society, Chicago.

Rosenberg, J. 1968. 1988 Survey of State Laws on Access to Adoption Records. *The Family Law Reporter* 14(14): 3017–3027.

Rosenzweig-Smith, J. 1988. "Factors Associated with Successful Reunions of Adult Adoptees and Biological Parents." *Child Welfare* LXVII [5]: 411–422.

Rubin, A., and B. Earl. 1989. Research Methods for Social Work. Belmont, CA: Wadsworth Publishing Co.

Sachdev, P., (ed.) 1981. Abortion: Readings and Research. Toronto: Butterworths.

Sachdev, P. 1984a. "Unlocking the Adoption Files: A Social and Legal Dilemma." In Paul Sachdev (ed.) *Adoption: Current Issues and Trends.* Toronto: Butterworths.

————. 1984b. "Breaking the Adoption Barrier: A Study of Record Disclosure to

Adoptees." Paper presented at annual meeting of Council on Social Work Education, Detroit, March 11–14.

Sachdev, P., (ed.) 1985. *Perspectives on Abortion*. Metuchen, NJ: Scarecrow Press.

———. 1989. "The Triangle of Fears: Fallacies and Facts." *Child Welfare* 68(5) (September/October).

———. 1988. "Reunions and Aftermath" [mimeograph]. Prepared for Parent Finders of Ontario, Canada.

Sants, H.J. 1965. "Genealogical Bewilderment in Children with Substitute Parents." *Child Adoption* 47:32–42.

Sauber, M., and E. Rubinstein. 1965. *Experiences of the Unwed Mother as a Parent*. New York: Community Council of Greater New York.

Schechter, M.D. 1965. "Adoption Research and Literature Review." A paper presented to Los Angeles Society for Child Psychiatry. Arrowhead, Calif.

Scheppers, R.C. 1975. "Discovering Rights of the Adoptee—Privacy Rights of the Natural Parents: A Constitutional Dilemma." *University of San Fernando Valley Law Review* 4 (1):65–83.

Schoenberg, C. 1974. "On Adoption and Identity." *Child Welfare* 53(9): 549–553.

Schumuck, R. 1965. "Concerns of Contemporary Adolescents." *Bulletin of National Association of Secondary-School Principals* 49:19–28.

Selltiz, C., L.S. Wrightsman, and S. Cook. 1981. *Research Methods in Social Relations*. 4th ed. New York: Holt, Rinehart and Winston.

Simon, N., and A. Senturia. 1966. "Adoption and Psychiatric Illness." *American Journal of Psychiatry* 122:858–868.

Simon, R.J., and H. Altstein. 1981. *Transracial Adoption: A Follow-Up*. New York: D.C. Heath.

Simpson, M., H. Timm, and H.I. Mccubbin. 1981. "Adoptees in Search of Their Past: Policy Induced Strain on Adoptive Families and Birth Parents." *Family Relations* 30(3): 427–434.

Smart, M.S. and R.C. Smart. 1972. *Children: Development and Relationship*. 2nd ed. New York: Macmillan.

Sobol, M.P., and J. Cardiff. 1983. "A Sociologocial Investigation of Adult Adoptees' Search for Birthparents." *Family Relations* (October): 477-483.

Sorosky, A.D., A. Baran, and R. Pannor. 1975. "Identity Conflicts In Adoptees." *American Journal of Orthopsychiatry* 45(1), 18–27.

———. 1978. *The Adoption Triangle*. Garden City, N.Y.: Doubleday Anchor Books.

Starr, J. 1976. "The Search for Biological Parents." Paper presented at annual meeting of American Association of Psychiatric Services for Children, San Francisco, California.

Statistics Canada. 1983. *Canada Update: 1981*. Census of Canada, April 26.

Stein, L.M., and J.L. Hoopes. 1985. *Identity Formation in the Adopted Adolescent*. New York: Child Welfare League of America.

Stevenson, P.S. 1976. "The Evaluation of Adoption Reunions in British Columbia." *Social Work* 44: 9–12.

Stoneman, L., C. Blakely, A. Douglas, and J. Webber. 1985. *Post-Adoption Service to Birth Parents* (mimeograph). Toronto: Children's Aid Society of Metropolitan Toronto.

Sullivan, M. 1977. *Task Force on Confidentiality in the Adoption Program.* A Report to the California State Department of Health.

Thompson, J., et al. 1978. *The Adoption Rectangle.* (mimeograph). Children's Aid Society of Metropolitan Toronto.

Thompson, J. 1979. "Roots and Rights—A Challenge For Adoption." *The Social Worker* 47(1): 13–15.

Tingley, B. 1978. *A Report on the Current Status of Search and Reunion Activity Amongst Principal Parties to Adoptions in Saskatchewan.* (mimeograph). Department of Social Services, Saskatchewan.

Toussieng, P.W. 1962. "Thoughts Regarding the Etiology of Psychological Difficulties in Adopted Children." *Child Welfare* 41: 59–71.

Triseliotis, J. 1973. *In Search of Origins.* London: Routledge and Kegan Paul.

———. 1980. "Counselling Adoptees." In John Triseliotis (ed.) *New Development in Foster Care and Adoption.* London: Routledge and Kegan Paul, 224–237.

———. 1984. "Obtaining Birth Certificates." In Philip Bean (ed.) *Adoption: Essays in Social Policy, Law, and Sociology.* New York: Tavistock Publishers, 38–53.

Weidell, R.C. 1980. "Unsealing Sealed Birth Certificates in Minnesota." *Child Welfare* 29(2): 113–119.

Weider, H. 1978. "On When and Whether to Discuss About Adoption." *Journal of the American Psychoanalytic Association* 26(4): 793–811.

Winkler, R., and M.V. Keppel. 1984. *Relinquishing Mothers in Adoption: Their Long-Term Adjustment.* Melbourne: Institute of Family Studies.

Yellin, L., T. Falasa, and D. Bobcean. 1983. *Adoption: Search, Reunion, and Aftermath.* (mimeograph). Lansing, Michigan: Michigan Department of Public Health.

Index

About the Author

Paul Sachdev, Ph.D., is professor and chairperson in the Department of Social Work at Cleveland State University. He is currently on leave from Memorial University of Newfoundland. He has taught and published in the areas of child welfare and reproductive health care. Among his previous books are *International Handbook on Abortion* (Greenwood Press, 1988), *Adoption: Current Issues and Trends* (Butterworths, 1984), *Perspectives on Abortion* (Scarecrow Press, 1985), *Abortion: Readings and Research* (Butterworths, 1981). Paul Sachdev is the recipient of several national and international research and travel awards. He received Memorial University President's Award for Outstanding Research. He is also an editor (domestic violence section) of the International Journal, Medicine and Law.